Exotic Botanical Illustration

Illustration

with the Eden Project

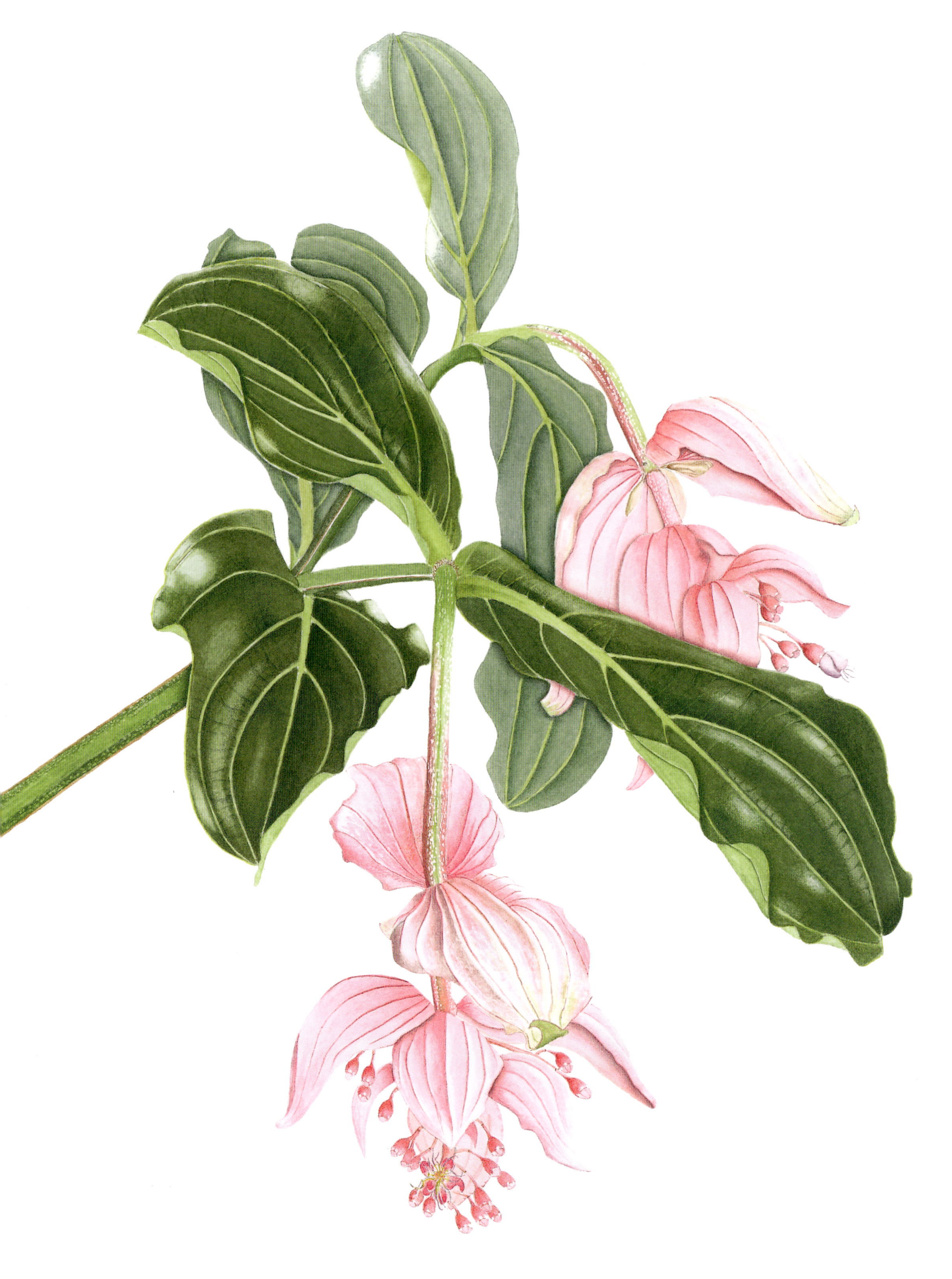

Exotic Botanical Illustration

with the Eden Project

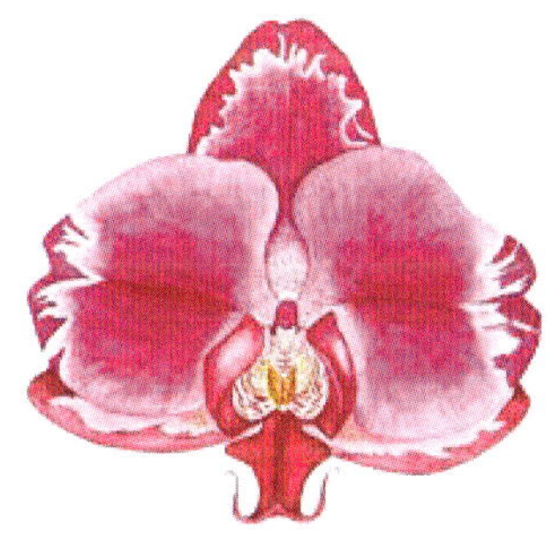

Rosie Martin &
Meriel Thurstan

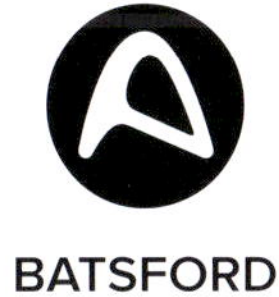

BATSFORD

First published in the United Kingdom in 2012 by
Batsford
10 Southcombe Street
London W14 0RA

An imprint of Anova Books Company Ltd

ISBN-13: 9781849940313

A CIP catalogue record for this book is available from the British Library.

10 9 8 7 6 5 4 3 2 1
20 19 18 17 16 15 14 13 12

Reproduction by Mission Productions Ltd, Hong Kong
Printed by Craft Print Ltd, Singapore

This book can be ordered direct from the publisher at the website: www.anovabooks.com,
or try your local bookshop.

Distributed in the United States and Canada
by Sterling Publishing Co.,
387 Park Avenue South, New York, NY 10016, USA

Page 2 The luminous pink and green of the chandelier tree (*Medinilla magnifica*) give great contrast.

Page 3 Orchids painted for identification purposes are shown 'full face'.

Right The purple and pink flower spike of the bromeliad looks almost artificial.

Contents

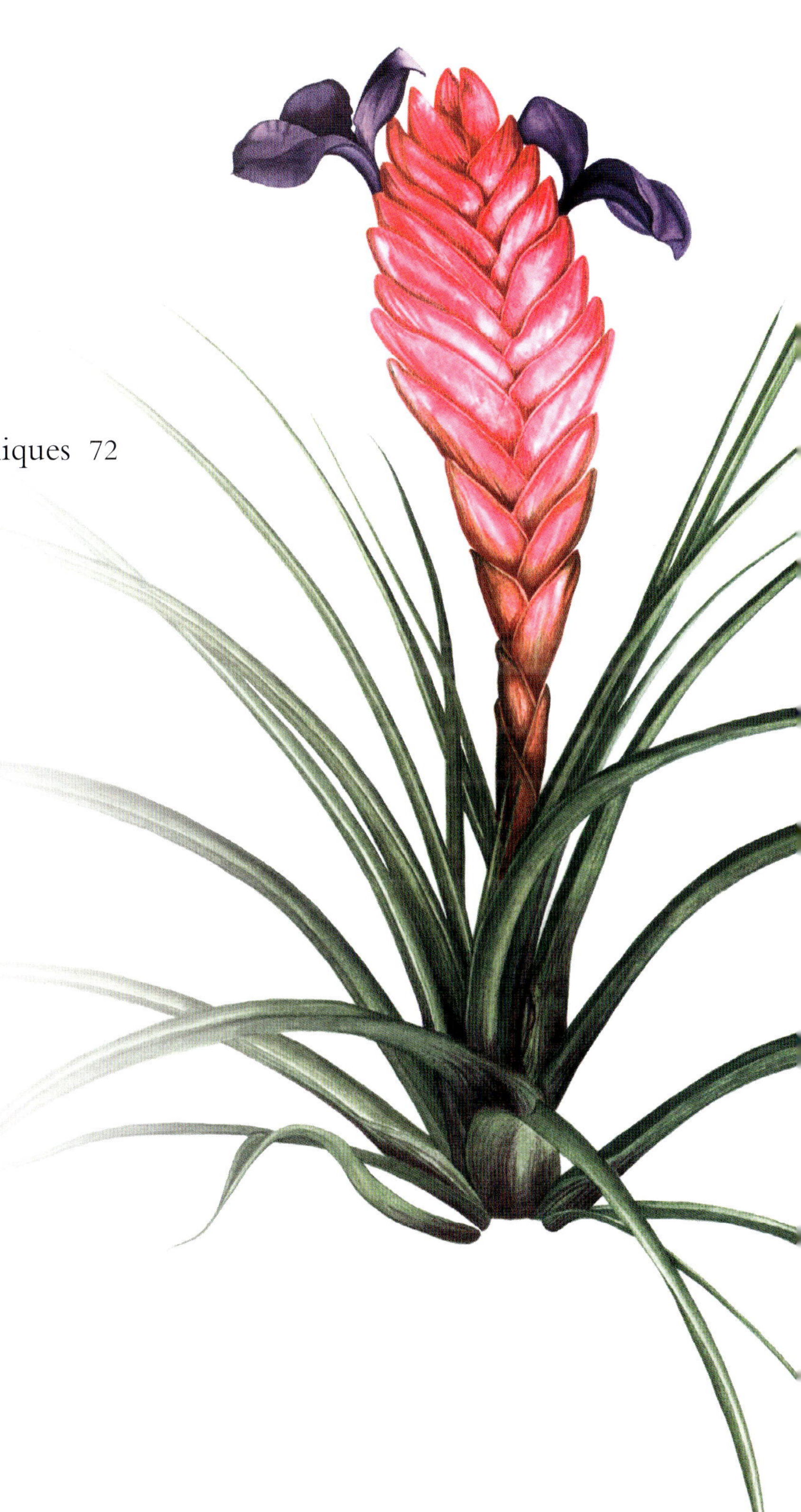

Foreword

Exotic botanical illustration as a phrase captures the imagination in some deliciously decadent way totally in keeping with the subject. Capturing the flamboyant, blowsy, 'in your face' foliage and flowers of the rainforest and the sub tropics is, in many ways, one of the greatest challenges in art.

My deep pleasure in the work of botanical artists is based on the revelation that science and art stem from the same root – observation. The beauty and exactitude of those observations are perfectly exampled by their work: delicate, yet muscular in the confidence of the artist's brush; disciplined, yet allowed a small artistic licence to convey the essence of all such plants rather than the particular.

I have known Meriel since the early days of Heligan and later as a driving force in the Eden's Friends team. From those modest early days a marvellous body of work has been created. It all began in a portakabin on Eden's eastern rim in 2003 – our offices at the time where she and Rosie Martin ran the very first botanical painting course here. I like to think that Eden was the perfect matchmaker for them because they have both flourished, written successful books (of which this is the fourth) and been publicly recognised for their craftsmanship and artistry, receiving awards from the Royal Horticultural Society for their paintings.

This is the fruit of their latest collaboration. Much of the work is inspired by the plants of the Rainforest Biome at Eden. The work is astonishing and beautifully observed and demonstrates, in the raw, the adaptive power of the plants of jungle and desert, plain and prairie. Understanding them is a life's work. It is powerful stuff and, for all those who care to pay attention and observe, an introduction to the wonderful variety of nature that should leave us all in awe.

I commend this book to you, written by two people whose greatest gift is the encouragement of others through the sharing of their talents. It is nice to think that the paintings contained in this book are a testament to the love of life in the painters themselves. We salute you all, and Rosie and Meriel. Long may your careers and generosity flourish because it gives so much pleasure to those who take part and those who, like me, only have the pleasure of observing from the sidelines.

Tim Smit KBE
Chief Executive, Eden Project

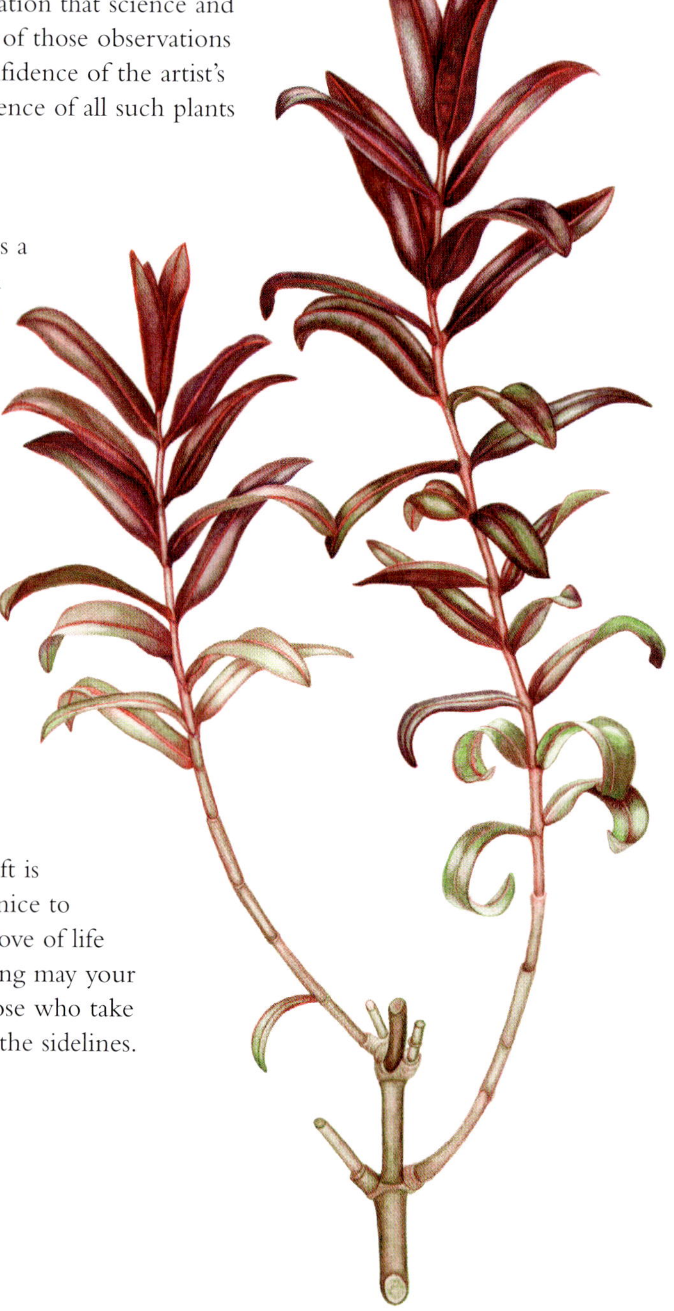

Below Layering colours one on top of another gives depth and resonance to this painting of a hebe.

Introduction

Some years ago, walking past the glorious summer flowerbeds at the Eden Project in Cornwall with a botanist who was visiting from the South Atlantic island of St Helena, we commented on how exotic the nearby arum lilies seemed. '*Zantedeschia aethiopica*?' said our companion. 'You may think so, but at home it has been declared a toxic weed and we are all trying to eradicate it!'

So what do you think of when you hear the term 'exotic'? Perhaps you consider the exotic to be a plant that is foreign to your country, as the native qualup bell, *Pimelea physodes,* (right) and the black kangaroo paw, *Macropidia fuliginosa* (below) of Western Australia are to Great Britain; or something that needs careful tending in a greenhouse; or a tropical bloom offered by your local florist. Maybe you visualize an exotic plant as striking, with hot, vibrant colours, or an unusual characteristic such as spikes or furry leaves – or maybe it could be a more commonplace plant that has been given an exotic artistic treatment. We show some of these in this book to inspire you to 'think outside the box'.

Whatever your interpretation, the ultimate question is 'What is available to me?' Botanical artists work best from a live specimen, which can be examined from all angles to see how it works and how best to portray it, so visit places such as the Eden Project in Cornwall, Kew Gardens in London, specialist nurseries and your local florist to find your source material.

Just as there are many meanings of 'exotic', so there are many ways to portray plants, from the scientifically accurate through to taking a botanical subject and turning it into more of a design than a portrait. We give examples of these throughout the book and hope that you will find it helpful and inspiring in your quest to paint exotic plants, even if you are reading it in a far-away part of the world and you find that – to misquote – 'One man's exotic is another man's weed'.

Above Qualup bell (*Pimelea physodes*).

Below Black kangaroo paw (*Macropidia fuliginosa*).

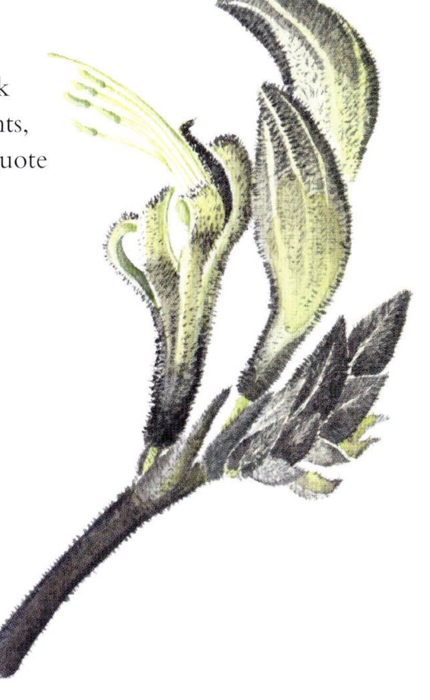

Equipping Yourself to Paint

Before you put pencil to paper, you need to consider carefully your environment, your light source and your materials. It is a common misconception by the student artist that 'my art is not all that important, therefore I can work anywhere'. You could not be more wrong. There is nothing more frustrating than, for instance, working in the kitchen and having to clear everything away at meal times, or trying to paint surrounded by other members of the household who are all going about their business, not always silently or discreetly.

Another misconception is, 'You are so lucky to be able to relax and paint.' Once more this could not be further from the truth. Painting is extremely hard work; you are constantly having to make decisions. Your art is important, and you need the right conditions to make it as easy as possible to concentrate and do yourself justice.

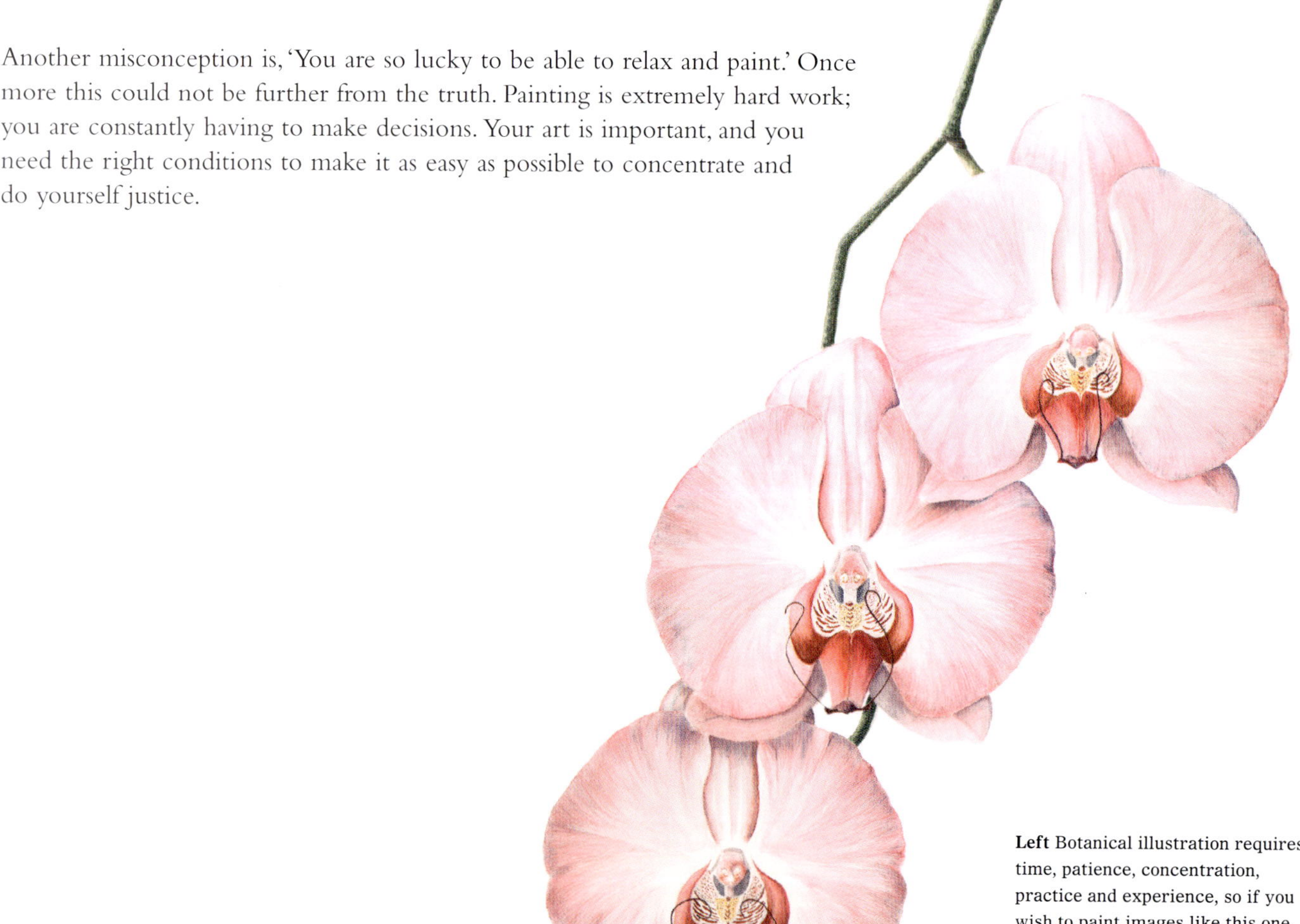

Left Botanical illustration requires time, patience, concentration, practice and experience, so if you wish to paint images like this one, of an orchid stem, consider carefully how and where you do it.

Your studio

Not all of us are lucky enough to have a whole
room that we can set aside to work in, or – the
ultimate luxury – a garden shed that can be
waterproofed, insulated and set up as a bona fide
studio. However, you should try to find a quiet
corner of the house where you can put a table
and a chair – and, more importantly, where you
can leave all your materials and your artwork
between sessions.

Lighting

Sometimes it helps to look at your subject in daylight in
order to establish which lighting would be most suited to
its colouring. Natural light is considered to be better than
artificial light, but either is better than poor light. Make sure
that your light source is consistent and consider the direction
– from the left for right-handed artists and from the right for
left-handers makes sense, as this will ensure that you are not
working in your own shadow.

In the northern hemisphere, sitting sideways-on to a north-facing
window is best of all; if your window faces south you are at the mercy of
changing levels of sunlight, which tends to be a misleading yellowish light.
North light is more neutral and not so affected by the vagaries of cloud cover.

Cast light on both your subject and your work. Even with a natural light source, you may
find that you need to augment it with a lamp. A desk lamp with an adjustable stem is ideal,
because you can then direct the light exactly as required. Normal light bulbs tend to cast
a yellowish glow, which can alter the colour of your subject, so it may be better to use a
daylight bulb. Try both and decide which you prefer. It may be that a normal bulb would
be better with a warm (red or yellow) subject, while a daylight bulb would suit a cool
(blue or green) subject. The decision is yours.

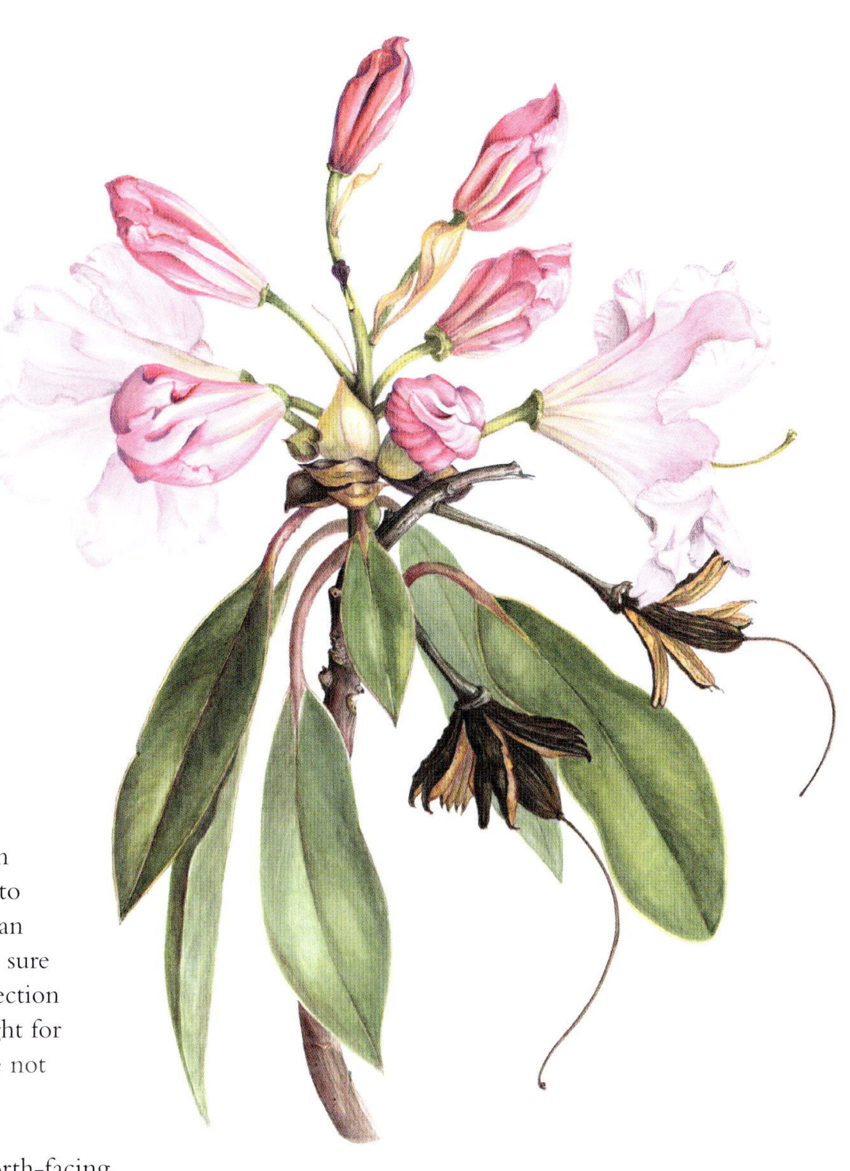

Above The standard of your work is
determined by your materials, so
give yourself every advantage in
terms of a place to work and the best
tools and equipment you can afford.

Furniture

A steady table and comfortable chair are essential. The table should be large enough for you to display your specimen to good advantage and to have all your materials close at hand, with room also for a lamp and possibly a magnifying glass on a stand. A typist's chair is useful as it swivels and is height-adjustable, but whatever type of chair you choose, it should give good support to your lower back. Arrange the position of your table and chair so that you can sit with your back as straight as possible; spending hours slumped over your work, or with your head propped on one hand, could cause back problems in the future.

Ensure that your materials are always laid out in the same way so that you get used to where everything is. Have your water container close to your paints and your mixing palette, and on the same side as your working hand so that you are not constantly stretching across your work with a loaded paintbrush.

Finally, shelves nearby are useful for housing art books, spare paper, pencils, paints and all the bits and pieces that you will collect around you.

Keeping your specimen fresh

Know your plant. Some specimens, such as dried seedheads, will stay the same for weeks or months, while some fungi deteriorate in half a day. Knowledge of the behaviour of your specimen will save you from unnecessary stress.

You would think that a magnolia seedhead, such as the one shown below, would be fairly straightforward, but the orange seeds soon lost their lustre and were therefore painted first. One or two fell out and had to be stuck back in. The rest of the seedhead changed very little.

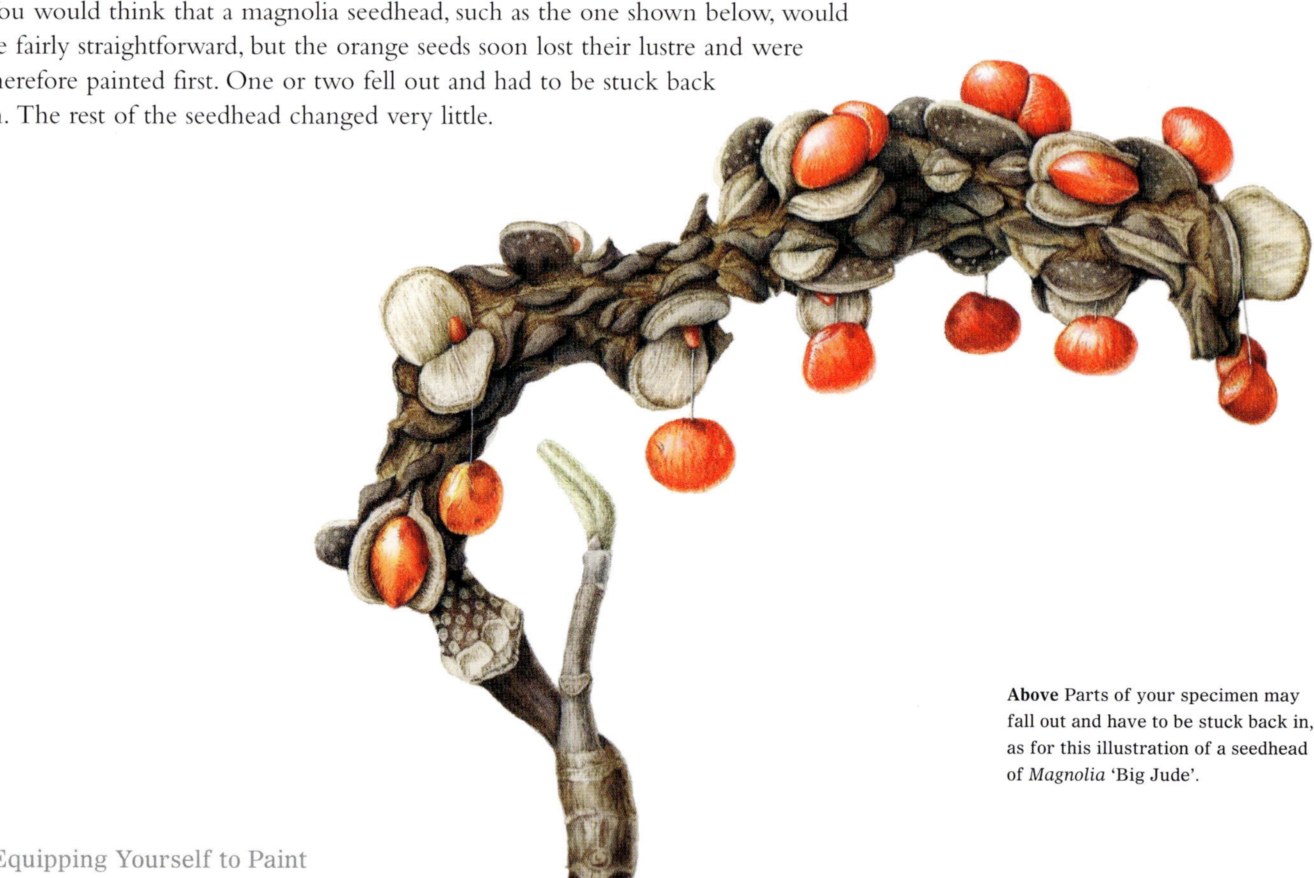

Above Parts of your specimen may fall out and have to be stuck back in, as for this illustration of a seedhead of *Magnolia* 'Big Jude'.

A certain amount of inventiveness is needed when working out how to keep a specimen in the same fresh condition as it was when you started. The life of cut flowers can sometimes be extended by adding sugar to the water in the vase; bulkier items can be stored overnight in a sealed container in a cool, dark place, possibly with a bit of moisture added; items that begin to wilt might be revived by spraying them with clean cold water.

If all else fails, and your preliminary notes and colour swatches (and photographs) are not enough to enable you to finish the painting, the only recourse is to wait until the following year when you can obtain another specimen. It has been known for a botanical painting to take up to six years to complete.

Materials

The quality, not the quantity, of your materials will determine the standard of your work. For this reason, we suggest a limited range, but insist that they should be of the very best – a much better allocation of your painting budget than a large quantity of poor-quality supplies.

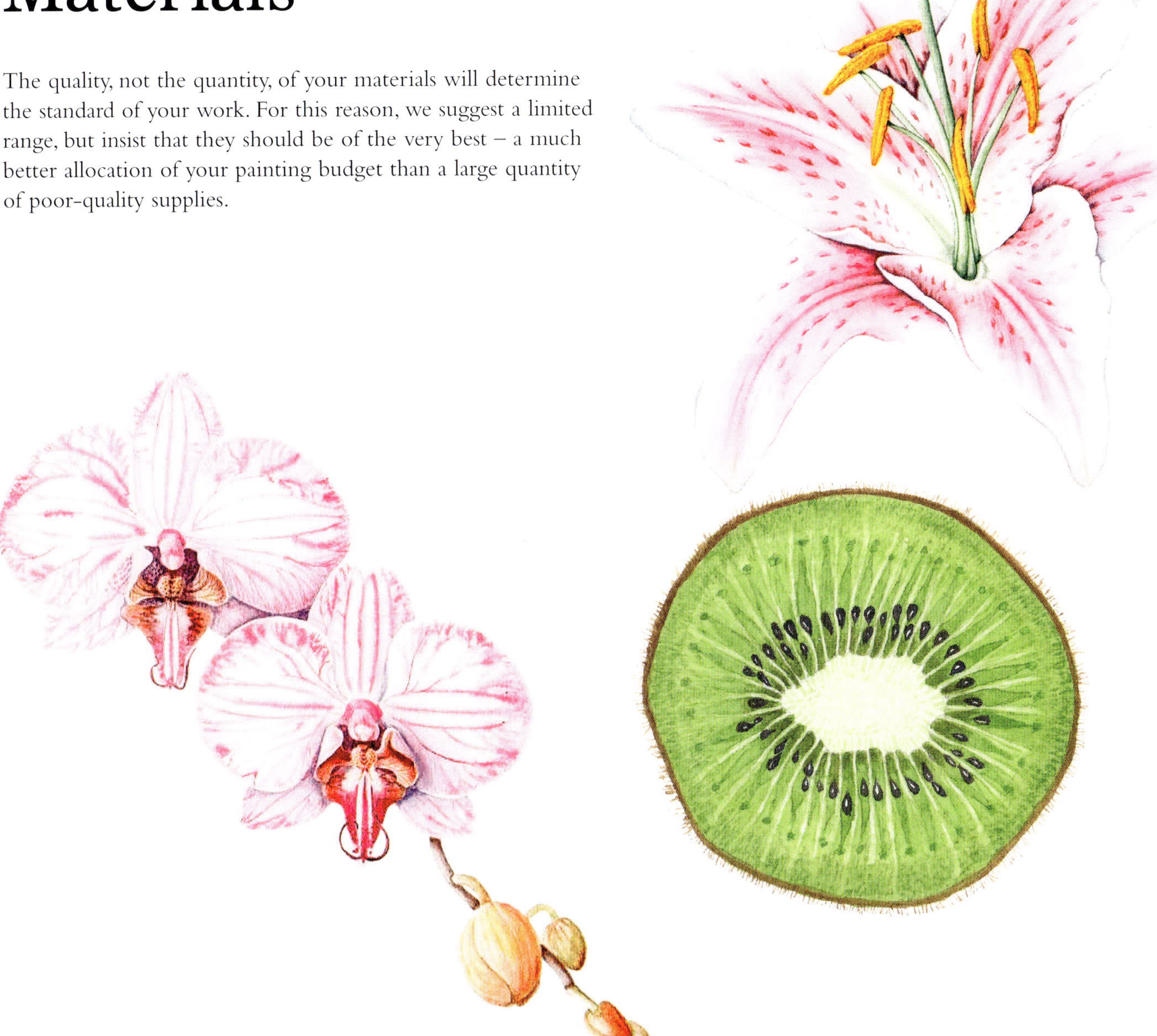

Paper

Most botanical artists use extremely smooth watercolour paper, which is sympathetic to very fine brushwork. This is known as Hot Press, or HP, a description of the manufacturing process that gives a hard, smooth finish. You will also find Not paper, which signifies that it is 'Not HP', and various types of Rough, but they are generally too textured for detailed work. The paper should be acid-free, an archival quality ensuring the longevity of the painting.

The papers we particularly recommend are shown on page 140. Watercolour papers come as full sheets measuring 56 x 76cm (22 x 30in), although most suppliers will cut the paper in half to 56 x 38cm (22 x 15in) or in quarters to 28 x 38cm (11 x 15in) for you. Most botanical artists prefer to use a heavy paper such as 300gsm (140lb). HP papers also come in 640gsm (300lb) for those who prefer a thicker, more board-like surface. Always store watercolour paper flat, not rolled. It's also possible to buy watercolour paper in a block, glued around all four sides, or as a pad, bound on one edge only. In each case, there is a variety of different sizes to choose from.

Testing the quality

Get to know your paper. Experiment with both sides – there is usually a difference in texture and paint-handling. Take a small sample of paper and write 'Front' at the top two corners. Cut it down the middle, turn one piece over and join the two bits together with sticky tape. You now have a surface of which one half is the 'front' and the other the 'back'. Try all sorts of washes, fine lines and other marks, as shown opposite, and you will see which surface is the most sympathetic.

Other papers

In addition to watercolour paper, you will need an A3 pad of **layout paper** for initial drawings. This is smooth and lightweight, 50gsm (35lb), and therefore relatively cheap, allowing you to try out techniques and different compositions, giving spontaneity in your preliminary drawings.

You will also find it useful to have a **small pad or sketchbook** of smooth watercolour paper in which you can make trial paint samples, carry out paint-mixing exercises and make notes on your subject before starting on the main artwork.

Once you have settled on a drawing that you like, it's easy to trace it from the layout paper on to watercolour paper. This is important, because you should endeavour not to use an eraser on the watercolour paper until the very end, as it can damage the surface of the paper and compromise the way in which it takes up the paint.

A good way of tracing is to fix your drawing to a sunny window, tape your watercolour paper over the top and trace carefully and lightly with a fairly hard pencil (2H). Don't press hard, otherwise you will score the paper.

Protection

To protect watercolour paper from splashes, smudging and the natural oils from your skin, place a **sheet of paper or acetate** under your hand while you work. Some artists like to use one that covers the whole area, with a hole cut in it to work through.

Right Test the quality of both sides of your watercolour paper because you may find that the back suits your style of painting better than the front. Simply try out a few washes and brushstrokes as explained left.

Front
Back

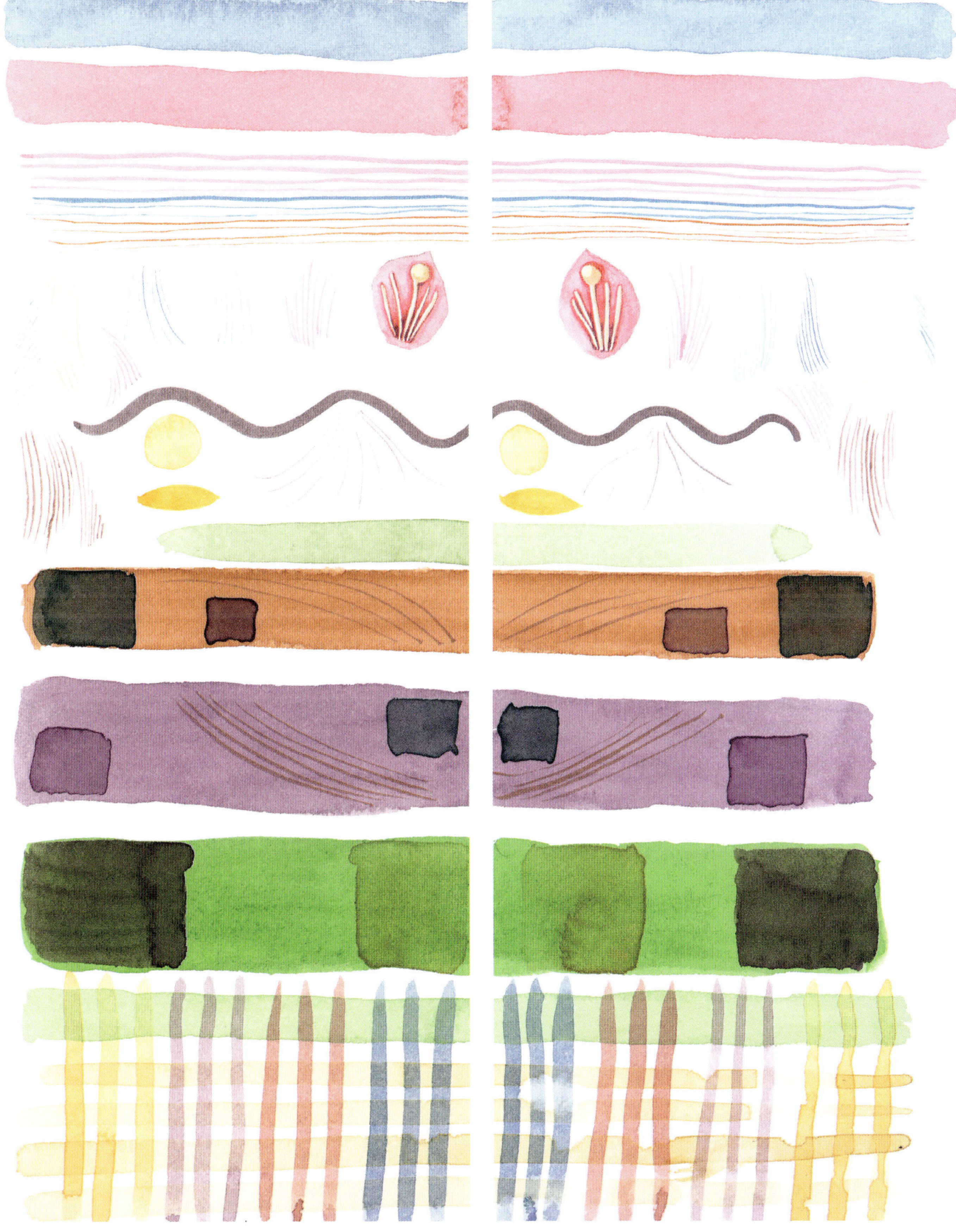

Graphite pencils

Usually only extremely experienced artists can start to paint without making any pencil marks beforehand. Use a range of graphite pencils from 4H (hard) to 2B (soft). Recommended makes are Staedtler Mars Lumograph 100, Staedtler 480, Faber Castell 9000 and Caran d'Ache Technograph. Derwent Classic pencils are popular but are generally much softer than the other makes mentioned here, so you would need to choose the individual strength of pencil for your work carefully.

Softer pencils (2B upwards) can deposit a dusting of graphite on the paper and for this reason need careful use to avoid smudging. Using a fixative isn't to be recommended as this can compromise the addition of further details.

Some artists prefer to use mechanical or clutch pencils, which have the advantage that they never become shorter and thus always retain the same balance in the hand. However, others maintain that the even marks made with them are, as the name suggests, 'mechanical' and rather characterless.

Watercolour paints

There are many different brands and qualities of watercolour paint on the market, but you will be doing yourself a disservice if you go for the cheapest. Always buy artists' quality paints – you can use a limited palette to keep the cost down.

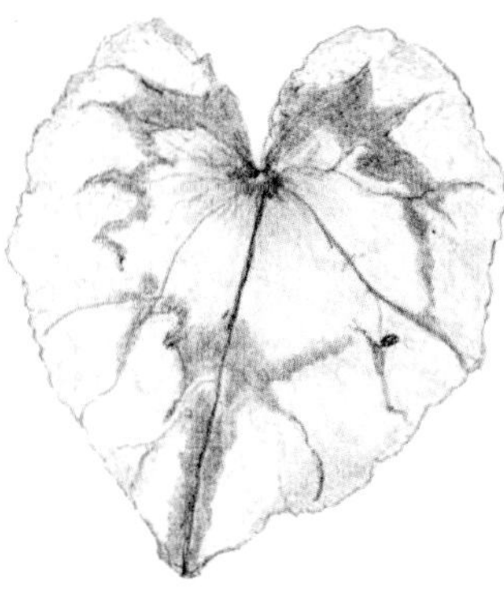

Above Use a range of graphite pencils from 4H (hard) to 2B (soft).

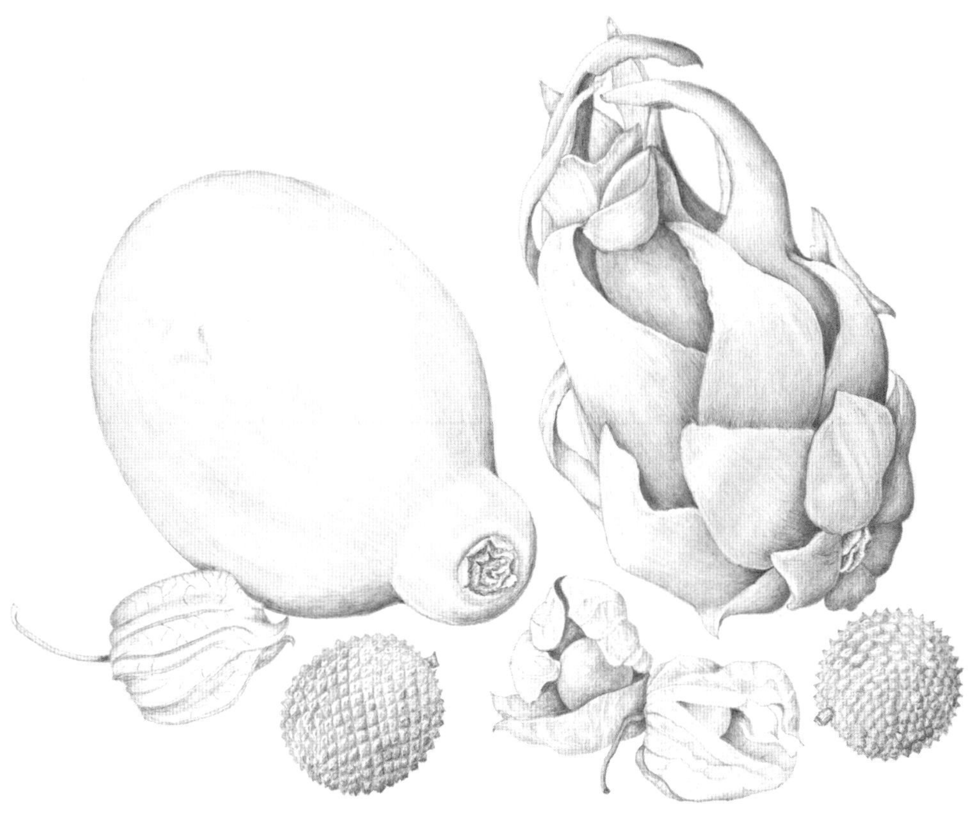

Below A pencil study of papaya, dragon fruit, physalis and lychees.

It's a good idea to buy an empty paintbox and fill it with your own choice of colours. The most basic colour palette, which has been used for most of the illustrations throughout this book, consists of just six colours, with another two or three optional ones.

Recommended paint manufacturers are Schminke Horadam and Winsor & Newton; other reputable makes are Holbein, Lefranc & Bourgeois, Sennelier and Old Holland Classic. Winsor & Newton colours are designed to favour the gentle tones of the British climate, whereas the others, which are by European manufacturers, provide strong, vibrant colours more in tune with sunnier countries. They are all very satisfying to use. If you prefer to buy some of these other makes of paint, check the manufacturers' colour charts carefully to ensure that they resemble as closely as possible the colours recommended on pages 16–17.

One cautionary note – it is not wise to use any paint with Cadmium as part of its name, as these tend to be dense colours which do not allow the white of the paper to shine through. For botanical painting in particular, the emphasis is on clarity and transparency.

White paint is useful for adding fine hairs on to a dark background, but for little else – except, possibly, adding bloom to fruit. A white gouache, Schminke Horadam Permanent Chinese White or Winsor & Newton Chinese White will all meet your requirements. There is no need to buy black paint; your own mixes will give you a far better result because in nature there are many different shades of black.

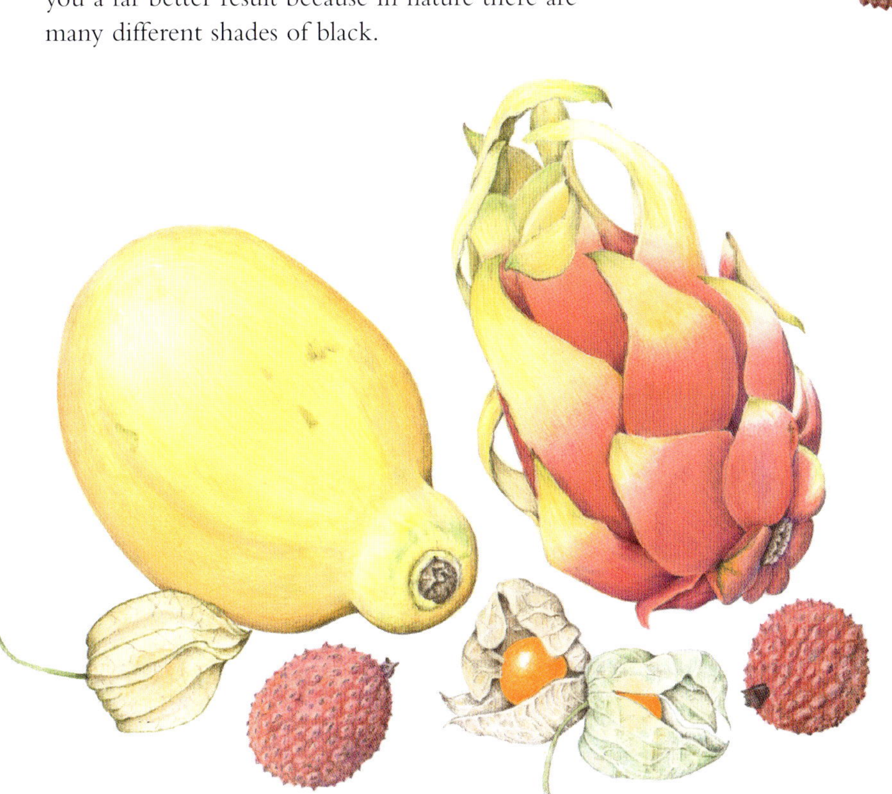

Left and above The same arrangement of fruit is shown here in coloured pencil (left) and watercolour (above).

Colours

The manufacturers' named colours given opposite have been divided into two categories – warm colours and cool colours. Throughout this book, we use either a particular name, for example Scarlet Lake, or its generic type, warm red. For your limited palette, choose just one warm yellow and one cool yellow, one warm red and one cool red, one warm blue and one cool blue. There is no harm in mixing different makes. Although using a ready-mix green is not recommended, you may find Sap Green useful as it is a good base from which to make a wide range of greens.

One of the newer, and controversial, colours favoured by botanical artists is Opera Rose. This is a fluorescent pigment that absorbs energy from the UV (invisible) spectrum and reflects it within the visible range, and has been enthusiastically welcomed for painting plants whose colours themselves look fluorescent, such as some fuchsias, orchids and pelargoniums. Believed by many to be fugitive, it has a B rating from its manufacturer, Winsor & Newton. This means that it is moderately durable, equal in permanence to Alizarin Crimson.

We use Opera Rose extensively. Similar pinks are Permanent Rose, also from Winsor & Newton, which is described as having unconditional permanence, and Brilliant Purple (Schminke Horadam). If you are preparing work for publication it is worth checking with your publishers as to which pink you should use, because some printers cannot reproduce fluorescent colours.

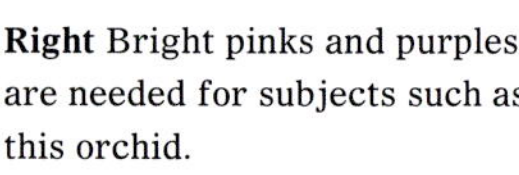

Right Bright pinks and purples are needed for subjects such as this orchid.

Schminke Horadam (SH) and Winsor & Newton (W&N) warm and cool primaries

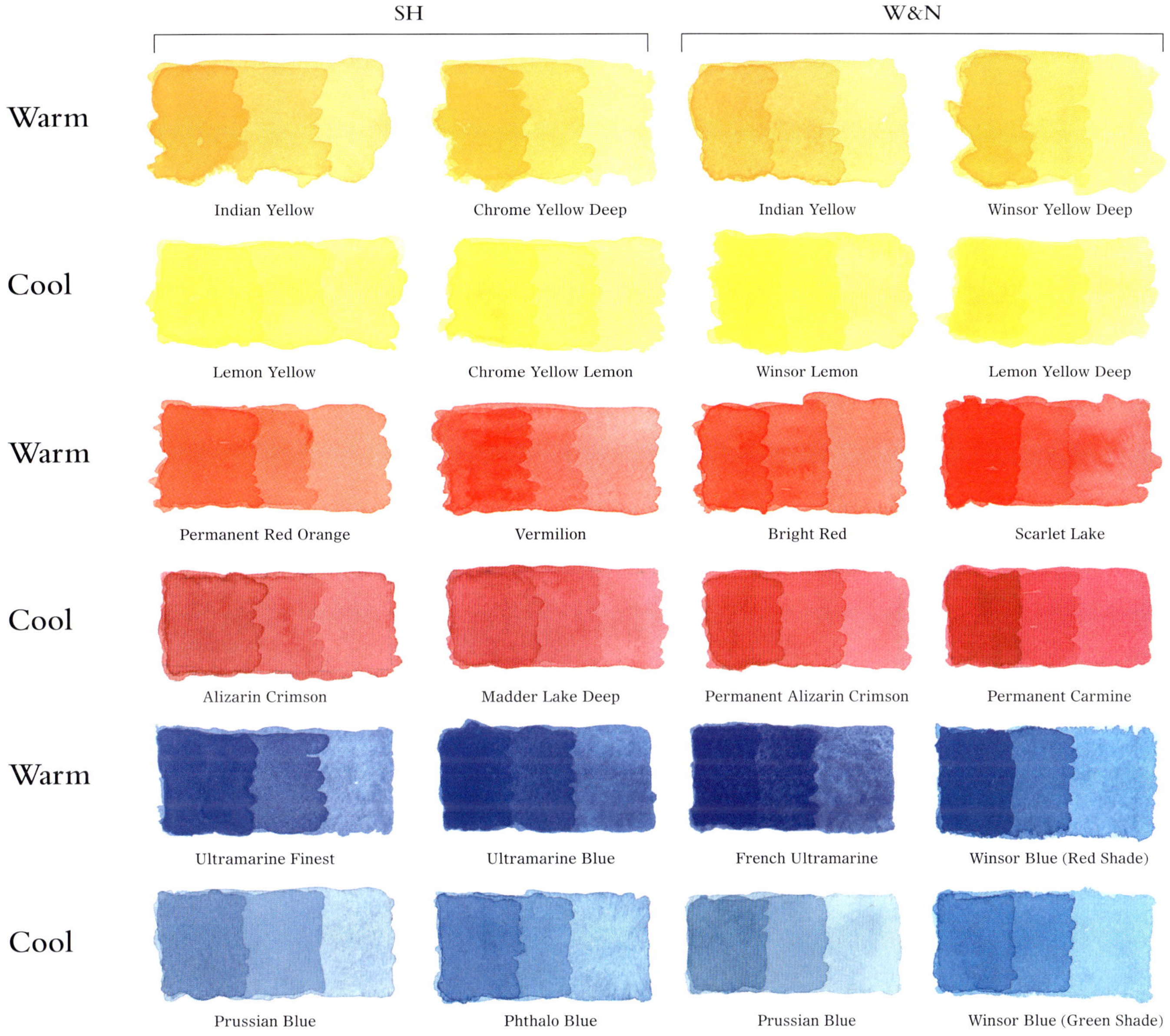

| | SH | | W&N | |

Warm — Indian Yellow — Chrome Yellow Deep — Indian Yellow — Winsor Yellow Deep

Cool — Lemon Yellow — Chrome Yellow Lemon — Winsor Lemon — Lemon Yellow Deep

Warm — Permanent Red Orange — Vermilion — Bright Red — Scarlet Lake

Cool — Alizarin Crimson — Madder Lake Deep — Permanent Alizarin Crimson — Permanent Carmine

Warm — Ultramarine Finest — Ultramarine Blue — French Ultramarine — Winsor Blue (Red Shade)

Cool — Prussian Blue — Phthalo Blue — Prussian Blue — Winsor Blue (Green Shade)

Pinks, purples and green

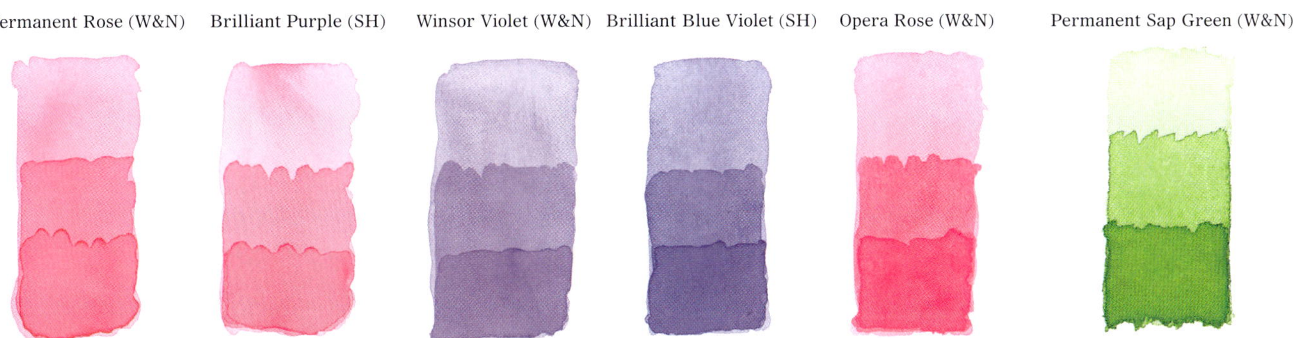

Permanent Rose (W&N) Brilliant Purple (SH) Winsor Violet (W&N) Brilliant Blue Violet (SH) Opera Rose (W&N) Permanent Sap Green (W&N)

Coloured pencils

Many artists are uncomfortable with brushes and paints and find that they work better using coloured pencils. These are covered fairly comprehensively on pages 90–95, with many examples of work done in this medium. It must be emphasized, however, that throughout this book the coloured pencils used are not the water-soluble kind (usually referred to as watercolour pencils), which necessitate altogether different skills from those given here.

Acrylics

While most of the coloured illustrations in this book are in watercolour, there's no reason why you shouldn't introduce other materials into your work. Acrylic pigments are thick, water-based paints that handle like oils but can also be used in much the same way as watercolours, allowing for washes and layered glazes, also known as superimposition (below). They are fast-drying but can be manipulated for a short period of time. The paints need to be kept damp on the palette to remain useable, and there are commercially produced palettes that achieve this. Otherwise, use a large, white china plate and keep the paints moist by misting now and then with clean water in a spray bottle.

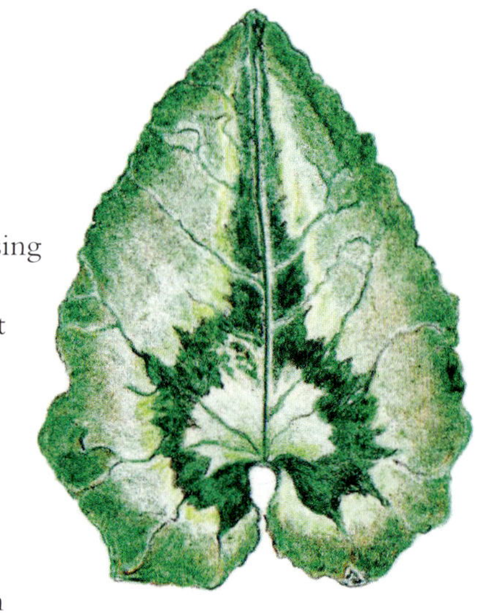

Above Coloured pencils skilfully used can give your artwork a painterly appearance.

Below Acrylic paints are probably more suitable for big, bold studies, such as this *Fascicularia bicolor*.

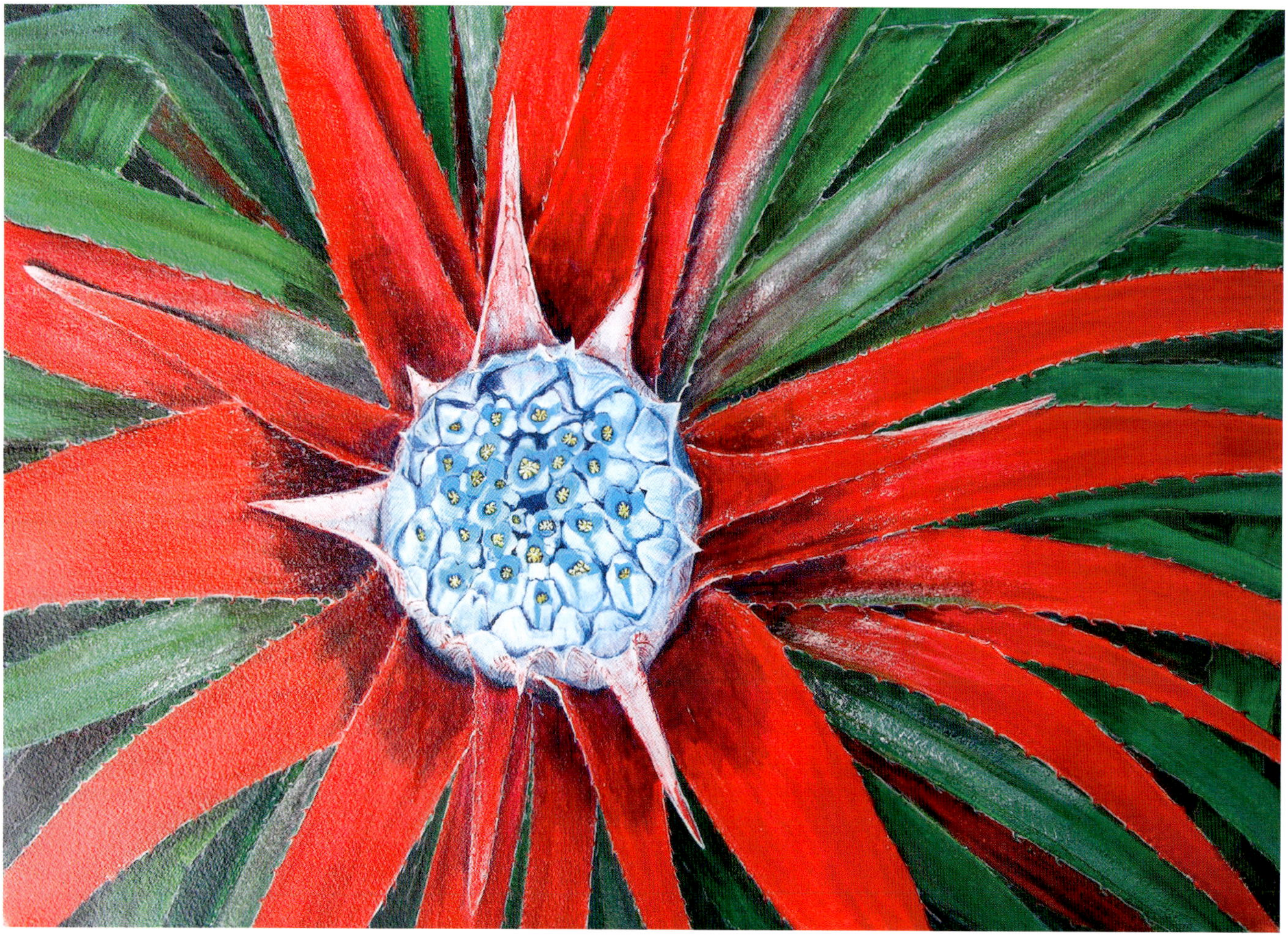

Tools and equipment

As with your paints and paper, you should always buy the best quality you can afford when it comes to tools such as brushes. However, much of what you need in this category comes from a range of everyday household items.

Brushes

Botanical art requires brushes which, while being full-bellied and holding a good quantity of paint, also come to a fine point. The finest brushes are made from Kolinsky sable. These qualities are met by several reputable manufacturers:

- Winsor & Newton Series 7 Round brushes (not the miniature range of the same name) are ideal for all levels of painter as they are of a high quality and reliable.
- The Da Vinci Series 10 Maestro range comprises high-quality watercolour brushes, more tapered than the Winsor & Newton series.
- Raphaël Kolinsky Red Sable Series 8404 are top-of-the-range brushes from France.
- Isabey Series 6228 Kolinsky Sable is another French brand of hand-made brushes and with a round, fine point.
- Escoda Kolinsky-Tajmyr Sable Series 1212 brushes are professional quality from Spain with round heads.

To start with, you will need just two brushes, sizes 1 and 3. You will also need a larger, cheaper synthetic brush for mixing paint – a size 6 would be ideal. Compare the prices of high-street art shops with those of online retailers. If you are buying in an art shop, it is perfectly acceptable to ask for a container of water so that you can check the point of the brush. Brushes from online retailers are less likely to have been handled as much as those in art shops, but retailers are usually happy to exchange goods if they are returned in the condition in which they were supplied.

Below Two Kolinsky sable brushes in sizes 1 and 3 will be sufficient to start with for most botanical subjects.

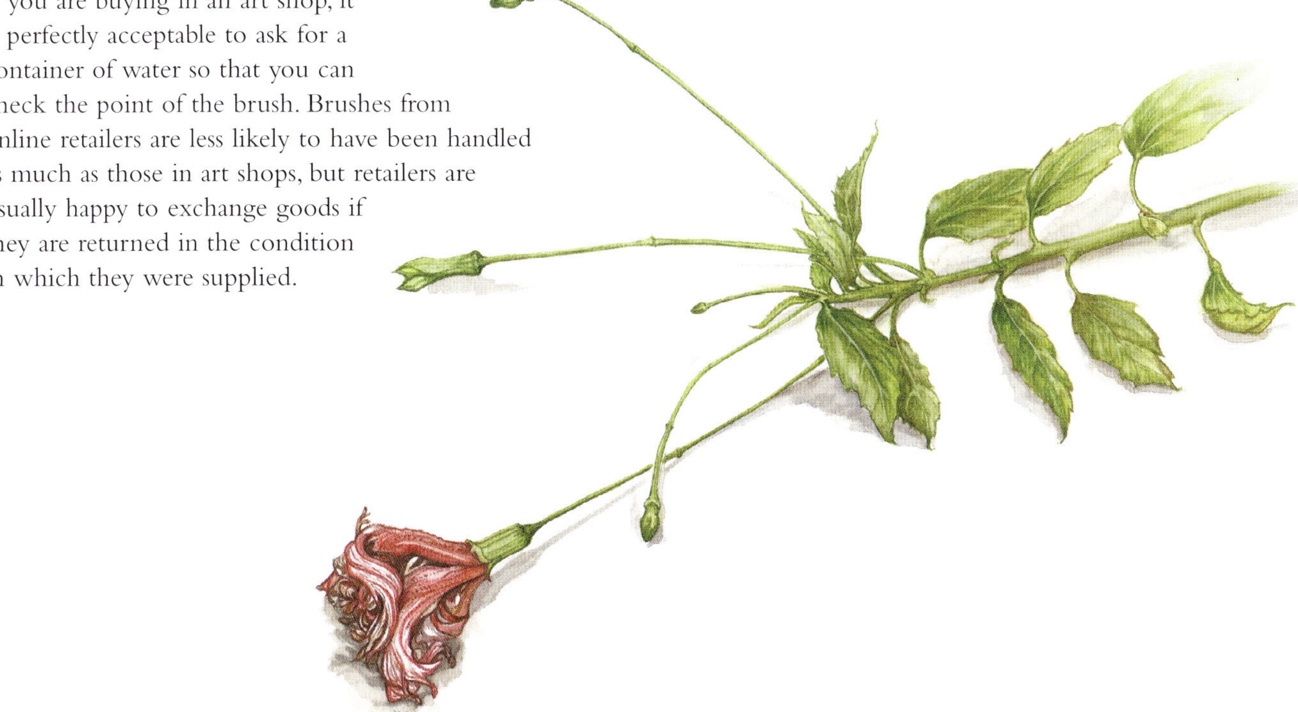

Taking care of your brushes

There are a few simple rules to ensure that your expensive brushes will give you many years of faithful service.

- Never leave brushes standing in the water pot; clean and dry them carefully and store point-uppermost in a dry jar. If travelling, keep them in a brush wallet – although a sheet of corrugated cardboard, rolled round the brushes and secured with an elastic band, makes a good cheap substitute.
- Don't use your brushes for anything other than watercolour. Never use with masking fluid – it's impossible to remove completely and your brush will never be the same again.
- After using white paint, wash the brush thoroughly in warm, soapy water and remove all traces of the paint, which can collect around the ferrule and leach out, making your watercolour opaque.
- Should your brush become damaged or lose its point, try gently working some soft soap into the hairs, form it into the correct shape with your fingers and leave to dry. Rinse thoroughly in warm water before use.

Pencil sharpeners

Keep your pencils sharp – so sharp that when the point is pressed into your fingertip, it hurts. You may be of the old school and like to use a sharp knife, or you may prefer a manual or electrically operated sharpener (see page 92). Whichever the case, sharpen your pencil little and often, and refine the point by turning it a few degrees off the horizontal and rotating it while rubbing gently on a sheet of fine sandpaper or an emery board. This is appropriate for mechanical pencils as well.

Erasers

While it's undesirable to use an eraser much, you'll inevitably need one at some point, even if it's only to rub out any remaining pencil lines once your painting is finished. The choice is between a putty eraser and a hard white one such as are made by Staedtler and Faber Castell. To achieve delicate erasing with a putty eraser, pinch it into a point; in the case of a hard white eraser, cut off a small piece or shave it to a point. Also available from art suppliers are eraser pencils and small battery-operated erasers, both of which can be sharpened to a point.

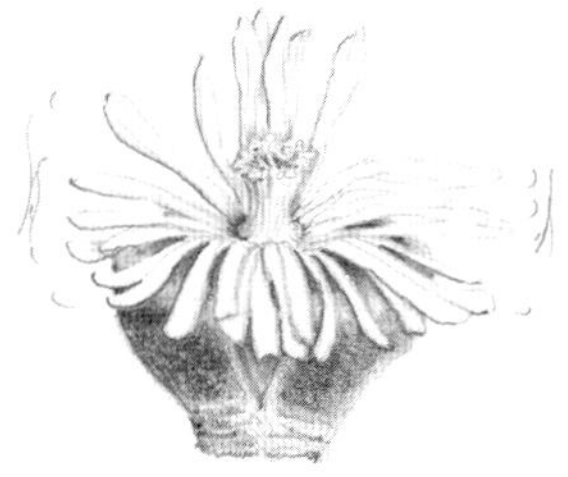

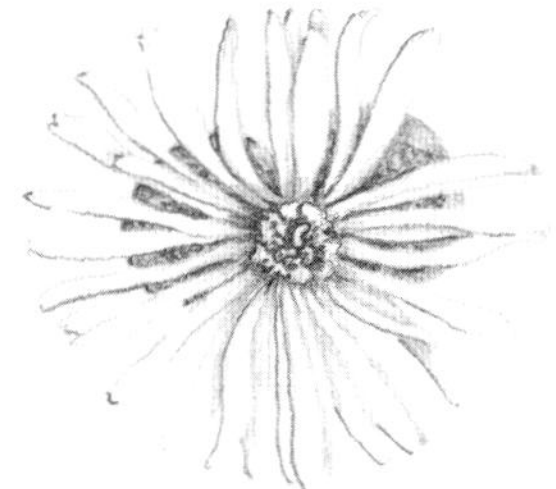

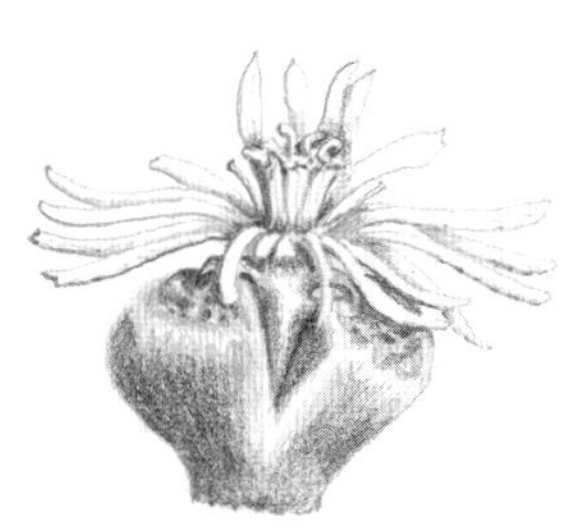

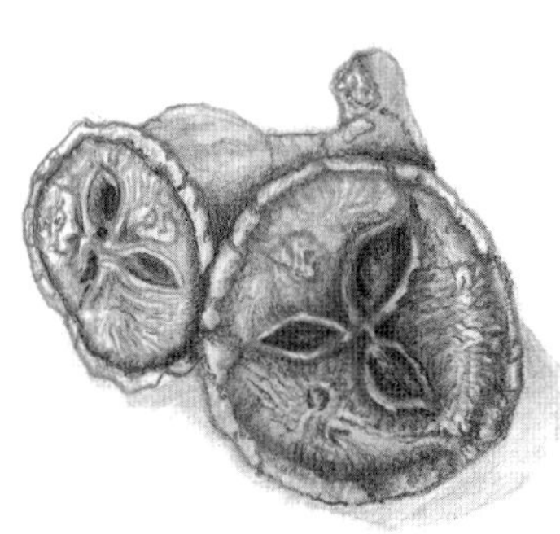

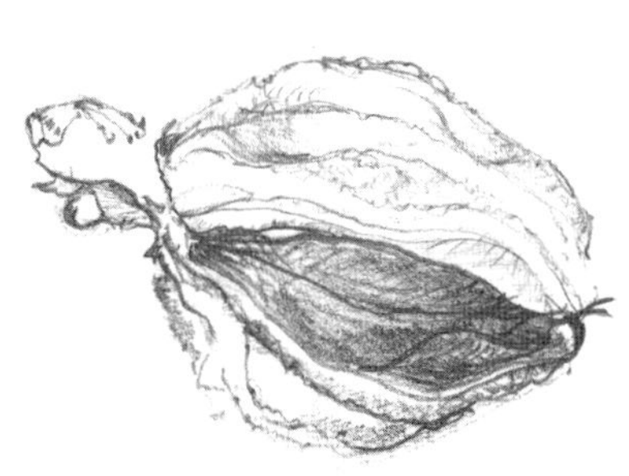

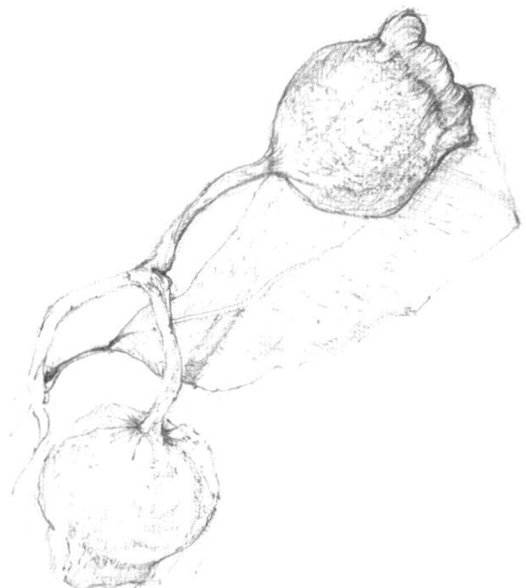

Exercise: Using masking fluid

This detail of a fern crozier (below) is a good example of the benefit of masking fluid (see page 22). First, draw the overall form and shape, then focus on any structures within the overall object that need shaping. Finally, consider and add detail.

Apply masking fluid using an adjustable ruling pen to give lines of differing thickness when masking all the hairs and scales. You will find that your drawing is more or less covered with masking fluid marks and squiggles at this stage.

You can use wet-into-wet washes to begin with, with various greens. Then build up the colours using deeper greens, blended with a damp brush to make the fern look three-dimensional. Once you are happy with it, rub off the masking fluid. The resulting white marks will look stark and will need softening with some appropriate subtle colours and further shadows added. Paint the scales brown at this stage and add further detail using an almost-dry brush.

Below An enlarged section of the fern crosier shown on page 31 demonstrates the skilled use of masking fluid to give fine furry detail.

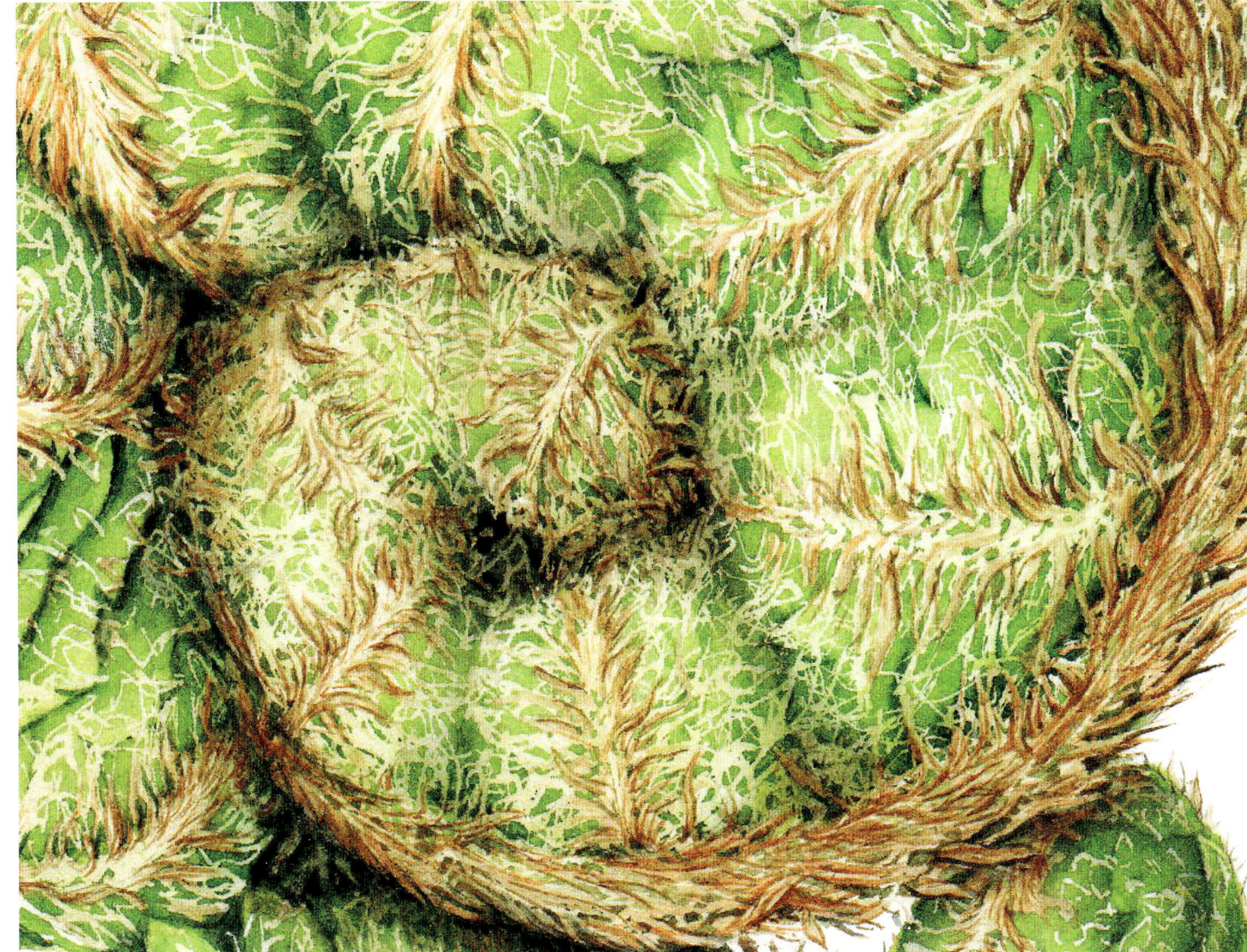

Other useful equipment

You will no doubt acquire a range of equipment that is particular to your tastes, but the following are useful for nearly every botanical artist.

- **Two large jars** for clean water – one to wash your brush, the other to mix your colours.
- **A magnifying glass** for seeing and painting small details. Hand-held magnifying glasses are available from opticians and other outlets, but the disadvantage of these is that your spare hand is fully occupied when it could be put to better use holding a paint rag. Use a free-standing one if possible.
- **A paint rag** or roll of kitchen paper has multiple uses – wiping your brush, blotting wet paint, cleaning up spills, and so on.
- **A tilted drawing board**, or a plain board with a 7.5–10cm (3–4in) block to raise the end, enables you to sit comfortably but ensures that your line of sight is roughly at right angles to your work surface.
- **Masking fluid**, a thick liquid latex which dries to a rubbery consistency and may be painted over once dry. Brands include Winsor & Newton Art Masking Fluid and Pebeo Drawing Gum. Use with extreme caution to block out small areas before applying a wash. Don't leave it on the paper for any length of time, and remove by rubbing gently with an eraser once the paint is totally dry. Do not apply it with a precious brush as it will be ruined; use a sharpened quill, a fine-nibbed mapping pen or a ruling pen as used by mapmakers. Ruling pens are adjustable and deliver lines of differing thickness, as shown at the top of the dried cardoon seedhead (right).
- **A large feather** or a **cosmetic brush** to clear your paper of eraser detritus – don't use your hand as this will deposit a fine layer of natural oils on the paper. Wash and dry the feather first, of course.
- **Mixing palettes** of various shapes and types, available from art suppliers, or a large white china plate. Having lots of space for colour mixing is important.
- **Masking tape** is useful for all sorts of things, from holding your paper in place to positioning your specimen.
- **A 'third arm'** – a contraption of adjustable arms and clips, available from model-making suppliers – is also useful for holding a specimen. Alternatives include a block of florist's oasis; some crumpled chicken wire; a plastic milk bottle with the top cut off (small items can go in the cut-off handle, larger ones in the main cavity); a bottle weighted with sand; a bulldog clip on the edge of your drawing board, and so on. Be inventive!
- **A ruler and a pair of dividers** for measuring. However, when you are a beginner draughtsman it is important to train your eye. Try to rely on your observational drawing techniques and use your dividers only as a back-up to check any measurements.
- **A razor blade**, craft knife or scalpel for dissections.
- **A microscope** will open up a whole new world for you but is not strictly necessary.
- **A digital camera** is useful for recording details, together with a computer and printer (see pages 26–29).

Right A large block of oasis or a piece of wood with a hole drilled in it would make a good 'third arm', able to accommodate a heavy object such as this dried cardoon (artichoke) head.

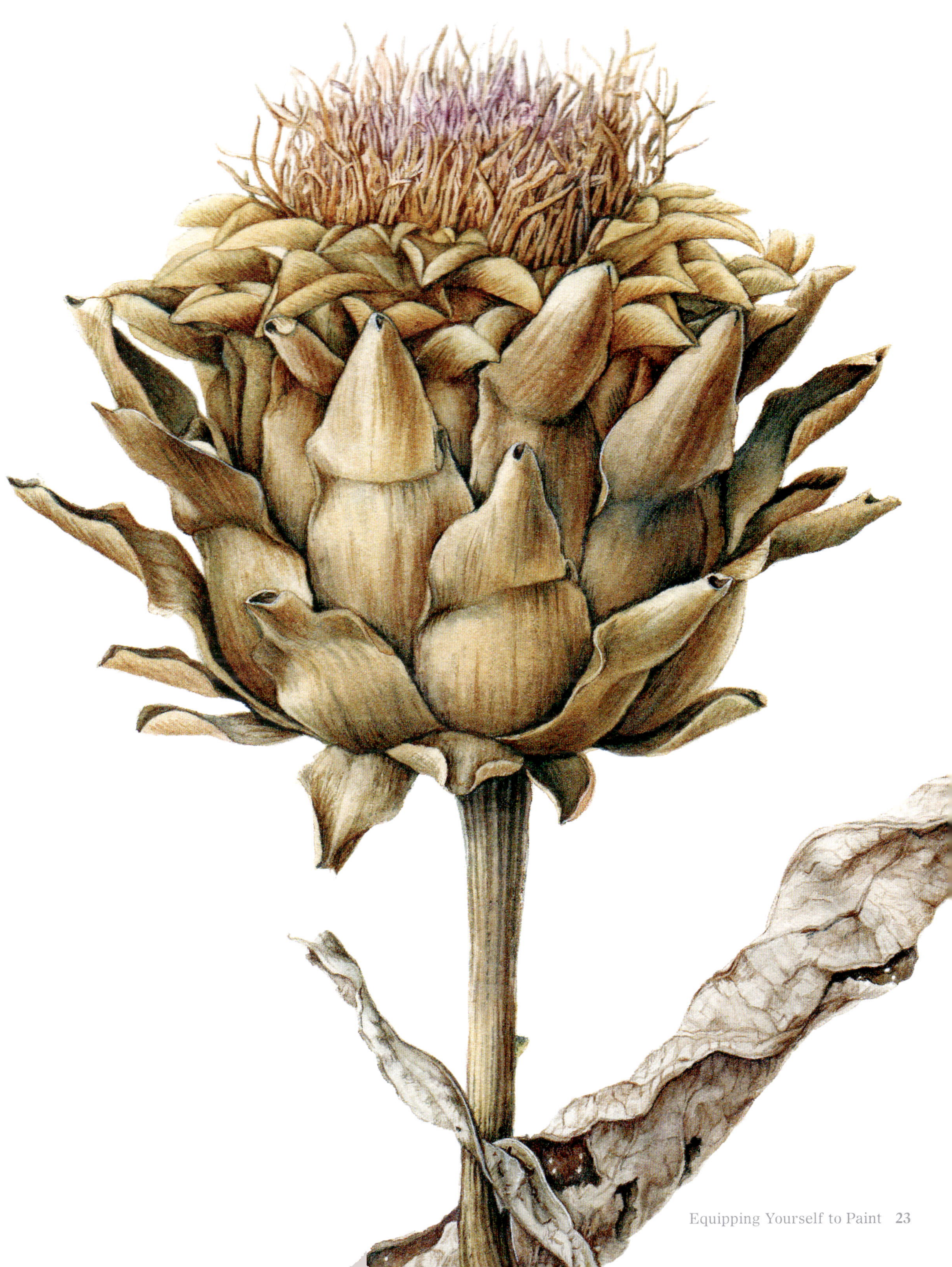

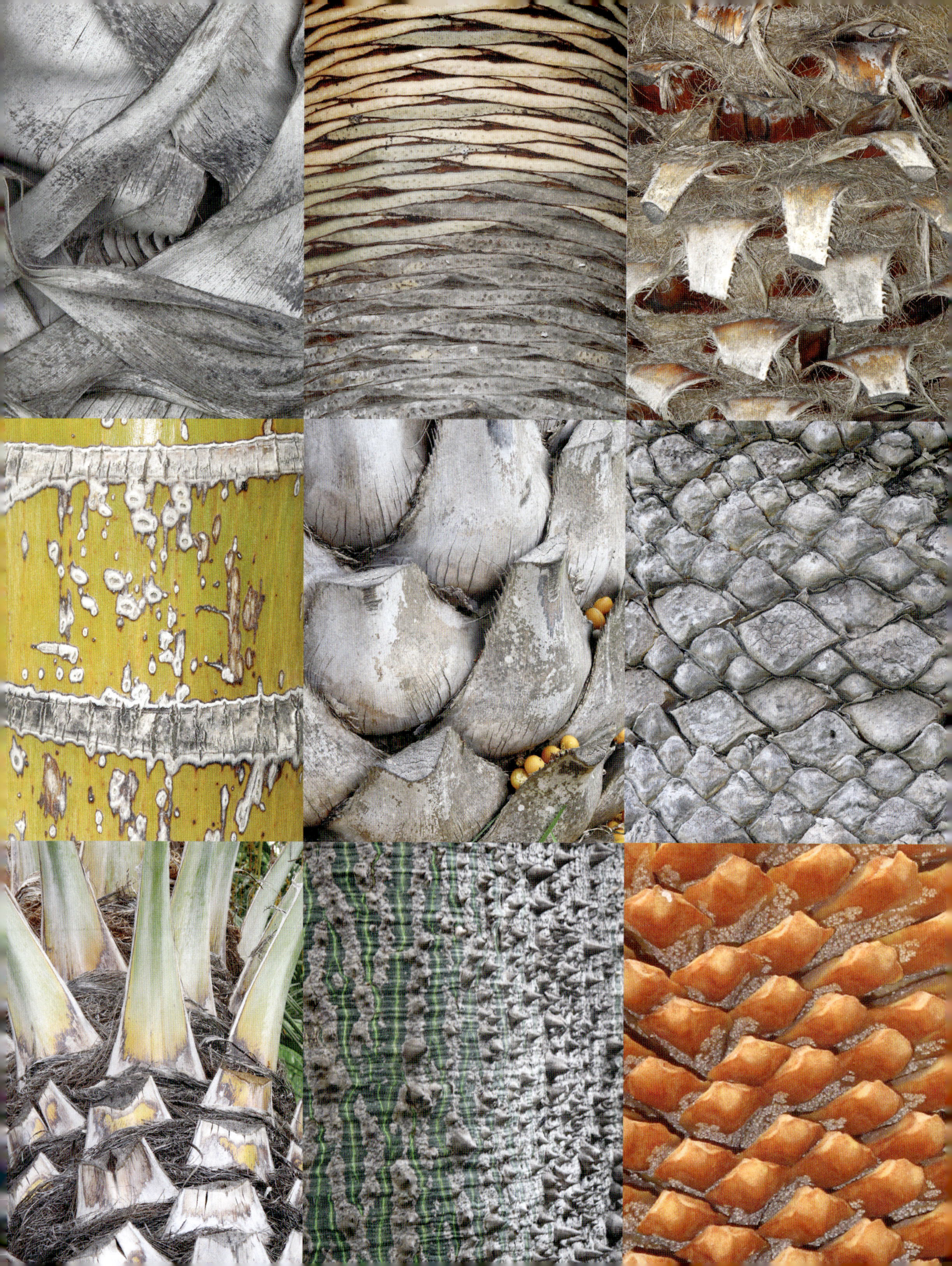

Harnessing Technology

Artists have always used the technology available at the time to make their job easier. It's widely believed that Old Masters since the early fifteenth century, such as Caravaggio, Holbein, Leonardo, Ingres and Vermeer, used mirrors and lenses to make projected images, enabling them to draw with great accuracy. In the early 1800s the *camera lucida* was invented, showing a reflected view of the subject on the drawing surface, and has been used by many artists since then. This theory is set out comprehensively and decisively by David Hockney in his book *Secret Knowledge* (2001).

In the first decades of the 21st century we have even more technology at our disposal, mainly in the form of computers, printers and digital cameras, which can be found in the majority of households. The overall pace of modern life is a lot faster than it was in the fifteenth century, but botanical illustration remains a slow and painstaking art. It therefore makes sense to give a bit of thought to how we can make things easier for ourselves by harnessing modern technology without compromising our work.

Yet it remains the case that every artist, and especially a botanical artist, should strive to be a competent draughtsman, as this is about far more than copying what you see. Draw every day if possible, because it is only by doing so that you will become a good draughtsman – and only then should you allow yourself to explore the use of technology. Remember, it's only an aid.

Left A camera can be a useful tool, recording subject matter and inspiring further work. Take pictures like these, showing different plant textures, and then try to draw them accurately in a sketchbook to help develop your technique.

Using photographs

Try to avoid working exclusively from a photograph of a plant. A photograph has already rendered your subject two-dimensional, and much information is lost. How does the plant grow? How do its various parts join together? What happens round the back? You need to study the three-dimensional subject before you can portray it two-dimensionally. The lack of in-depth knowledge of your subject means that copying from a photograph can make your subject appear bland and uninteresting.

Photographs also often reduce the size of the subject. How will you be able to show a large plant at life-size if it is constrained by a sheet of A4 photographic paper? It is essential to have the physical plant in front of you, or at least to have studied it and made copious notes, not least because photographs are simply not reliable as a record of colour. Neither the camera nor the printer can be guaranteed to give an accurate rendition of colour. The asparagus photograph and watercolour shown here demonstrate this.

Having said that, now consider trying to paint *Hymenocallis speciosa* or the spider lily (right). This is a plant of about 2ft (60cm) in height and the flowers are about 18cm (7in) in diameter, but quite flat. It is native to the United States, Mexico, Central America, South America and the Caribbean. Each plant bears between two and nine fragrant flowers. The anthers are on very long stalks, away from the centre of the flower.

You are unlikely to have a plant like this in your studio for the length of time it would take to draw and paint it, therefore sketches, colour notes and photographs are of prime importance to keep the image fresh in your mind. This is where photographs do come into their own.

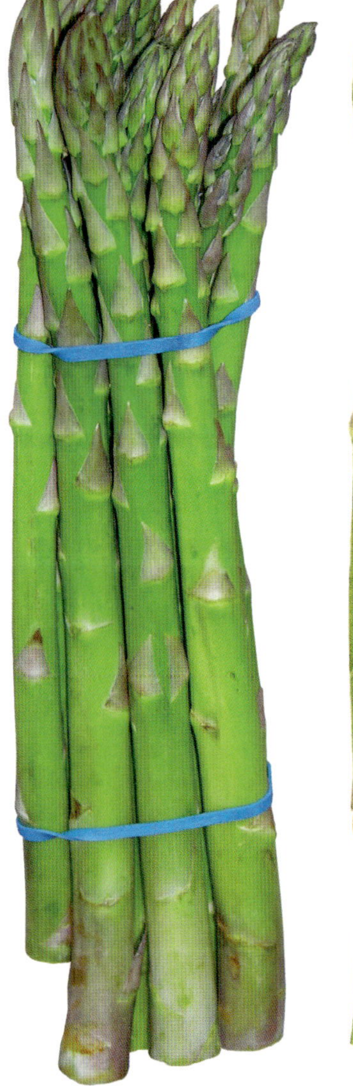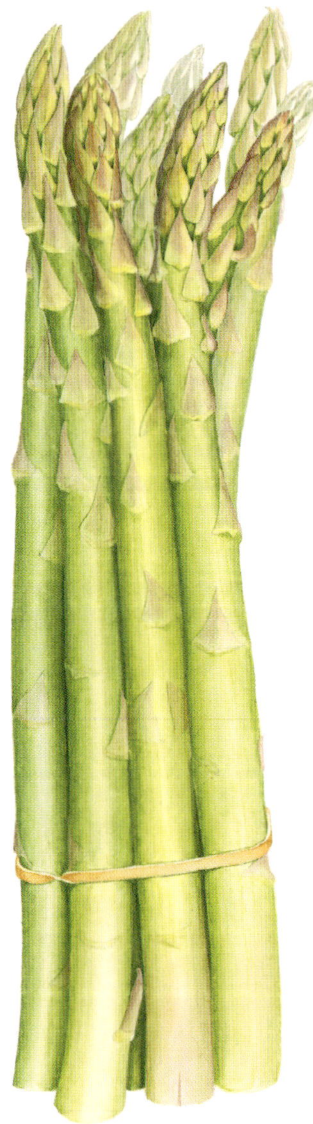

Right Use a photograph as an aid only – it is still essential to have the plant in front of you, or to have studied it in detail. This is especially true when it comes to reproducing colour accurately.

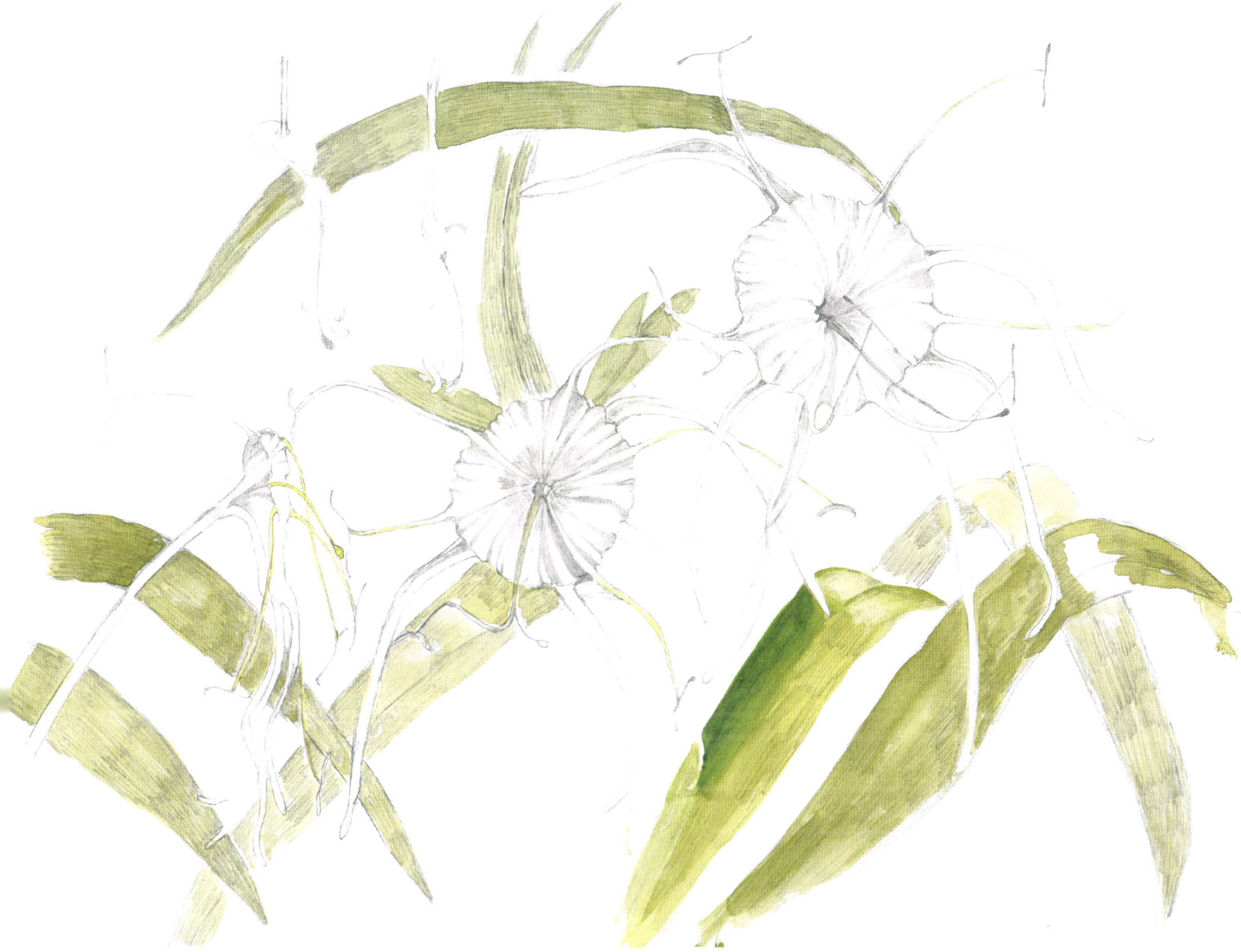

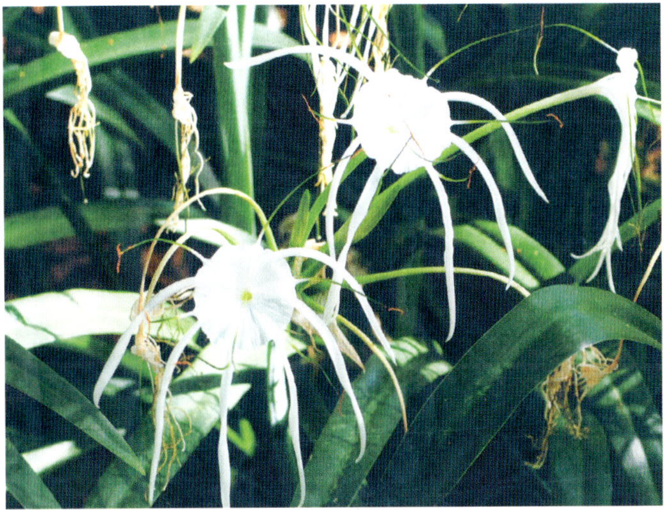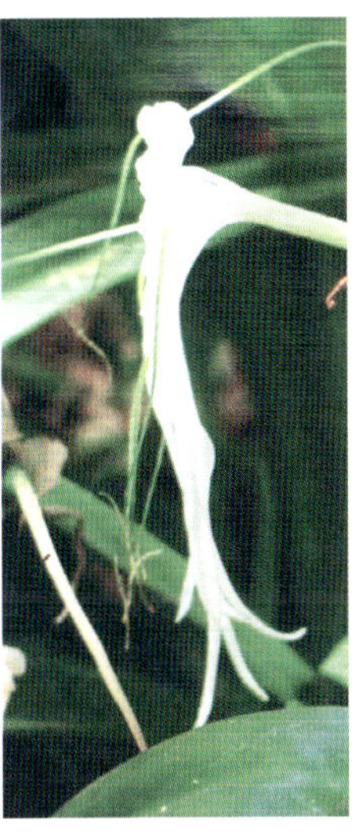

Above and left Photographs are useful if your plant is short-lived or you are unable to have it in your studio for long enough to complete your painting, as would be the case with this spider lily (*Hymenocallis speciosa*).

Using a photograph to suggest a design

You may wish to use a photograph for a design, rather than a botanically correct painting, and here digital technology is very useful as you can easily see what happens when you crop and zoom in on a photograph on screen, looking for different views and effects.

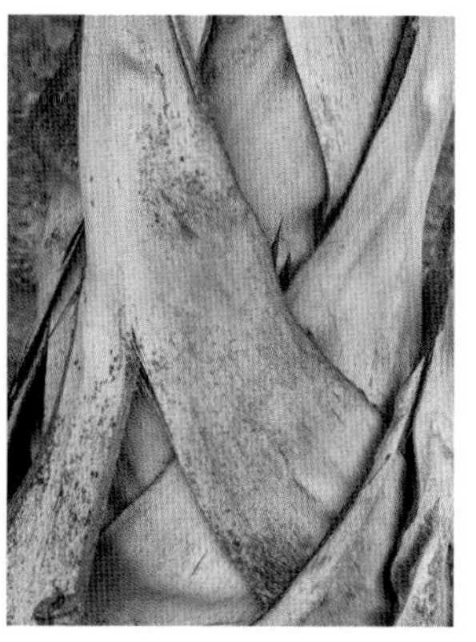

Palm tree

Page 24 shows a series of photographs taken of different barks with geometric shapes found on the island of Madeira, all of which could be used to make exciting and unusual designs. A similar one (shown right) has been painstakingly worked up into a sophisticated pencil drawing (below right) via a diagrammatical line drawing and a rough, simplified version (below left).

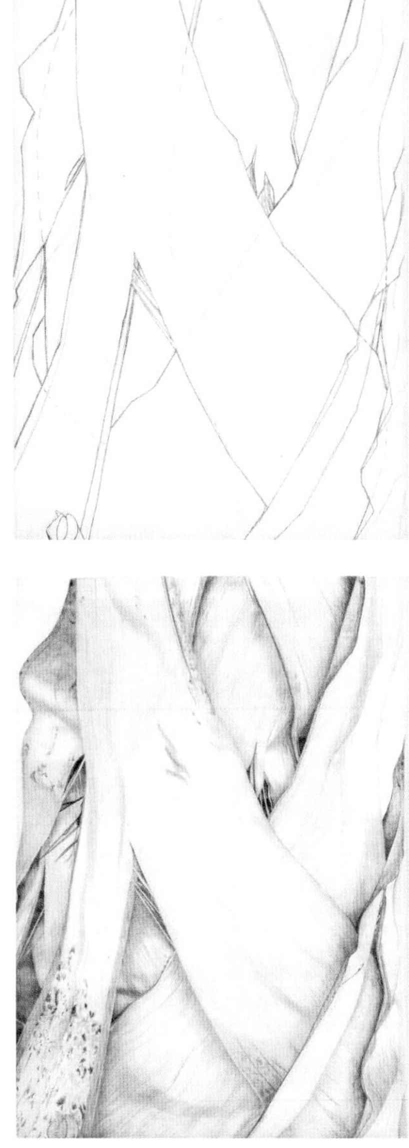

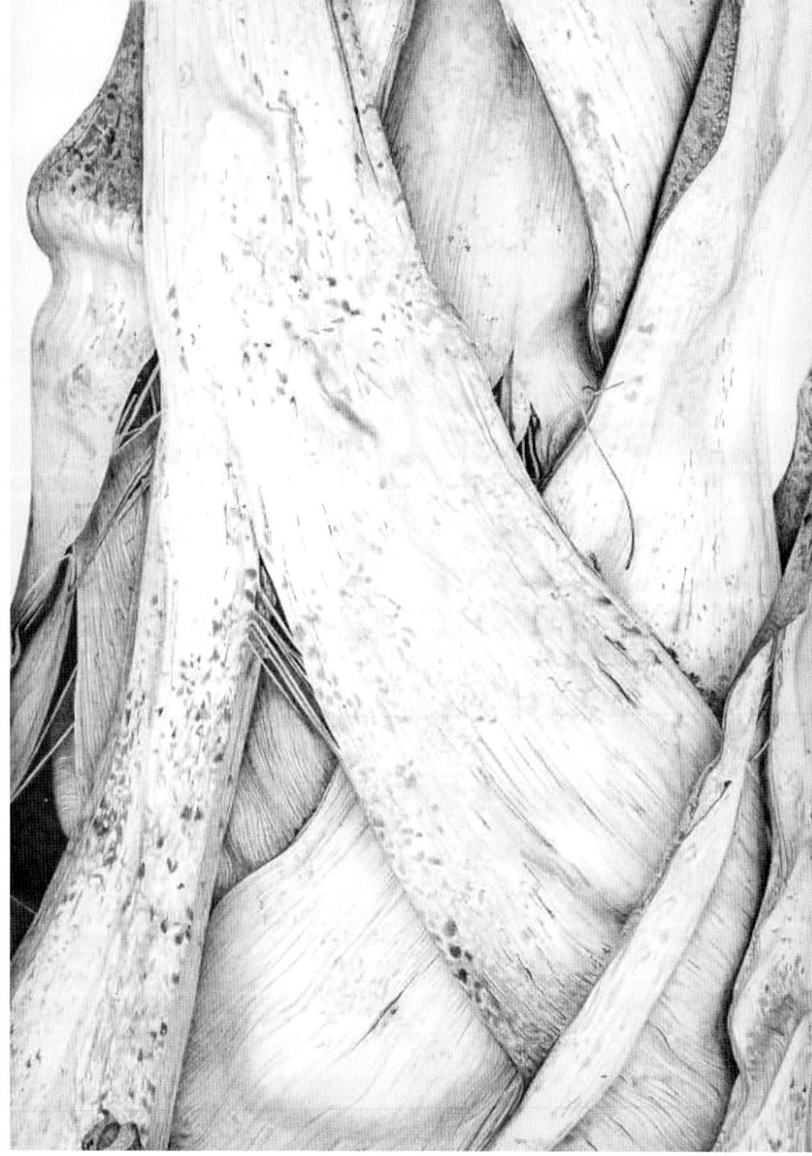

Pineapple design

For this design, a section of pineapple was photographed (right). From this a simple outline drawing was made (below the photograph), which was used for various treatments, some involving the whole square of design, others simply extracting just a part. The basic shape of one small segment was used for designs such as the psychedelic colours, the green 'bird', the 'aboriginal' treatment, the pen-and-ink doodle and the blue and violet 'iceberg' (below). How would you interpret the pineapple design?

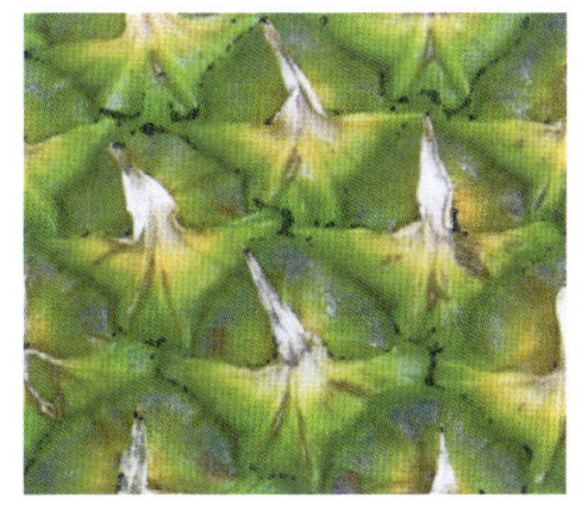

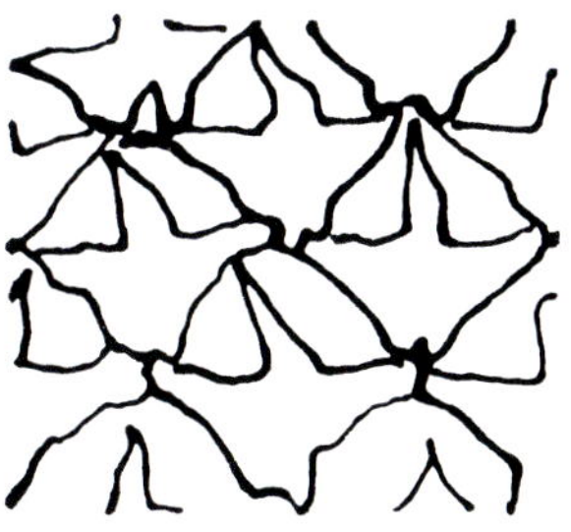

Above and left Make an outline drawing from a photograph of a section of pineapple (above) and use it to suggest different treatments (left and below).

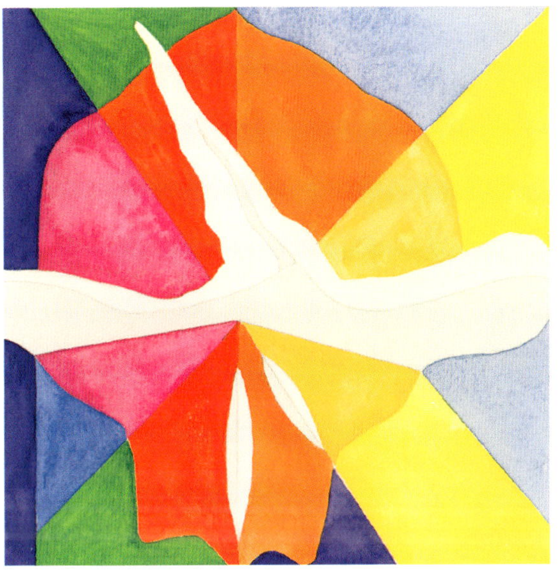

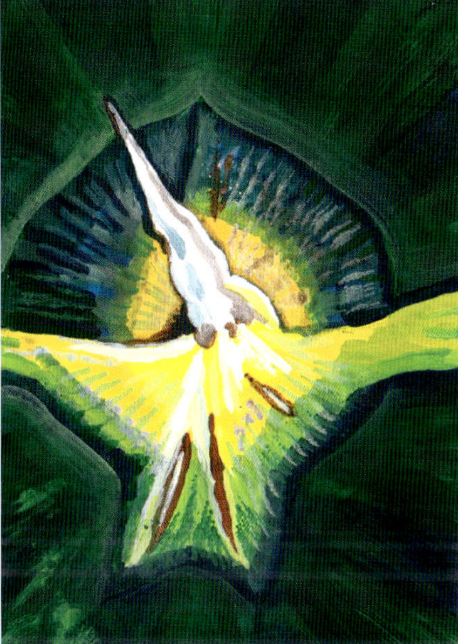

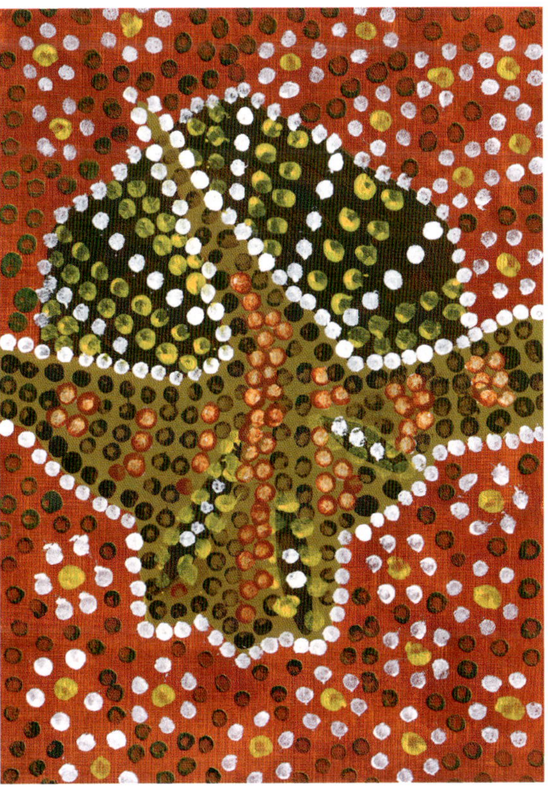

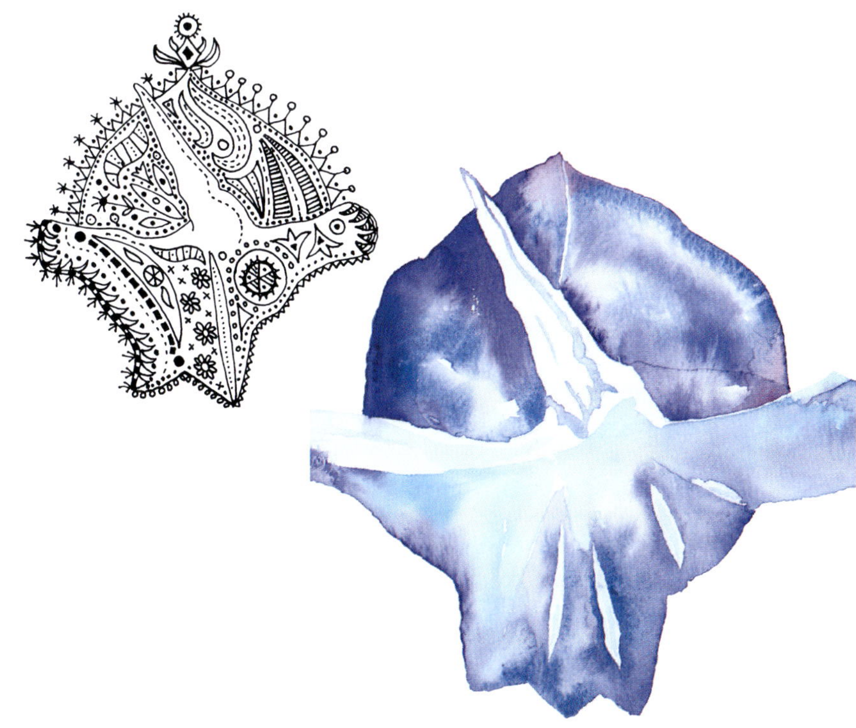

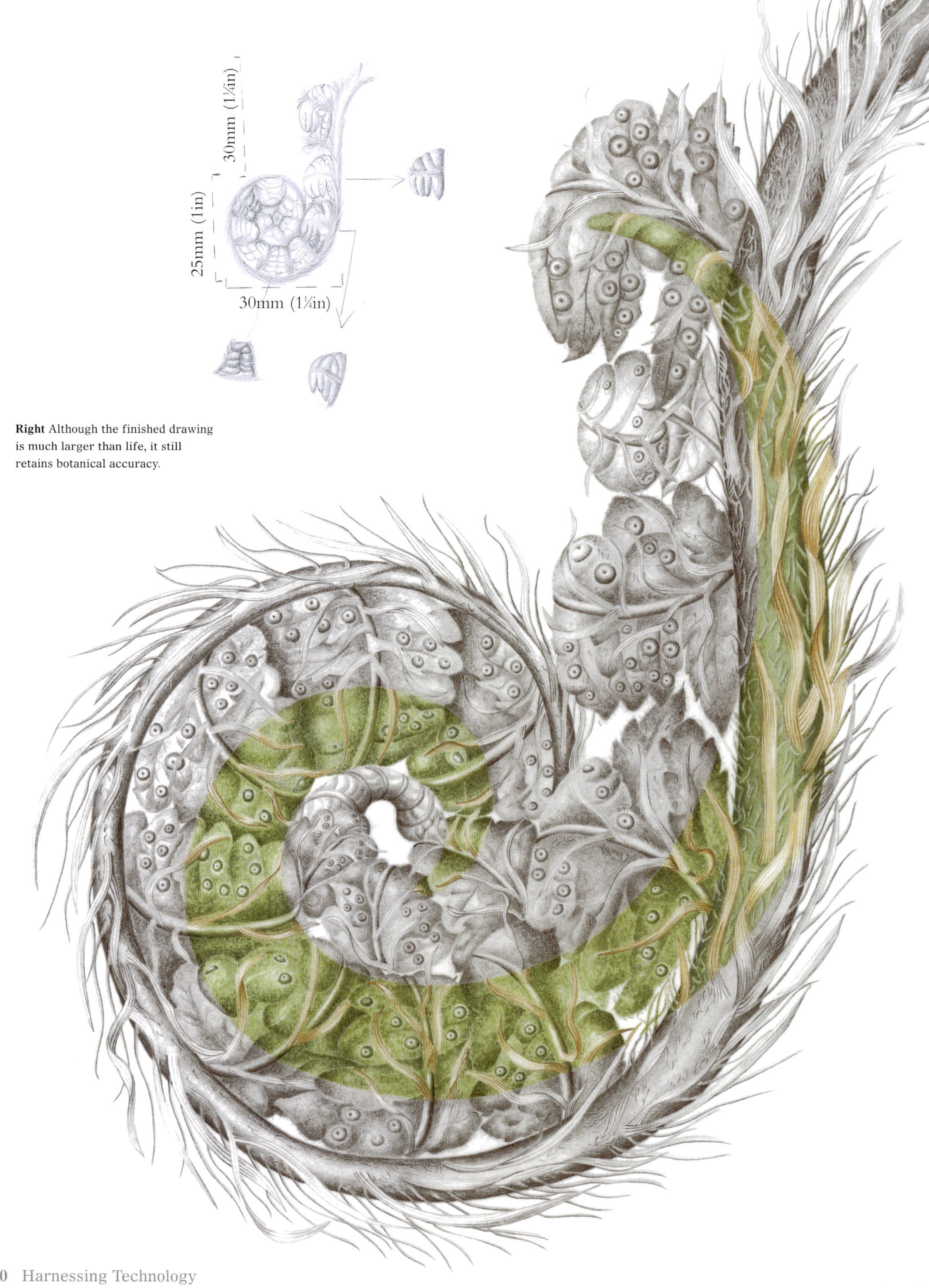

Right Although the finished drawing is much larger than life, it still retains botanical accuracy.

Enlarging your subject

These very different versions of an unfurling fern frond (left and below) have both been enlarged dramatically. Scaling subjects up not only represents nature in a true and accurate way, but allows us to see each specimen's structure in an era when most of us lack the time to stop and admire plants at their best. Where a subject is small, like the unfurling fern, magnifying it makes it easier for us to study its fascinating structure.

Enlarging on the computer

If you are reasonably skilled with a computer, it is possible to shrink or enlarge your subject on screen.

Start by measuring your plant material. Then photograph it, download the image on to your computer and use photo-editing software to enlarge it to the size needed. The fern crosier (below) was enlarged x5 in this way. Use a combination of the enlarged photograph and the real thing, and study it under a magnifying glass to draw it to the desired size.

There is no substitute for having the living material to check structure and detail and, certainly when painting, you should refer primarily to the subject. You might find a digital microscope useful for checking finer detail. Even if the detail is too small to include in the final painting, it can inform the texture and detail that you can see at your chosen enlargement. In this way you can make sure you know how the subject 'works' before you start painting.

Below If you are skilled with a computer, try shrinking or enlarging your subject on screen to enable you to paint it the way you want.

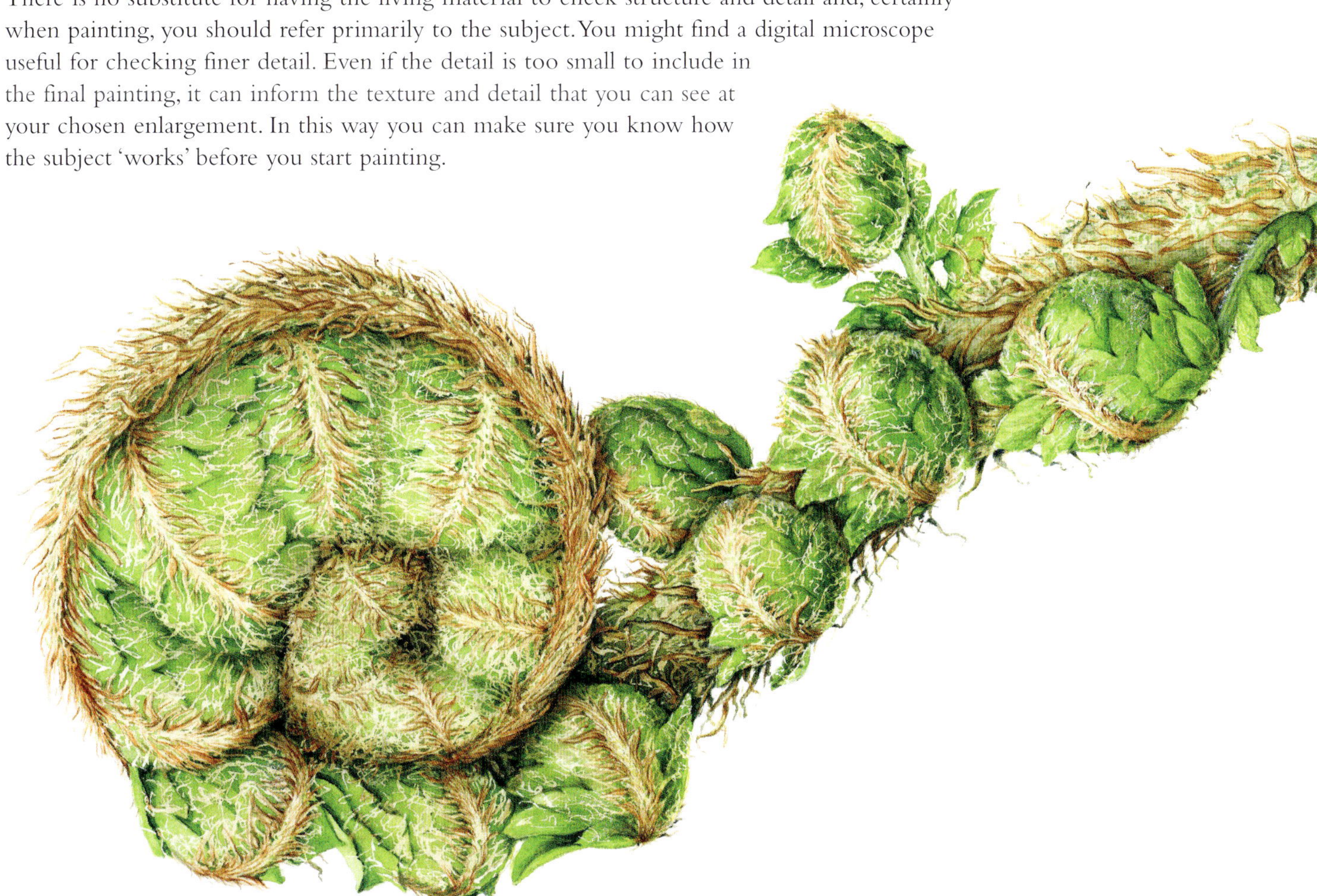

Exercise: Enlarging using a ruler

The cut section of a banana stem (shown opposite) was worked from life. It is enhanced by the coloured spiral, which, while being an idiosyncratic treatment, seems to be particularly apt for this subject. The actual stem section measured 40 x 35mm (1½ x 1⅜in). This was scaled up by x8.1, giving a width of 324mm (12¾in) and a height of 291.6mm (11½in). To do this, the artist drew a line 8.1cm (3in) long to represent 1cm (⅜in), and measured all parts of the drawing against this.

Step 1

Draw the subject actual size.

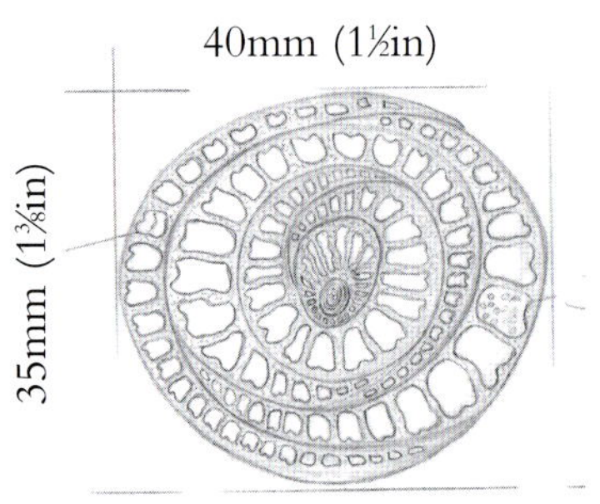

Step 2

Study the different parts of the subject, such as the cell structure, and make drawings of what you see. At this stage you might like to scale up small elements of the design and make notes. Try different grades of pencil to see which one is best suited to which section.

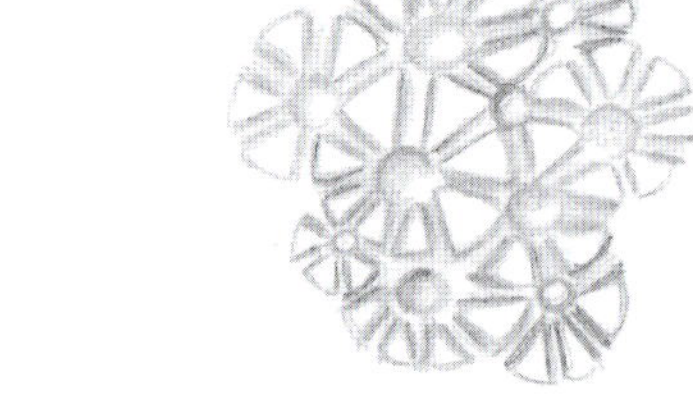

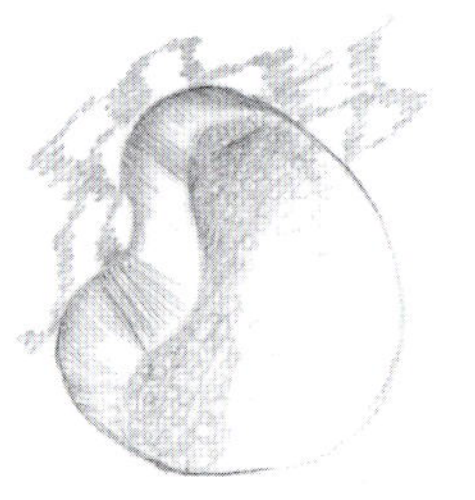

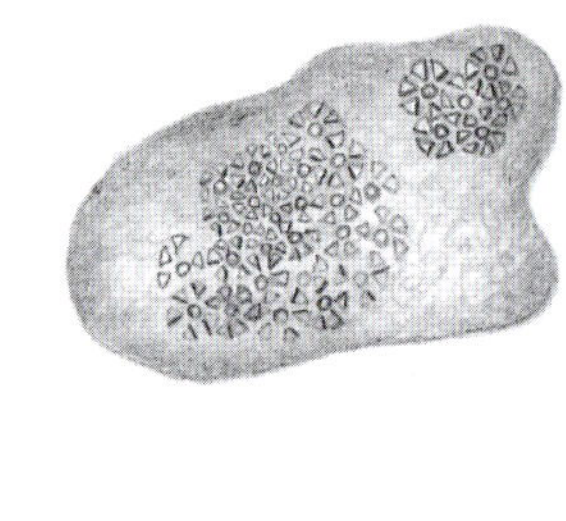

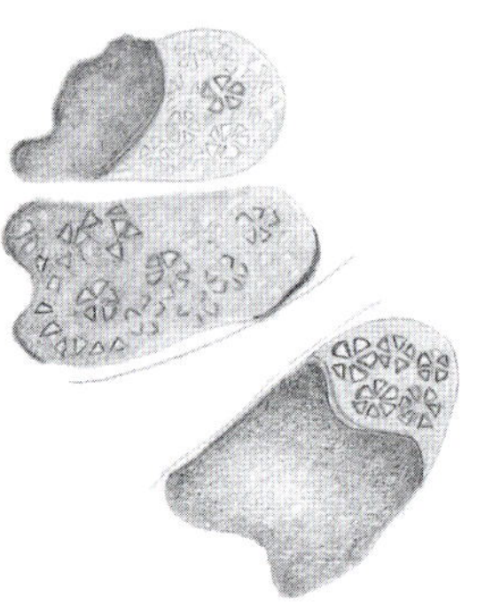

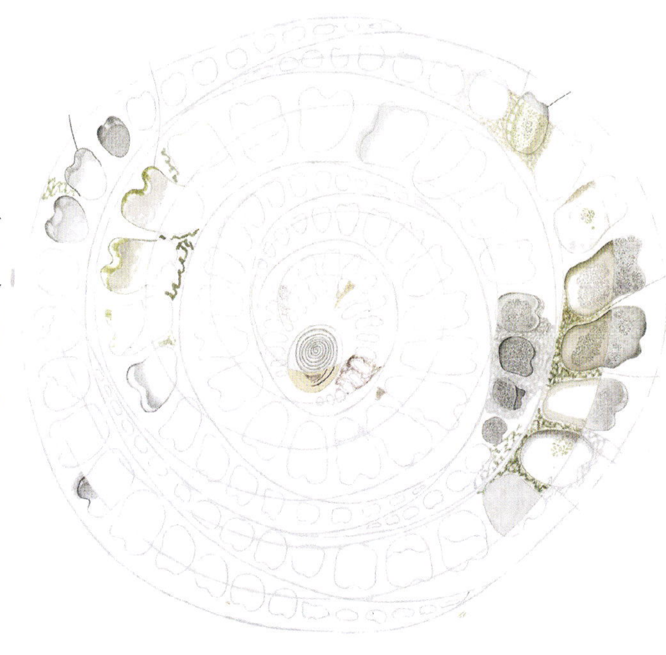

Step 3

Scale up the subject as an accurate pencil drawing by multiplying your original measurements by the amount you wish to enlarge – here x8. Use this to test colours and how you will apply them, as well as different techniques of shading and painting, to find the best way to achieve the true form and textures. Make notes on the worksheet to remind yourself that certain elements may be darker, or to list the colours that you may need (greens, greys, creams); that some greys might need a little blue added, others a little pink. This is the time, also, to work out how you are going to show the minuscule patterns and textures in the different parts of your subject.

Step 4

Keeping your practice piece by you at all times, start
to work on your final piece in pencil and paint. Assess
your work throughout.

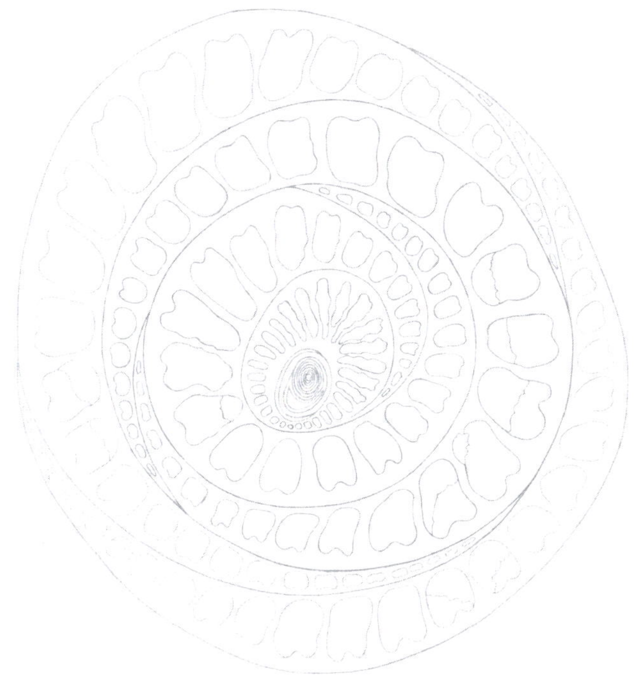

Step 5

Make a final assessment and put in the final touches,
such as deeper tones and sharper lines.

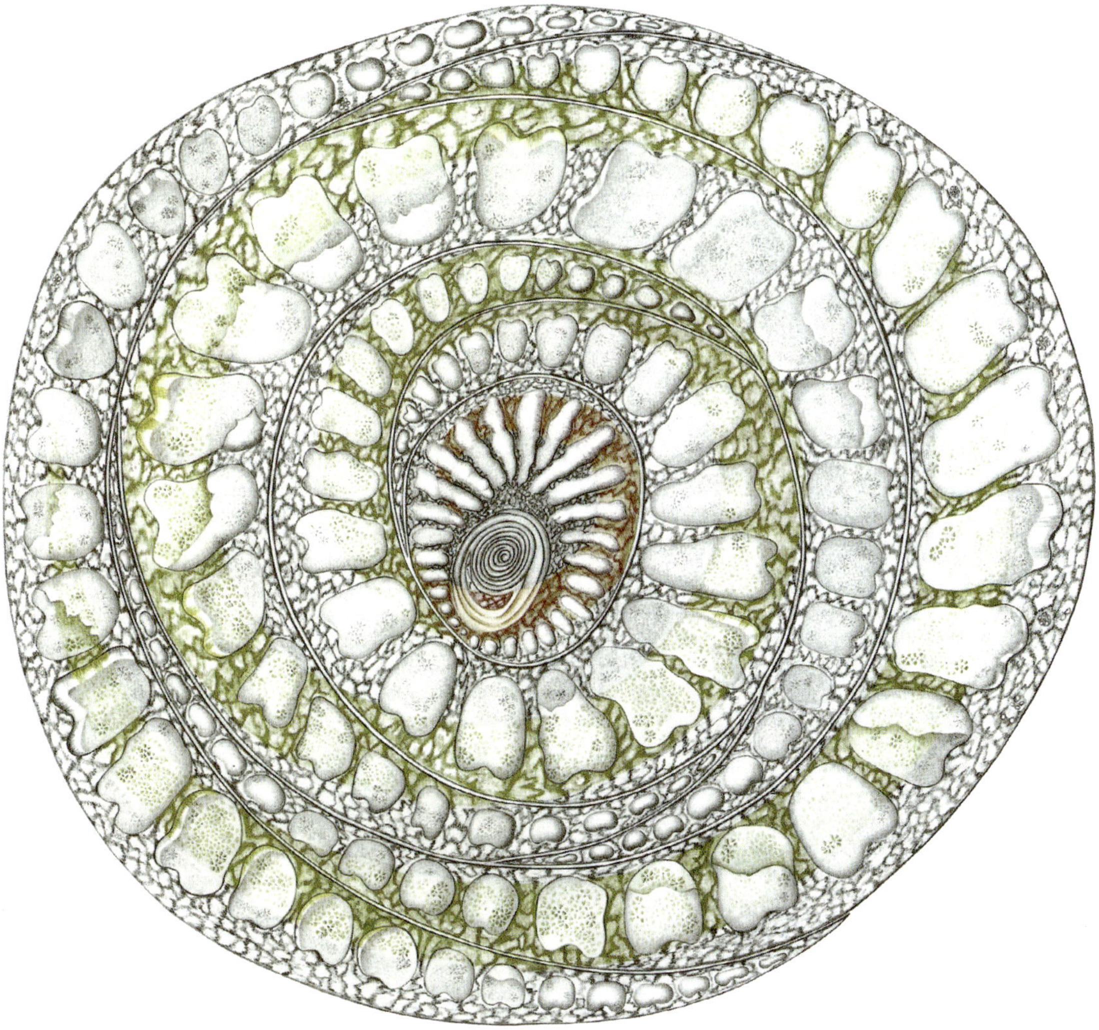

Composition

The art of composition is all about placing your subject on the paper in a way that makes your illustration attractive to the viewer. There is, after all, no point in making a painstakingly accurate record of a plant if the viewer's eye passes quickly over it.

The first thing to consider is how you are going to show your subject. For example, you could choose to do a simple portrait or a complex arrangement such as the floral cornucopias seen in 17th-century Dutch paintings; you might prefer a design in which large subjects are cropped at the edges, or where several specimens are arranged with no apparent relationship to one another, as painted so beautifully by the late Rory McEwen; or maybe subjects shown in their natural environment as portrayed by Margaret Mee or, conversely, scientifically based breakdowns and diagrams of an individual specimen.

Once you have decided upon your subject and your approach to it, the next thing to think about is the format that will be suitable. Is it going to be portrait (upright) or landscape (horizontal) in shape, or maybe square? For instance, it would be uncharacteristic to put a tall, thin flower into a landscape format. Two very different compositions are demonstrated by *Micranthus junceus* (right) and *Arisarum proboscideum* (below), known as the mouse-tail plant because of its long, tail-like spathes. The first is tall and thin, while the second is shown in its typical attitude, curling randomly over the paper.

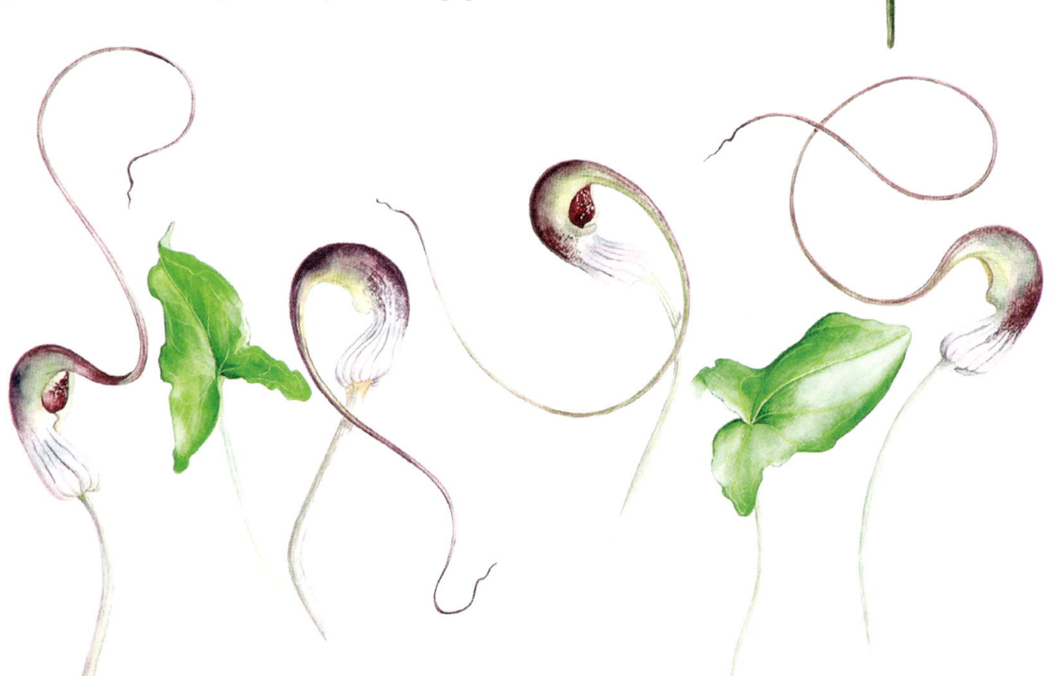

Above and left *Micranthus junceus* is tall and thin (above), while *Arisarum proboscideum*, the mouse-tail plant, curls randomly across the paper (left).

Some other points to consider when planning your composition are:

- The space around the specimen.
- The distance from the top, bottom and sides of the page.
- The focal point, to which you wish to draw the viewer's eye, such as a fine flowerhead.
- The dynamics of a group, for example making sure that the painting is not too top-, bottom- or side-heavy. Packing most of the interest into one small area can easily draw attention away from the most important element.

One of your objectives is to show how the plant grows. To do this, make sure that you have chosen a specimen that is typical of its type, with consistent characteristics – the correct colour, undamaged, and so on. If you are uncertain, research your plant before you start to draw it, and if you know any botanists, exploit their knowledge shamelessly.

Make a list of things to look at before you begin: the way the leaves grow off the stem; any particular characteristics of the leaf margins; the arrangement of veins on the leaves; the number of petals, stamens and other parts. You might even like to show the roots, as in the case of the *Micranthus junceus* (left). Paint the plant life-size, unless it is very small or very large. If you paint it other than life-size, you might like to indicate this by use of a scale bar (see pages 51 and 52), depending on the purpose of the picture.

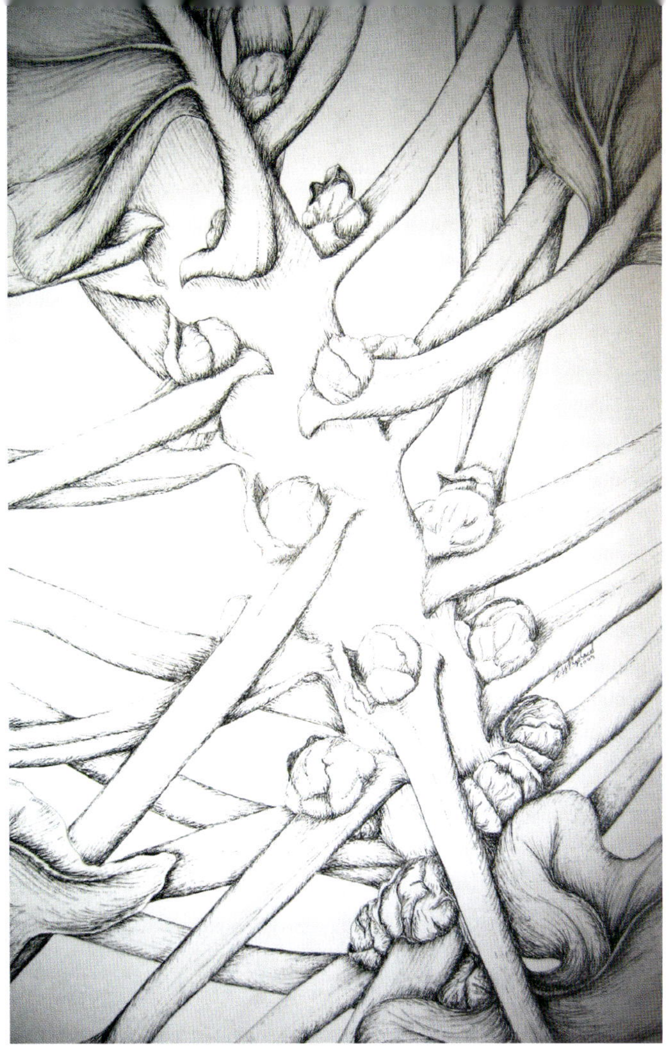

Above Brussels sprouts, a common garden vegetable, are given an amusing and exotic treatment. The illustration has a skeletal look about it and a resemblance to early medieval drawings. Rather than leave plenty of white paper around the plant, the artist has cropped it to fit into a much smaller space.

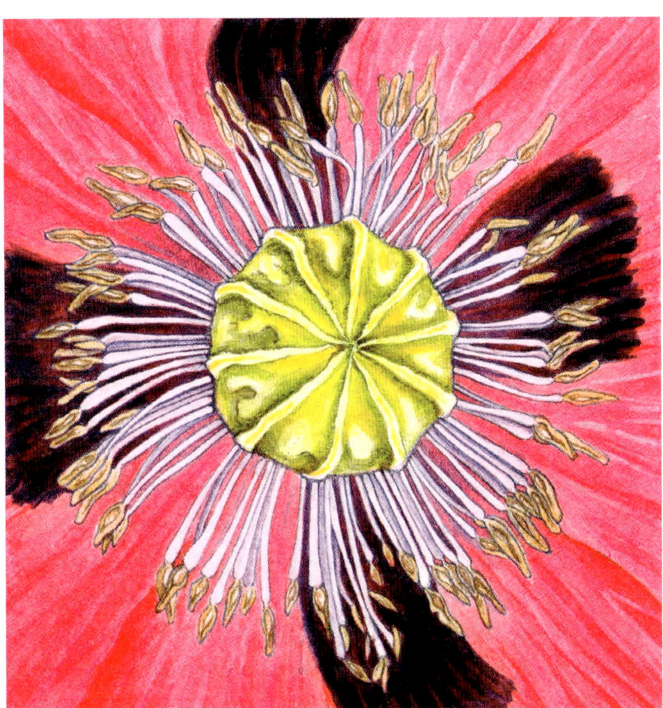

Left This poppy heart was painted from a close-up photograph, which showed very clearly the yellow-green centre, the stamens and the petals. While it's tending towards abstraction, the image is based upon an accurate representation of the plant. For such a complex drawing, in which the stamens are multi-layered and the flower itself may not last the time it would take to create the initial drawing, a photograph can be a valuable source of inspiration.

Deciding on a composition

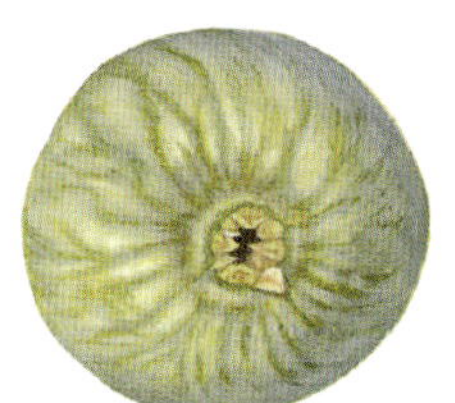

Spend as much time as you can planning your composition before you begin to work on what will be your completed illustration. In nature there are always beautiful compositions that occur naturally, without any manipulation or help from the artist, but don't just accept your first thought – explore as many different possibilities as you can, experimenting with different formats to see which one suits your subject in a variety of arrangements.

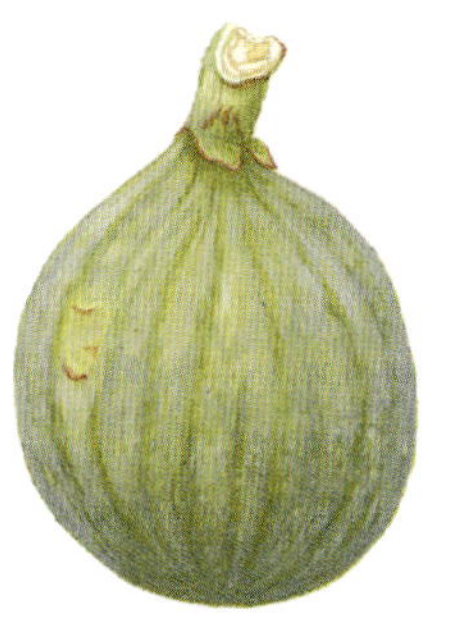

Using cheap layout paper and an HB pencil to draw small samples – about postcard size or less – is a quick and easy way to embark on this; if you carry out your experiments on a larger scale, it's useful to prop your compositions against a wall, since mistakes as well as successes will become apparent as you re-enter the room and see them afresh.

When composing your picture, don't forget that you will probably want to place it in a mount and maybe a frame too. Leave enough blank paper around your subject to give plenty of scope for this (see page 43).

Compositional choices

To help you to gain some ideas on how to tackle compositions for a range of botanical subjects, study the decisions that lie behind the treatment of the plants shown in this section.

Figs

The figs are shown in two different ways. While the pencil work surrounding the purple figs has enough impact to prevent it from fading away completely when viewed as a whole, it should not dominate the figs. The balance between paint and pencil should be such that neither steals focus from the other.

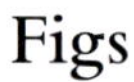

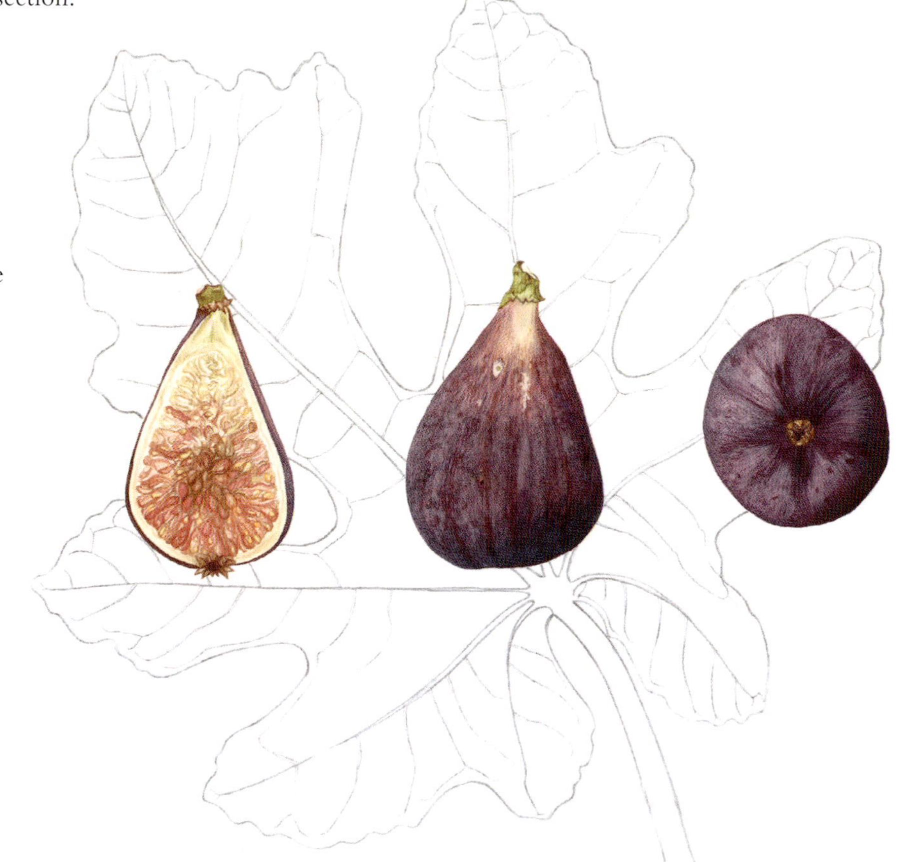

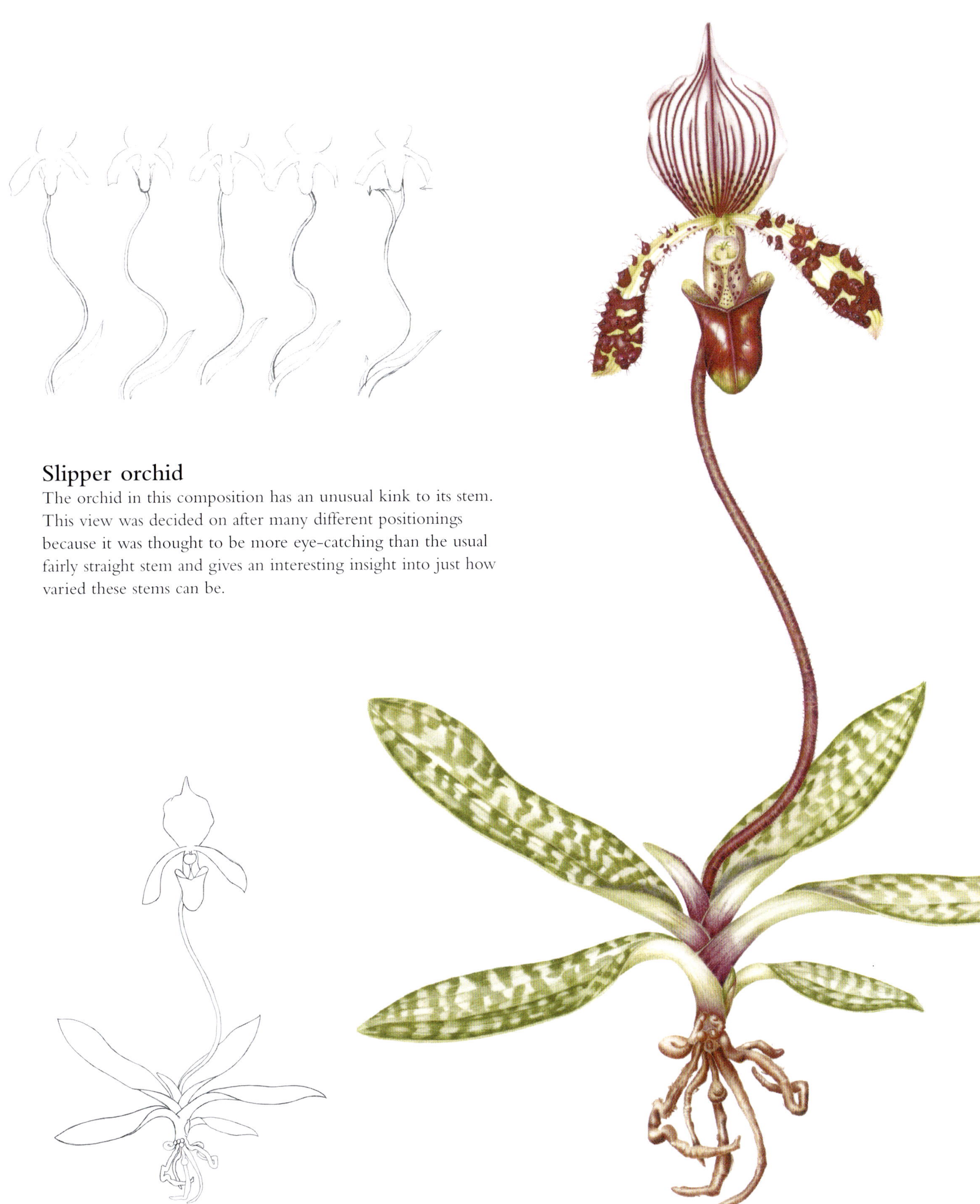

Slipper orchid

The orchid in this composition has an unusual kink to its stem. This view was decided on after many different positionings because it was thought to be more eye-catching than the usual fairly straight stem and gives an interesting insight into just how varied these stems can be.

Arums

This composition shows finished coloured elements against a backdrop of pencil work. It is one way to show the different parts of the subject without it becoming overcrowded and fussy, and avoids all the different shapes vying for attention with one another. A composition such as this would also allow you to show different varieties of the same species together on the same page, thus 'telling the story' of that particular plant.

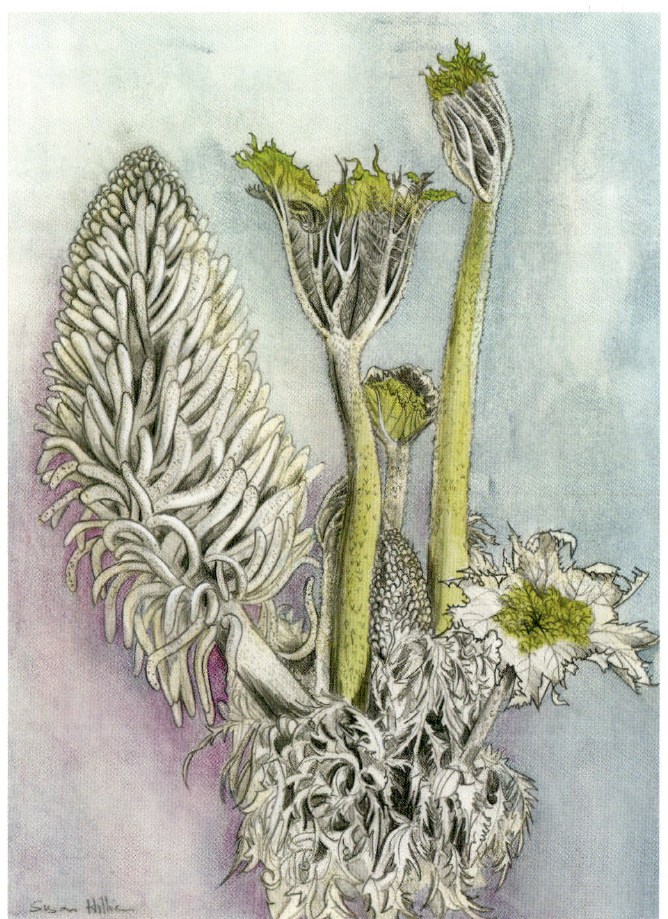

Gunnera

The gunnera is shown here on a coloured background, giving a jungly, steamy impression. The different parts of the plant are shown to great effect because the colouring of the plant blends in with the background, resulting in the painting taking on a slightly surreal character.

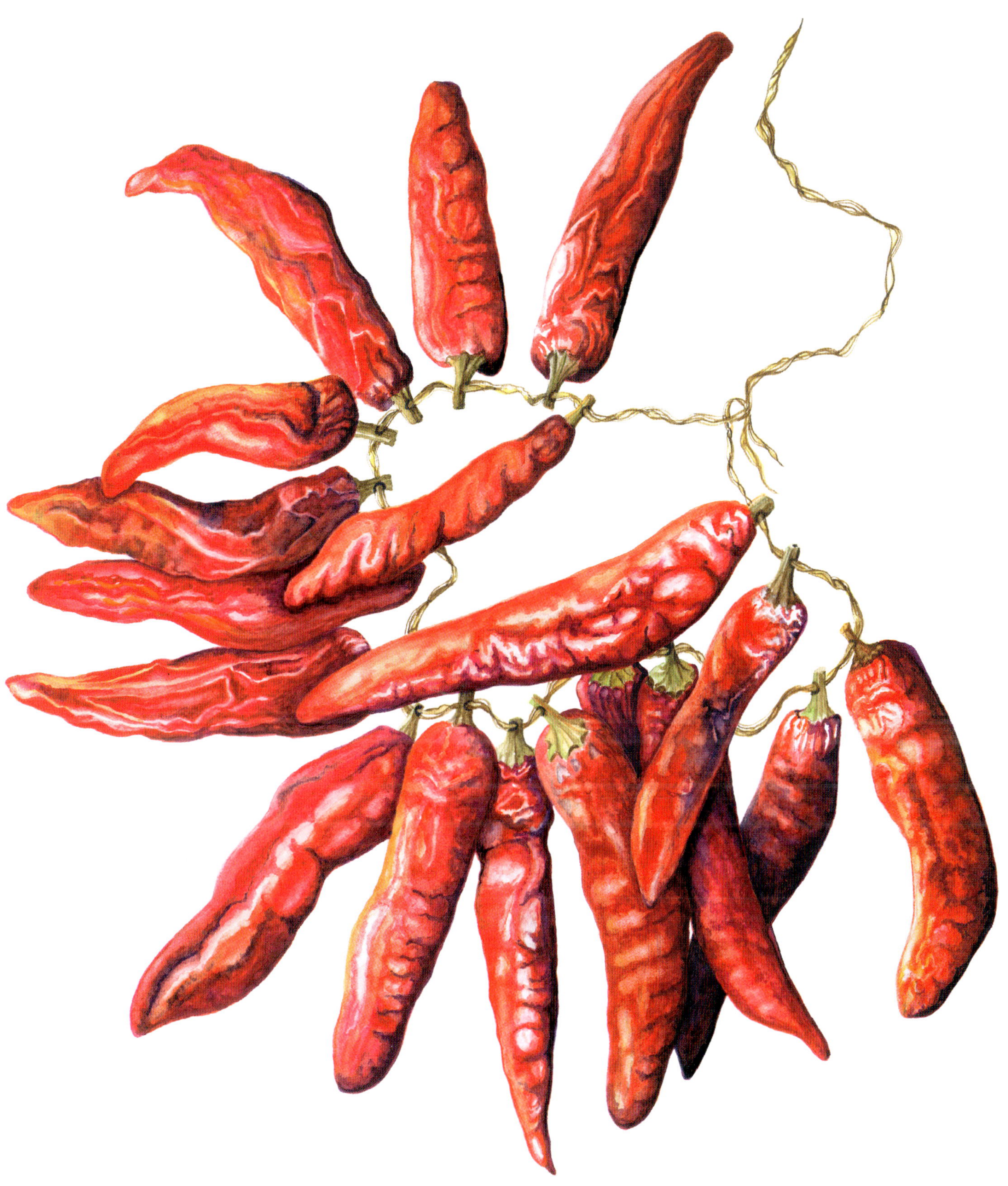

Chillies

In this very pleasing idea for a composition, the chillies are arranged like a necklace, unusual and colourful, with a slightly wild flavour. Notice how the painting contains many different reds from orange through to deep purple, echoing the strong, hot flavours of the chillies. The finished painting glows.

Passion flower

While accuracy has been carefully maintained, the centre of this passion flower has been expanded to such an extent that it assumes a life of its own. The different parts of the relatively small centre can be examined at close quarters without losing sight of the flower as a whole.

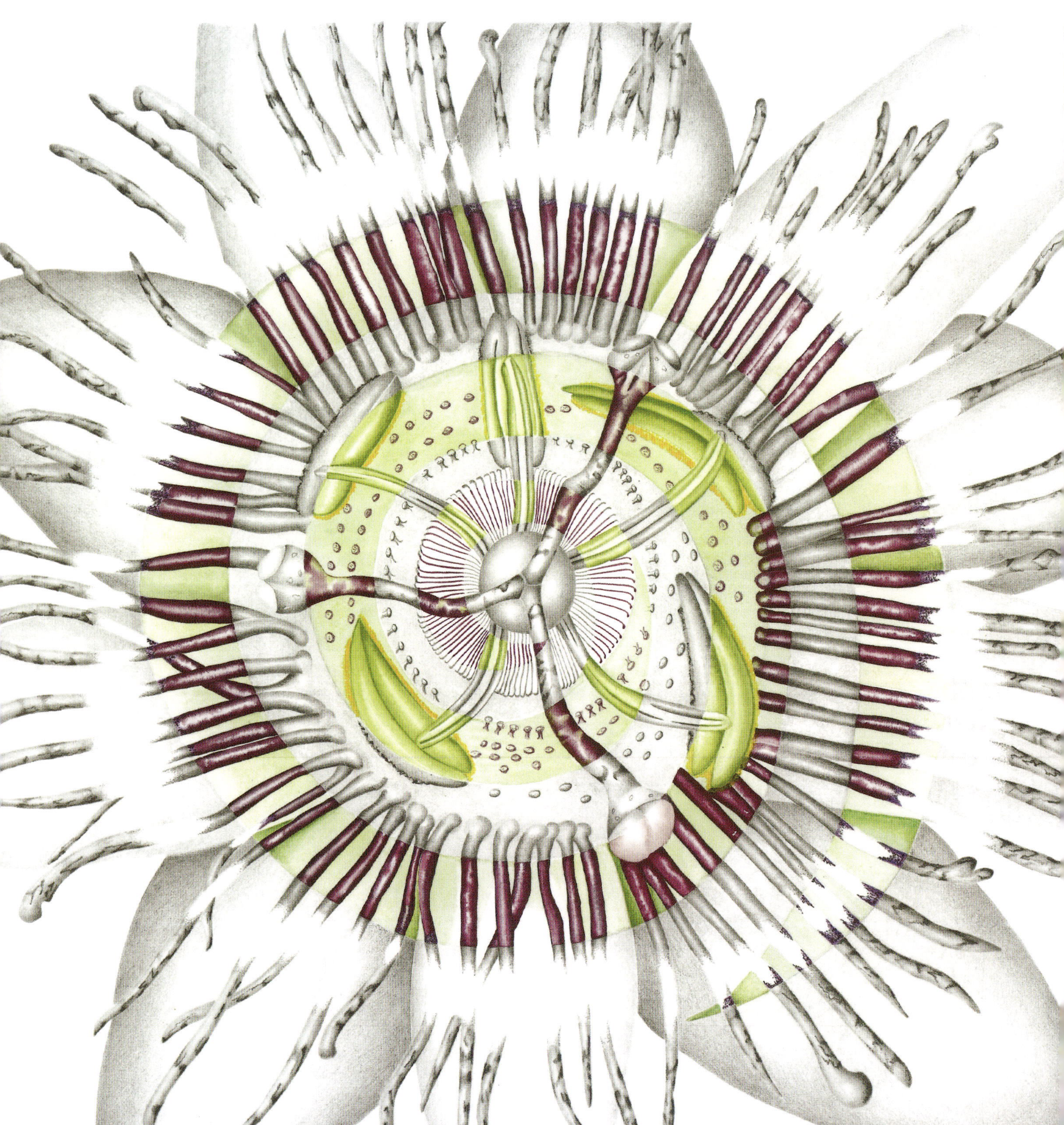

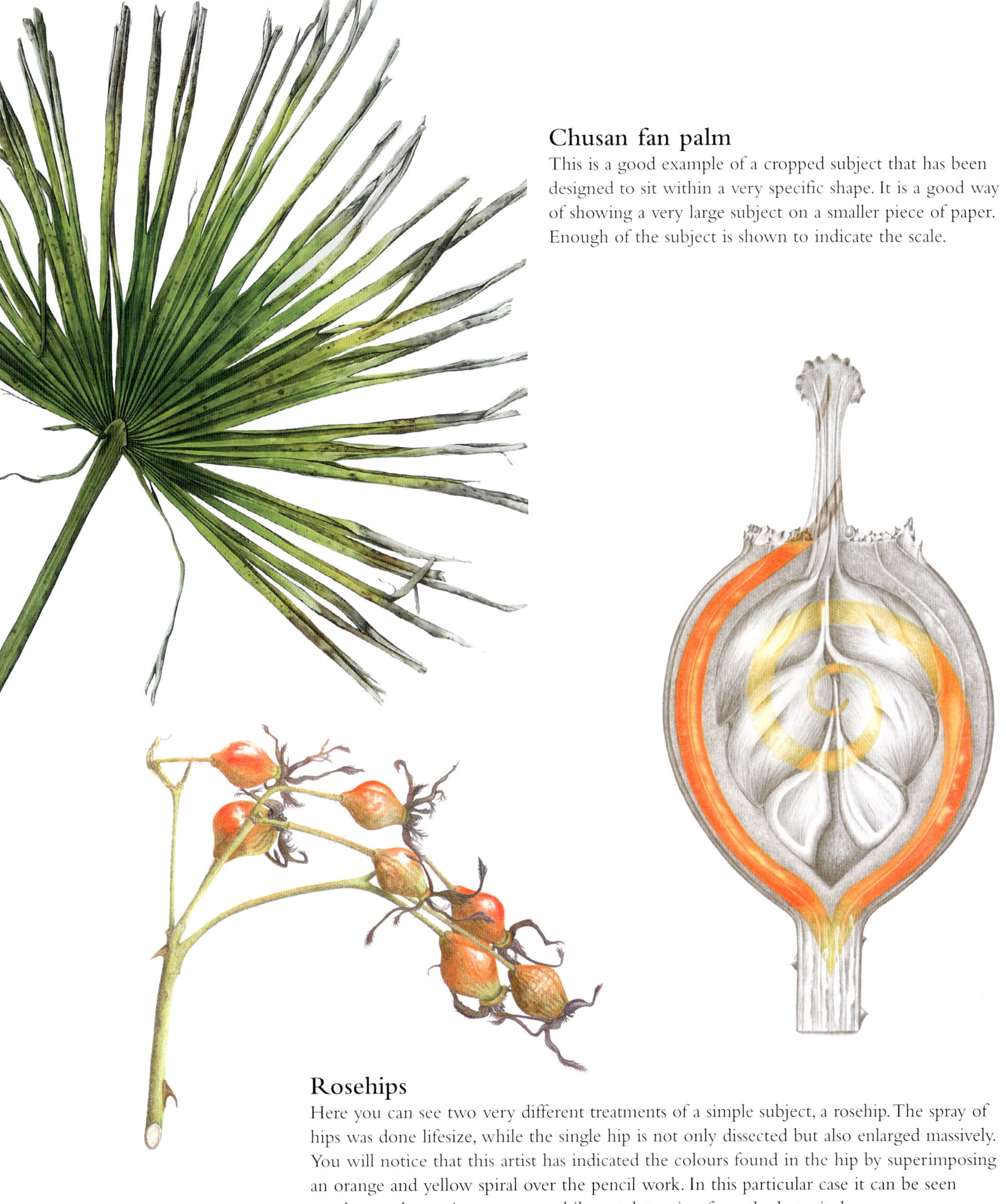

Chusan fan palm

This is a good example of a cropped subject that has been designed to sit within a very specific shape. It is a good way of showing a very large subject on a smaller piece of paper. Enough of the subject is shown to indicate the scale.

Rosehips

Here you can see two very different treatments of a simple subject, a rosehip. The spray of hips was done lifesize, while the single hip is not only dissected but also enlarged massively. You will notice that this artist has indicated the colours found in the hip by superimposing an orange and yellow spiral over the pencil work. In this particular case it can be seen purely as a decorative measure, while not detracting from the botanical accuracy.

The spray of hips demonstrates clearly the growth habit of these attractive seedheads. Worked in coloured pencil, they cascade energetically across the page, in glowing reds, yellows and oranges.

Plectranthus

This picture presents a traditional formation on the page, showing the
classic cut flower stem crossing over the leaf spray. This format allows you
to manipulate an unwieldy subject into a more acceptable arrangement.

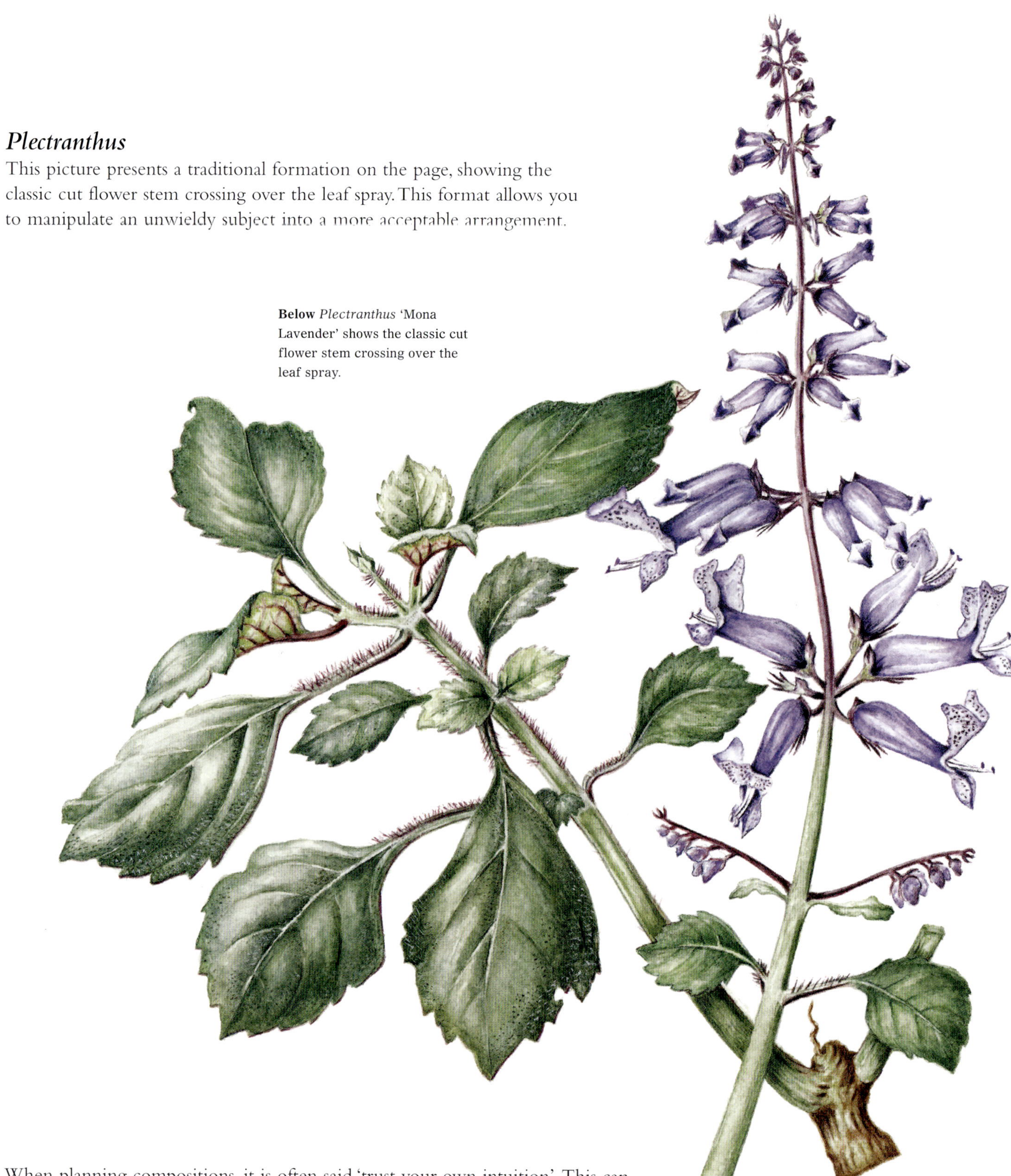

Below *Plectranthus* 'Mona
Lavender' shows the classic cut
flower stem crossing over the
leaf spray.

When planning compositions, it is often said 'trust your own intuition'. This can
be very true; we often know when something looks out of place, but we may not
always know why. If you feel that something does not look quite right in your
picture, try running through some of the whys and wherefores set out in this section
and the answers to some of your questions should become clearer. Another option
would be to look at the work of experienced and acknowledged botanical artists
and see how they have made up their compositions.

Framing your work

Having spent hours, if not days or even weeks, completing your pictures, you will no doubt start considering how best to set them off with a mount and frame. This is entirely a personal choice, although many botanical artists feel that pale colours are most sympathetic to the delicate nature of the genre. Most picture framers are extremely patient people who will give help and advice as you deliberate over different options.

Ready-made frames tend to be more economical than custom-made ones because they are usually made from offcuts. If you want to go down this route, you will have to organise your painting from the outset to fit a standard frame size. It's generally accepted that a mount sets the painting off well, but some artists prefer to dispense with the mount. Either way, take care that you leave the right amount of space between the frame (or mount) and the picture, so that it does not look cramped.

These three studies of a fig (below) were painted on separate small sheets of paper then float-mounted together, fixed to a foam core and set in a deeper frame than usual so that the pictures create interesting cast shadows. The rough paper edge was achieved by placing an ordinary ruler along a previously pencilled line, then pressing firmly on the ruler with one hand and ripping off the excess paper with the other. This has to be done carefully as once ripped there is no return. Inexpensive deckle-edged rulers are available to purchase, and you might like to experiment to see which suits you. This technique is best done before the painting is started, because to make a mistake on the finished picture would be catastrophic.

All artworks on paper fade in time, and some watercolour paints fade faster than others. Most manufacturers indicate the degree of permanence of all their colours, so you can select the most lightfast if you wish. Even so, take care about where to hang your artworks, siting them away from strong or direct light. That way they will give you many years of pleasure.

Below Three small individual studies of figs are mounted together in one frame.

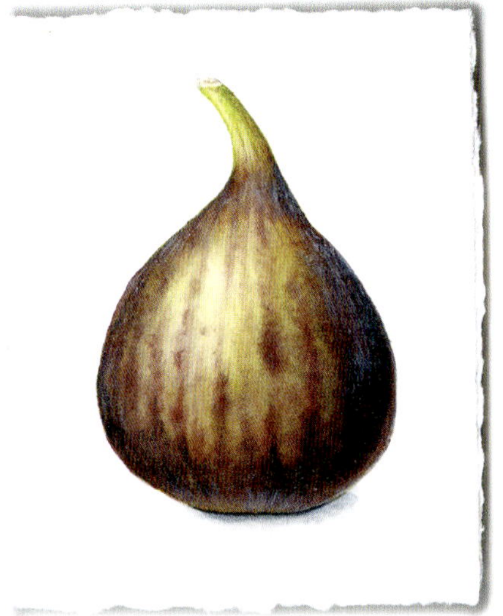
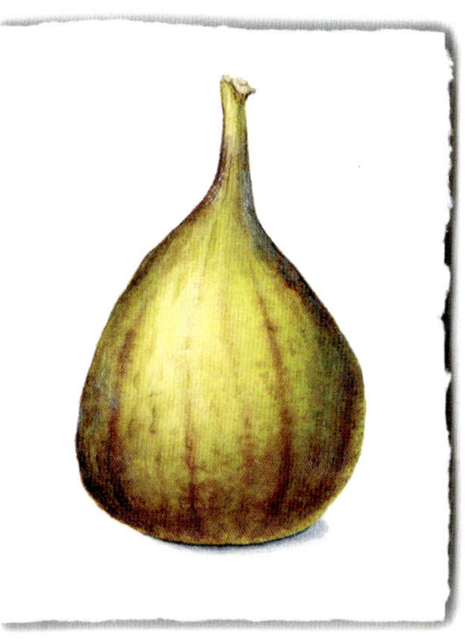
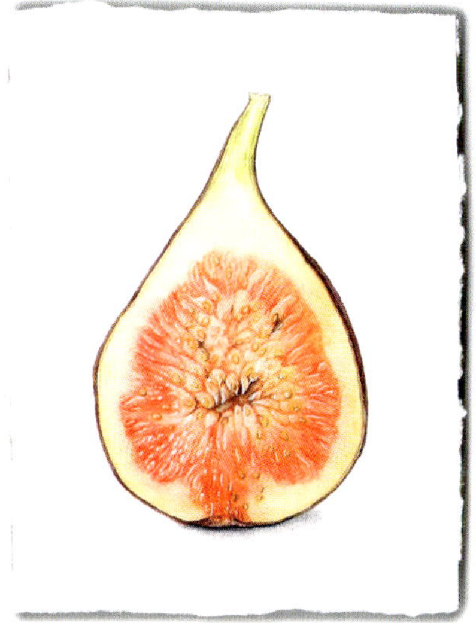

Drawing

In botanical illustration, drawing needs to be clear and accurate, describing a three-dimensional plant on a two-dimensional surface in such a way that its structure and distinctive features are clearly shown. This remains true whether you are drawing as a preliminary stage of a painting or making a drawing that is an illustration in its own right, as shown right and below. If you have an ideal light source, as described on page 9, some of the work is done for you, since good lighting will show you the variations in tone that describe the individual nature of very different subjects.

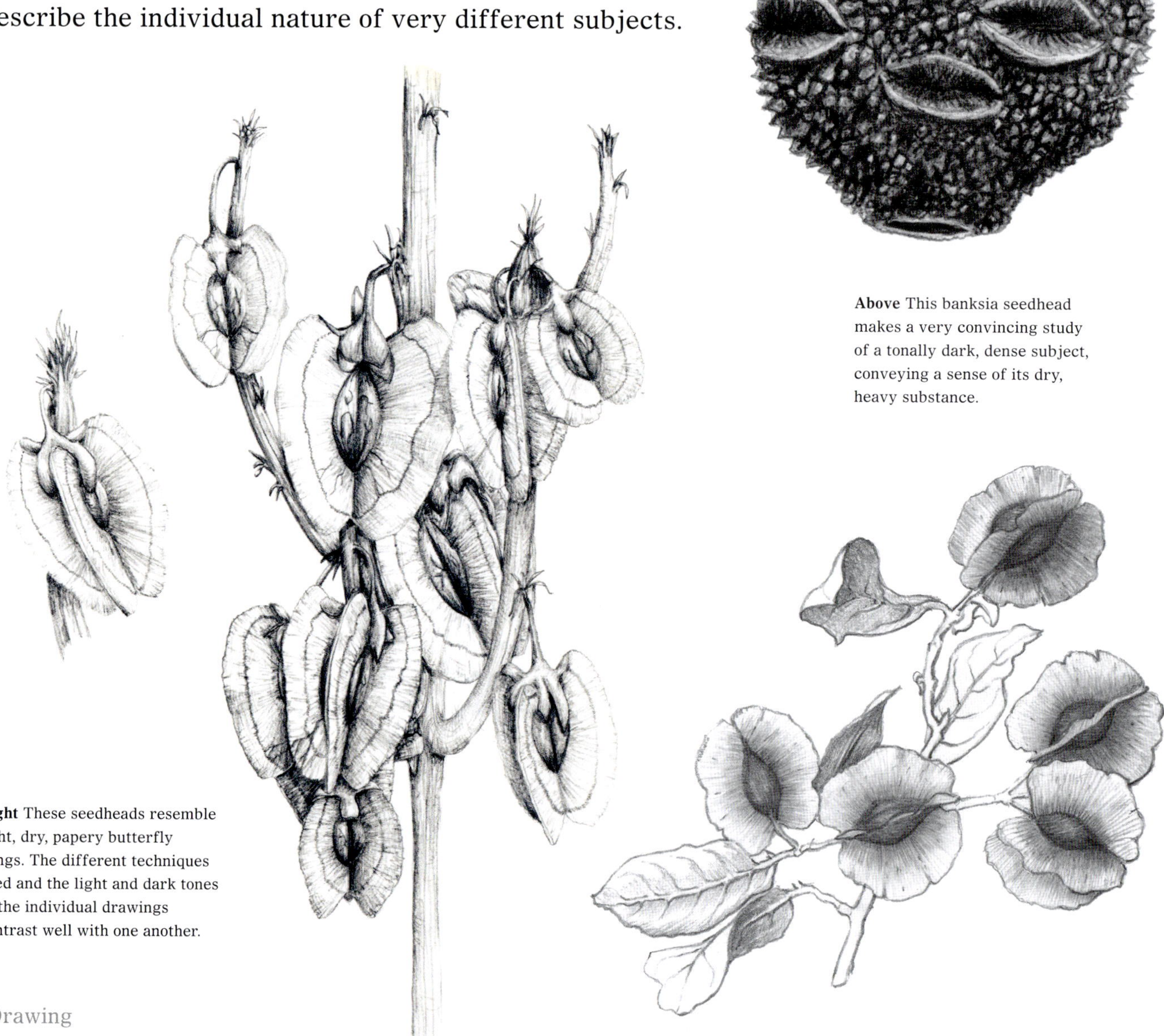

Above This banksia seedhead makes a very convincing study of a tonally dark, dense subject, conveying a sense of its dry, heavy substance.

Right These seedheads resemble light, dry, papery butterfly wings. The different techniques used and the light and dark tones of the individual drawings contrast well with one another.

It's tempting to grab a pencil and make elaborate and highly decorative drawings without fully understanding the structure, form and habit of the plant, so before you start, set aside some time to study it. Botanical knowledge will help you to identify your plant and to recognize the diagnostic features that need to be illustrated, but if you lack this, just look carefully at the overall shape, height and width and the distances and relationships between the individual elements as a way of establishing familiarity with the plant. You are then more likely to end up with an image on your page that closely resembles the actual subject.

Choose a specimen that is a good representation of its species and contains as much information about the plant as possible. Labouring over a diseased or misshapen plant is a waste of time, unless that is the message you wish to convey. Your picture should show the upper and under surfaces of leaves and the different angles of the flowers, or of any buds or seedheads. In fact, botanical paintings are often worked on over a period of months, depicting the parts as they appear.

So your summing-up study should establish important points such as size, proportion, growth pattern, attitude, angles, and any geometric or other shapes present. Also make sure that you are aware of the negative spaces – that is to say, the space around and between the different parts of the subject (below right). These will determine the relative positioning of all elements of the plant to the whole. If your drawing does not fit together correctly, then systematically check the negative spaces.

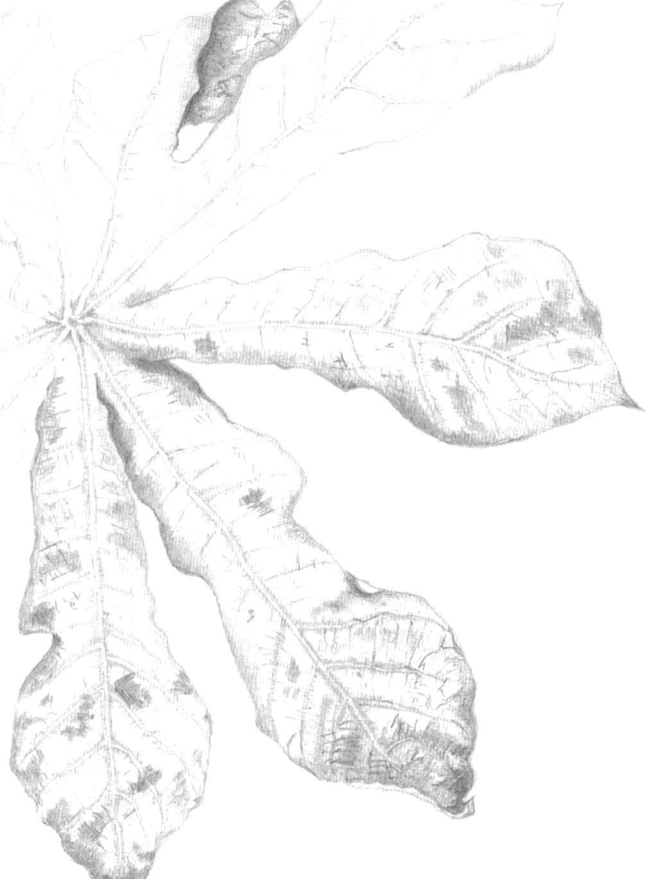

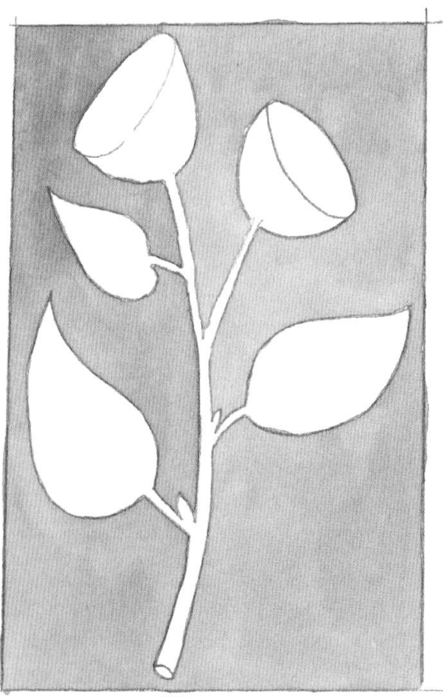

Left Understand the form and structure of your plant before beginning to draw.

Below The negative spaces around and between the parts of your subject are as important to the draughtsman as the subject itself. If something looks wrong, check the forms of the negative spaces.

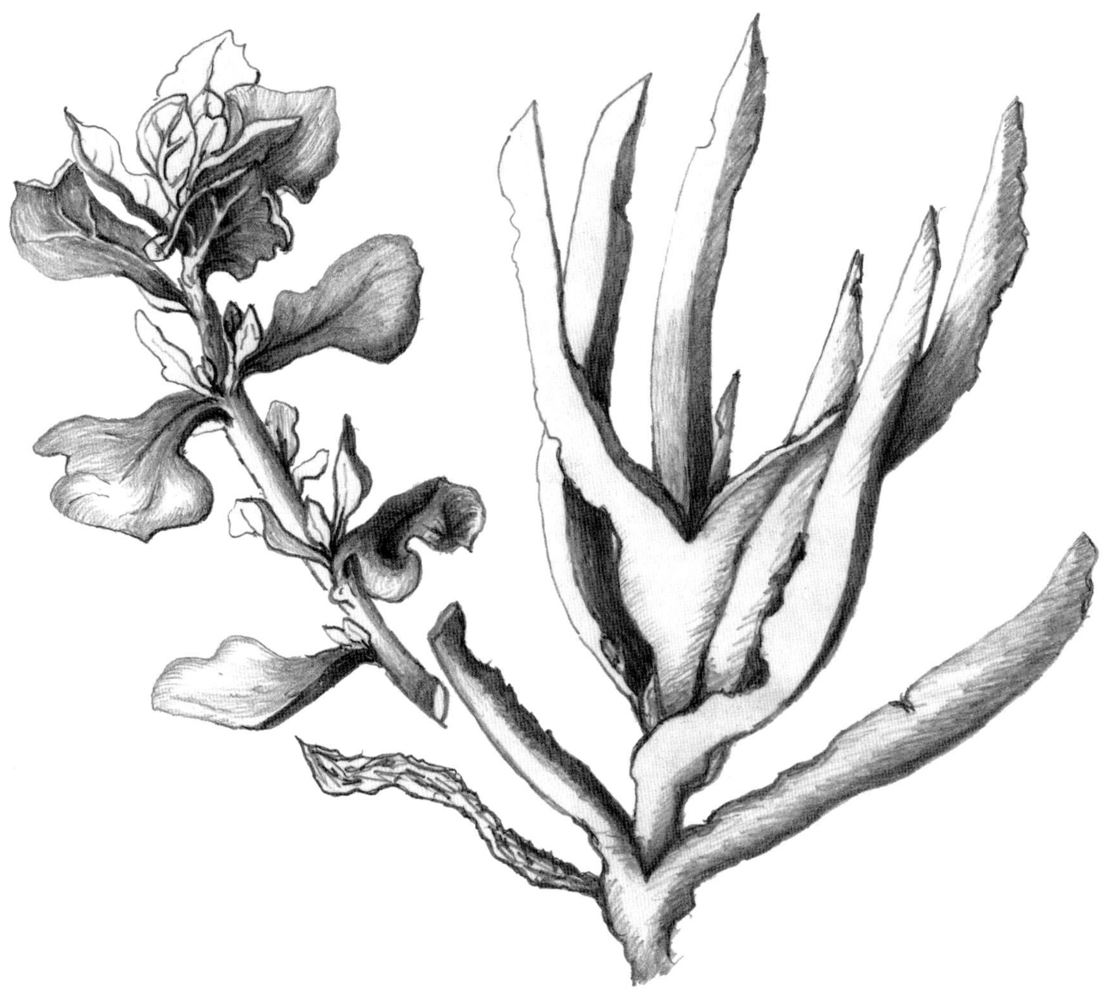

Establishing detail

In order to understand your subject further, write a list of adjectives describing it – hard, glossy, woolly, thorny, sharp, soft, fluffy, dry, papery, brittle, and so on. Refer to this list frequently, and if you find that your apple, for instance, looks soft and woolly when it should be hard and crisp, think again. The study of *Carpobrotus* (above) is a good example of how the artist has captured the fleshy and angular character of the plant.

Stems are particularly important; they are often portrayed as too thick or too narrow, in which case the whole character of the plant can be lost. A diagnostic feature of all good botanical drawings is also the internal construction of the stem, demonstrating whether it is round, square, hollow, pithy, and so on. For this reason, do not give stems a 'fuzzy' ending – if appropriate, show at least one in cross section and others clean cut.

On your worksheet, indicate the direction of your light source. Also make a note of the 'keying-in' spot on the plant – this is the place that you always look back to before adding any new marks to your drawing. For example, the 'keying-in' spot on the *Carpobrotus* (above) could be the v-shaped angle formed by the two upper leaves in the foreground. If you move or change your position, checking the keying-in spot ensures that your viewpoint doesn't shift.

Above *Carpobrotus* has fleshy and angular leaves, portrayed convincingly in this pencil study.

Familiarity with your pencils

Before starting to draw your first subject, familiarize yourself with your pencils and what they can do. It's a good idea to make a tonal exercise for each grade and make of pencil, so that you are aware of the full range of light, medium and dark tones that you can achieve (below). Your initial attempts may otherwise lack the contrast that would have been possible. The tonal scale shown here also demonstrates non-directional shading, which, as it suggests, has no markings in any particular direction and is therefore primarily used in botanical illustration because it shows the form of the subject in a realistic manner.

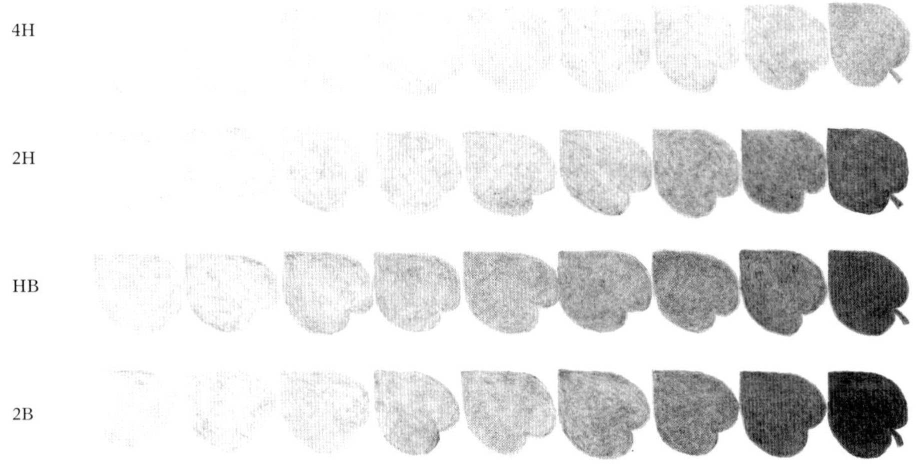

Left See how many tones you can achieve with each of your pencils. Here are just four grades: 4H, 2H, HB and 2B, also demonstrating non-directional shading.

Below Hatching and cross-hatching are not suitable ways to depict shadow on botanical subjects.

The illustrations below show examples of hatching and cross-hatching on a pair of mushrooms. These forms of shading are suitable for other kinds of artwork, but can be too intrusive and misleading for botanical subjects and are not recommended.

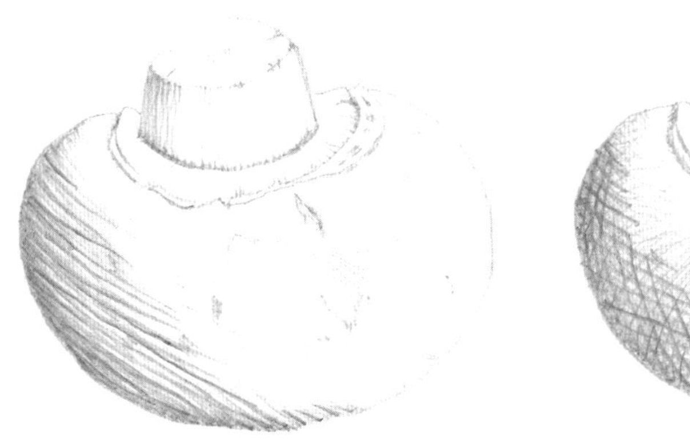

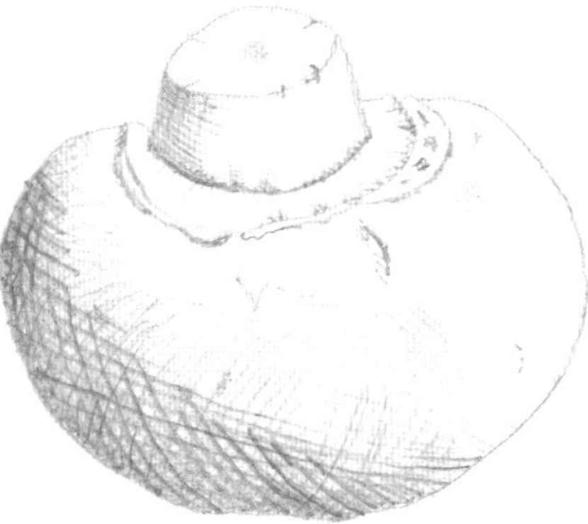

Foreshortening

For the following exercises, use cheap layout paper or smooth cartridge paper. Your initial drawings should be simple, using lines and tone to illustrate the most basic construction. For example, when you are starting a drawing, use single lines to indicate direction, angles, and basic shapes such as cones, squares, circles and so on (below left and opposite).

To help you understand how to draw a foreshortened leaf, take a sheet of clear acetate or flexible plastic such as a file cover. Draw a leaf shape on to it with a black felt-tip pen, marking the midrib and secondary veins and leaving a length of stalk. Cut it out and twist it in different directions, drawing what you see. You will be able to see through the clear material exactly what the stem and midrib are doing.

The basic construction of three different leaves is shown below right. The continuation of the midrib and some of the veins are shown, while disappearing midribs are indicated by a red dotted line.

Below left Use single lines to indicate basic shapes.

Below right Disappearing midribs on foreshortened leaves are shown here using red dotted lines.

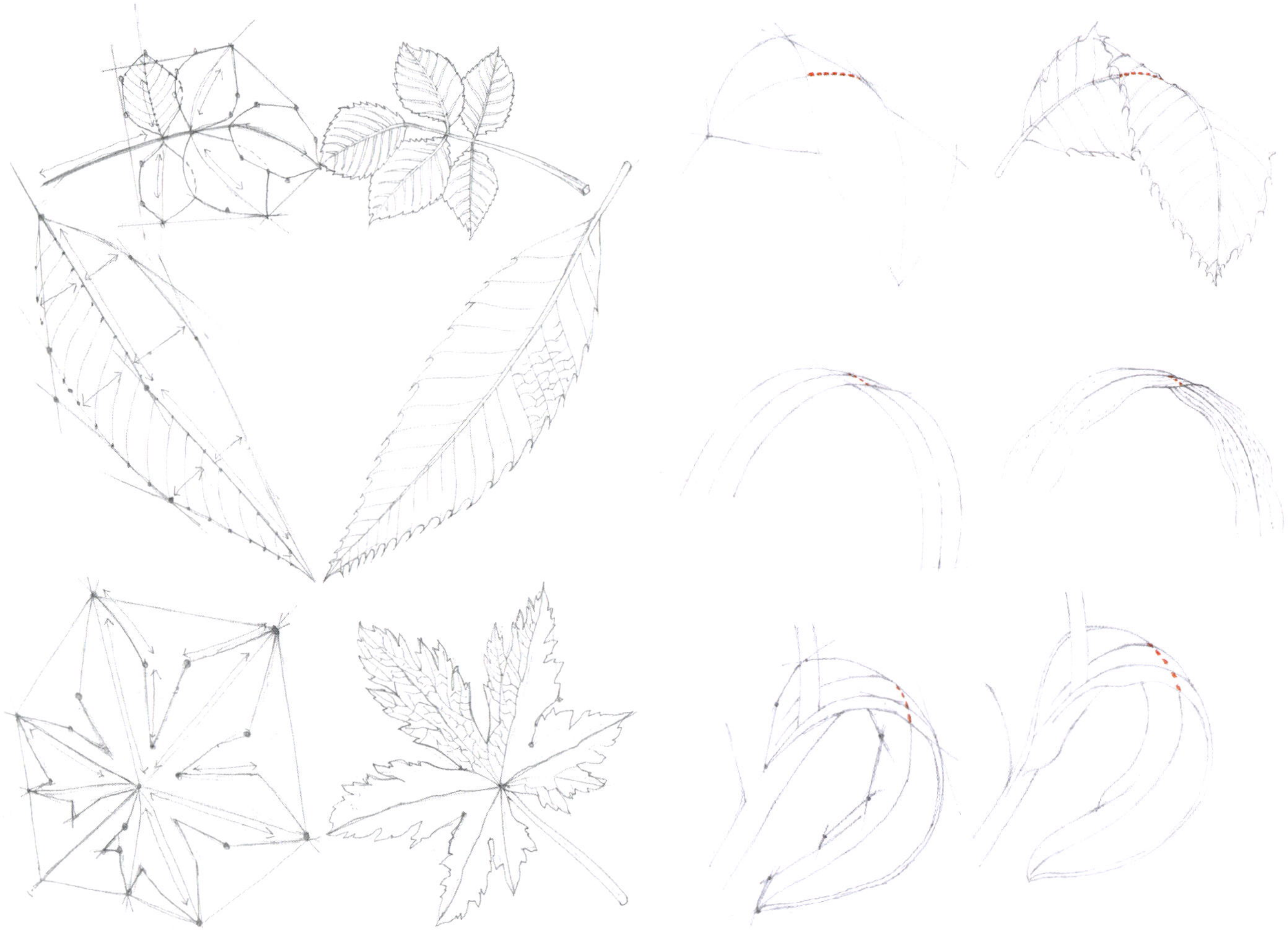

Structural drawing

The structural drawing of an iris (below right) shows you how to organize the irregular shape of an iris flower. The group of standard (upright) petals and the individual fall petals divide roughly into squares and rectangles. Draw the boxes and fit the floral elements into them, using only straight lines and angles. It is much easier to follow this drawing formula and to add detail after the basic shapes are accurate. The overall rectangle contains all parts of this complicated three-dimensional flower.

Notice how there are dots on the basic construction drawings. These indicate changes of direction in the angles and the point-to-point distances to help you identify the negative space and the overall shape of a subject. If you run your eye around the outside shape from dot to dot or point to point and keep looking from plant to drawing, your powers of perception and correct interpretation will be greatly improved. You can mark various important points with dots wherever you feel they may be useful while your drawing is under construction. The finished drawing is shown below.

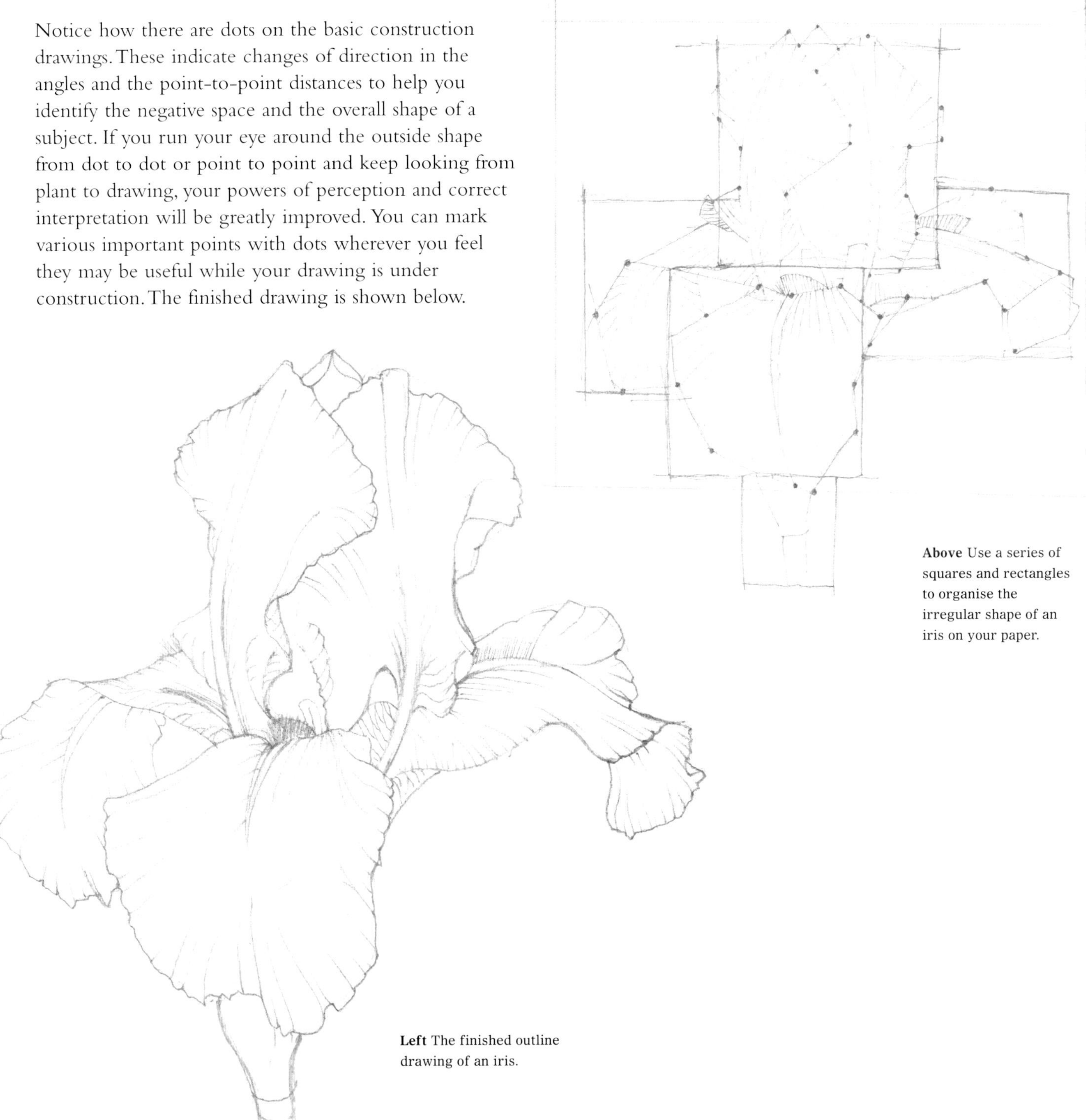

Above Use a series of squares and rectangles to organise the irregular shape of an iris on your paper.

Left The finished outline drawing of an iris.

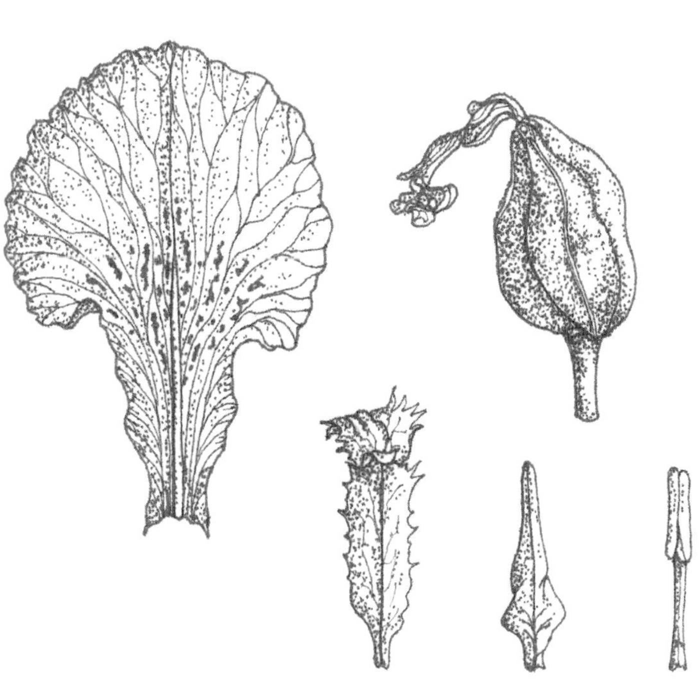

Drawing a dissection

Before you start, you might like to make separate drawings of different parts of the plant
– a dissection of the flower, perhaps, together with a seed or seedhead, a bud, and a section
of stem showing how the leaves grow. These should be accurate, so study the specimen
carefully, if necessary using a magnifying glass, before starting to draw.

It is a good idea to dissect one or two flowers, so that you know what goes where (above).
To do this, you will need a sharp craft knife or razor blade and a steady hand. Use smooth
cartridge paper, a sharp HB pencil, an eraser and a hand lens or magnifying glass. You might
also find one or two pairs of very fine forceps or tweezers useful for separating the small
parts of the flower.

Dissection drawings are usually diagrammatic, and done in pen and ink, but you may wish
to draw in pencil first so that you can make corrections.

Points to look for are:
• The number of petals and stamens.
• How the leaves grow from the stems.
• Whether the stems are the same thickness at the top and bottom.
• The shape of the leaves, and what the veins and edges are like.
• Whether the plant is hairy and, if so, whether the hairs all grow
  in the same direction and are of uniform length.

In each case, draw what you see and label the various parts. There is no need to add colour
unless you particularly want to. Make notes to yourself, such as 'too thick', or 'not hairy
enough', which will help to get the plant firmly lodged in your mind's eye. Should you
wish to make it into a finished drawing rather than a painting, you will already have done
much of the preliminary work as described.

Above Sometimes it is helpful
to make separate drawings of
different parts of the plant.

Indicating size

Botanical artists are usually advised to draw or paint life-size. But what if your subject is very small, like the tiny caladenia orchid (right), which measures only about 2cm (¾in) across? This orchid was discovered near Perth, in Western Australia, in 2003, at which time only 100 plants were known and it still had to be formally named. The dark tips to the petals are comprised of hundreds of tiny glands which release pheromones only at the time of atmospheric depression, attracting the wasps that pollinate the orchid. Some of the tiny waxy hairs on the stem ends terminate in miniature dark grey knobs, possibly to deter pests.

Alternatively, you might wish to draw a shrub or a tree, which you would have to make much smaller to fit on to the paper. The question of size is particularly relevant if you are making a drawing or painting of botanical significance rather than working purely for aesthetic purposes.

Indications of the plant size can be given in various ways. It is common to include a multiplication sign with a number, for example x2. This loses its value, however, if the image is enlarged or reduced in printing, so adding a scale bar (as shown above and overleaf) is undoubtedly better. In printing, the scale bar will always be magnified or reduced by the same amount as your drawing.

Scale bars can be horizontal or vertical and should be added to fit in with your overall composition. Make certain that your line, whether horizontal or vertical, is parallel to the edge of the mount, and straight – a line that is slightly diagonal or wobbly lets down the finished drawing or painting. Take care not to let a scale bar interfere with your drawing by putting it too close to the image or making it too large.

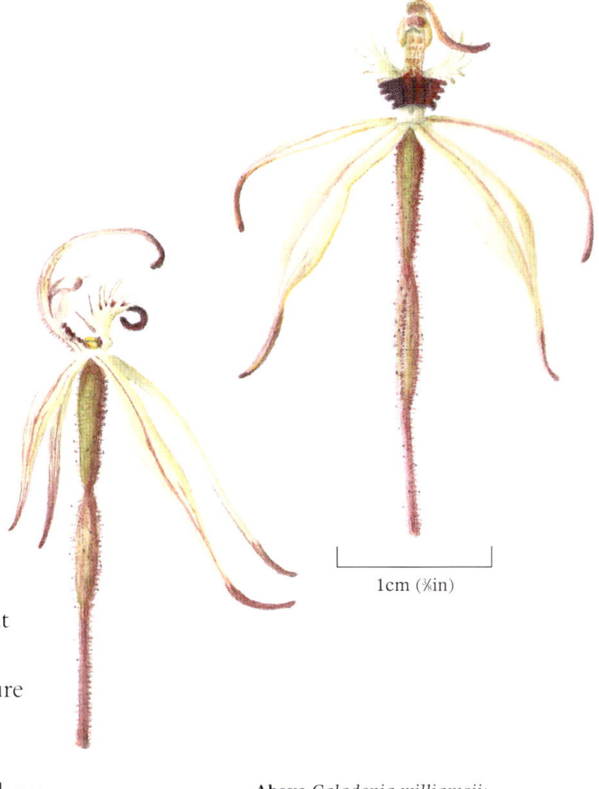

Above *Caladenia williamsii:* 'Caladenia' means beautiful glands and refers to the two yellow egg-shaped glands in the heart of the flower.

Below Each section of this tiny birdsnest fungus (*Cyathus olla*) is no larger than a little fingernail. It was painted life-size, but would have benefited from being enlarged and shown with a scale bar.

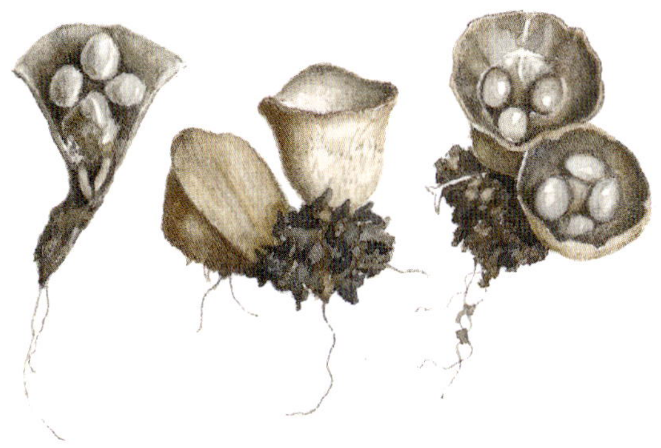

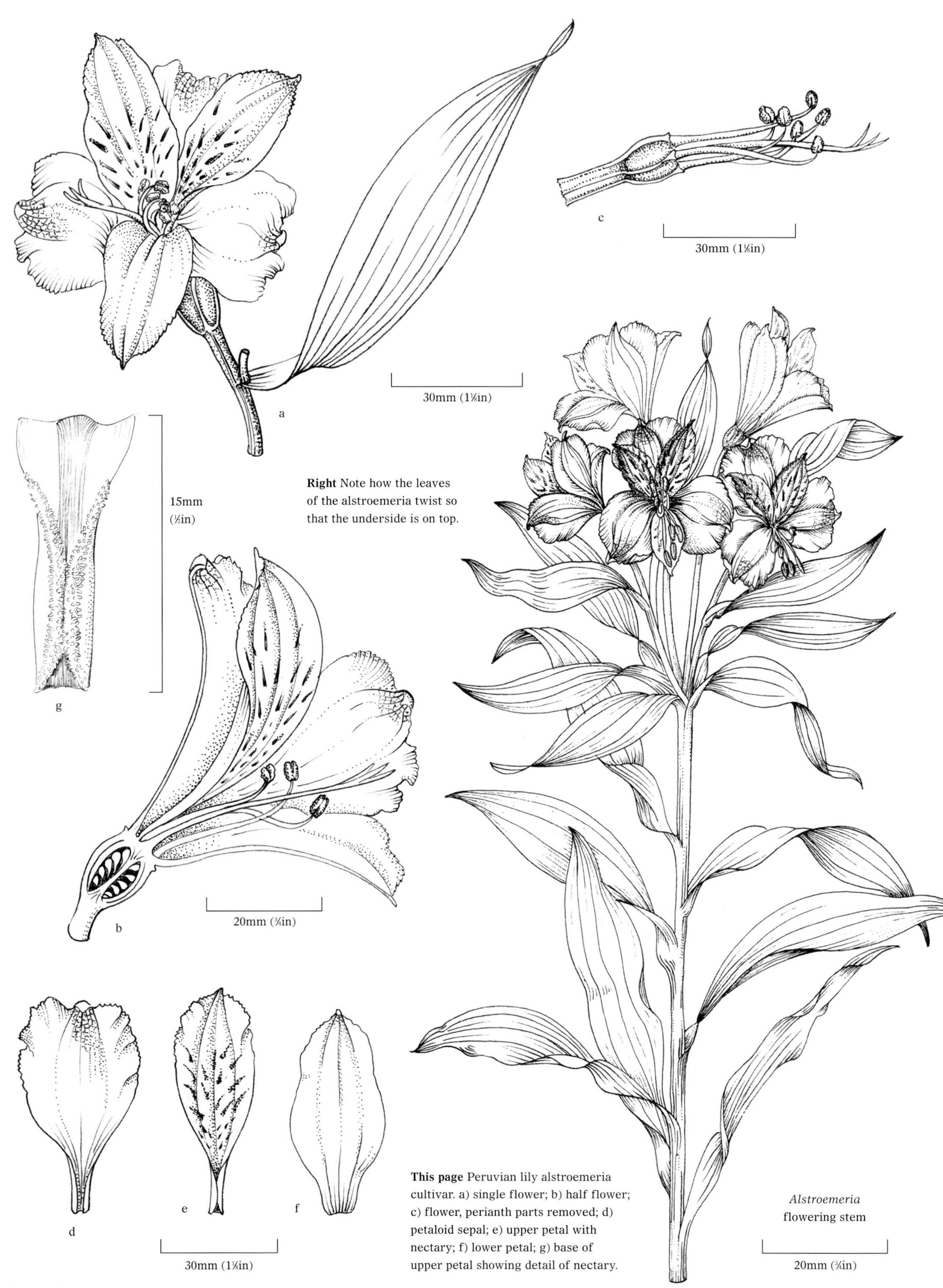

Right Note how the leaves of the alstroemeria twist so that the underside is on top.

Alstroemeria flowering stem

This page Peruvian lily alstroemeria cultivar. a) single flower; b) half flower; c) flower, perianth parts removed; d) petaloid sepal; e) upper petal with nectary; f) lower petal; g) base of upper petal showing detail of nectary.

Exercise: Pattern and texture

It's great fun to portray pattern and texture using just graphite pencils. Find a dozen or so examples with different surfaces. They need not all be botanical – below you will see some knitting, a shell, a basket and part of a shuttlecock – but they should all be very different in style and character.

These line and tone drawings illustrate the clever use of non-directional shading together with pattern and tonal changes. The drawing of wicker shows clearly how cast shadow occurs and how to draw it, while the drawing of a lemon slice shows the texture of citrus flesh and the fir cone is an example of overlapping planes.

Once you have mastered how to draw accurately, and how to portray tonal shades using graphite pencils, you will be ready to go on to explore the fascination of colour.

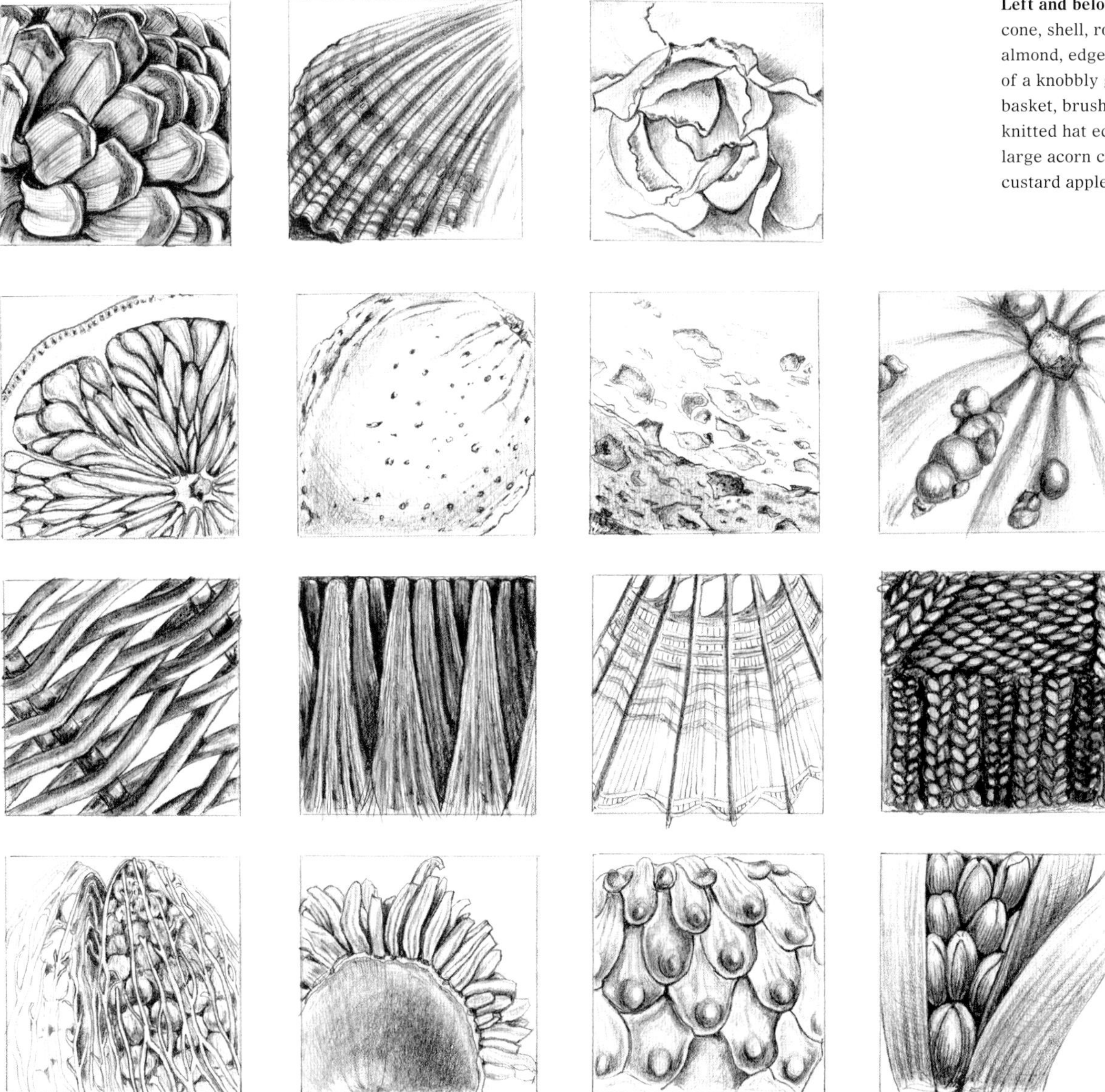

Left and below from top left: fir cone, shell, rose, slice of lemon, almond, edge of a sponge, bottom of a knobbly gourd, wicker basket, brush, shuttlecock, knitted hat edge, tropical seed, large acorn cup from Corfu, custard apple, hyacinth.

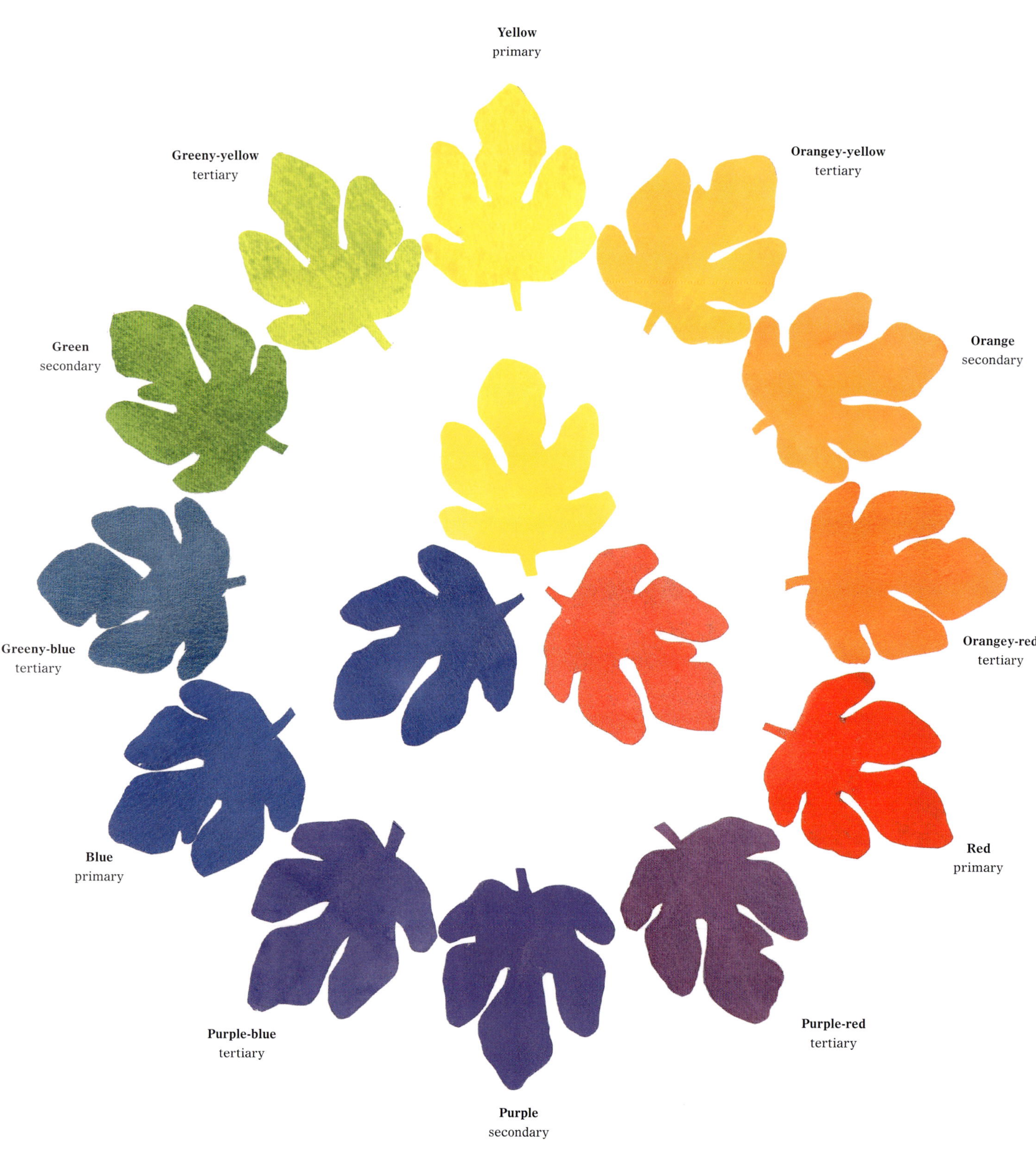

Yellow
primary
Greeny-yellow
tertiary
Orangey-yellow
tertiary
Green
secondary
Orange
secondary
Greeny-blue
tertiary
Orangey-red
tertiary
Blue
primary
Red
primary
Purple-blue
tertiary
Purple-red
tertiary
Purple
secondary

Understanding Colour

You will find that it's possible to buy as many ready-made colours as your heart could ever desire, but unless you understand their properties, the more colours you have the more likely you are to become confused and frustrated. You will also waste a lot of time mixing paints without much idea of how to achieve a specific colour. There's nothing wrong with experimentation – rather, it's to be encouraged – but a knowledge of basic colour theory will enable you to make informed choices regarding which paints to buy and how to use them.

Most colours in nature can be made easily from six basic colours. Knowing how to use a limited palette will enhance your mixing capabilities and instil confidence in your ability to select and recognize colour.

Primary, secondary and tertiary colours

The 12-hue colour circle shown left indicates the relative positions of the three primaries, three secondaries and six tertiaries on the colour wheel. The primaries – yellow, red and blue – cannot be mixed from any other colour; the secondary colours – orange, purple and green – are mixed from the primaries, while the tertiaries are a mix of a primary and its closest secondary colour, for example *primary* blue + *secondary* green = *tertiary* greeny-blue.

Because paint manufacturers rarely produce 'pure' primaries and because bought colours often vary, it's better to identify colours rather than relying on manufacturer's names. Colours are generally recognized as being either warm (reds, oranges and yellows) or cool (blues and greens). However, there are variations in colour temperature within those classifications – for instance, warm yellow leans to orange and red; cool yellow leans to green and blue. The same applies to the other primaries: red leans towards orange and yellow (warm) or purple and blue (cool); blue leans towards purple and red (warm) or green and yellow (cool). If you think this is complicated, Delacroix, widely regarded as a colour master, kept a 72-hue colour circle on his studio wall.

Left The leaf colour circle indicates the relative positions of the three primaries, the three secondaries and six tertiaries.

Complementary colours

The secondary colours are each the complementary colour of one of the three primaries Yellow's complementary is purple; red's complementary is green; and blue's complementary is orange. Among the tertiary colours the complementaries are greeny-yellow with purply-red; orangey-yellow with purply-blue; and greeny-blue with orangey-red. All complementary colours lie opposite each other on the colour wheel and mix to a neutral grey-black.

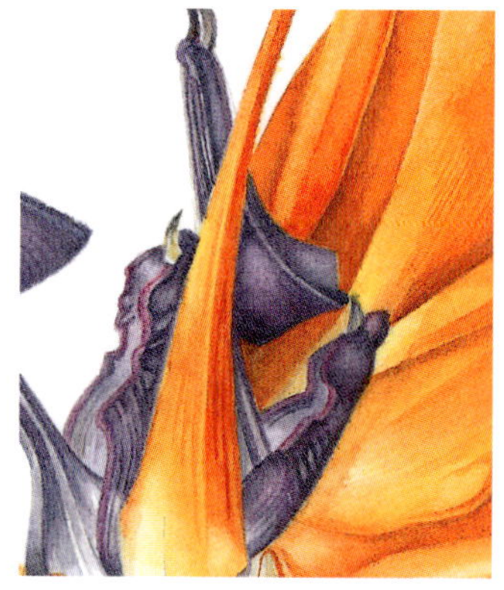

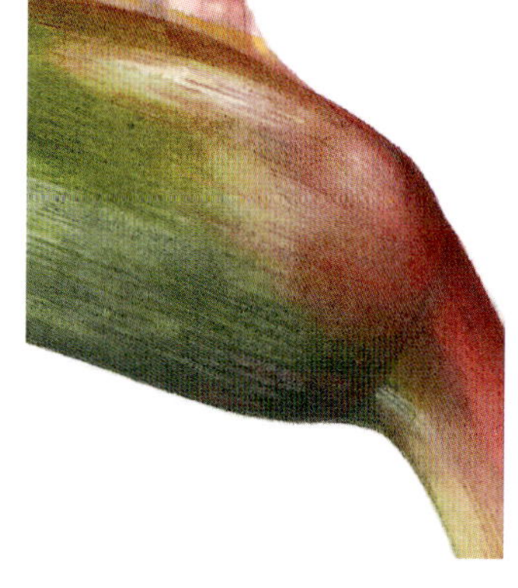

Above left and right These details from the strelitzia on page 102 show complementaries blue and orange (left) and red and green (right).

Below The complementaries purple and yellow can be found in this painting of yellow narcissi on a purple background.

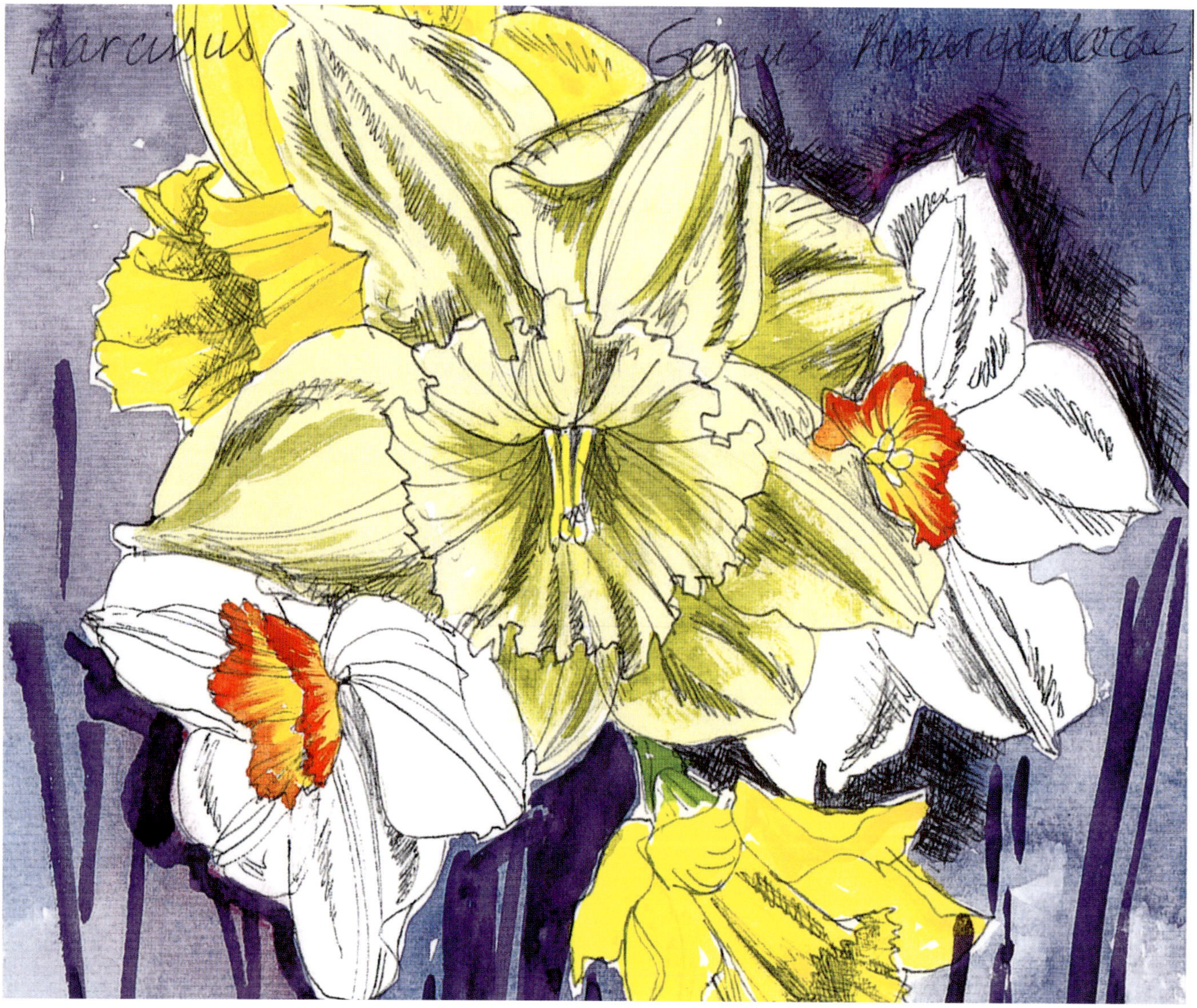

The importance of green

The importance of green for the botanical artist cannot be overestimated, but greens are generally regarded as the hardest colours to get right. Mixing your own is by far the best policy. There are so many colours on sale that deciding which to get can be a veritable minefield – and a time-consuming and very expensive one at that – and if your bought greens don't quite match those in your subjects, how will you know how to alter them successfully? Sap Green is one ready-made green that is useful, but even so you will often need to change it to provide the exact hue you need (see page 62).

When mixing green, it's vital to identify what kind of green you're seeing and to reproduce it accurately. There are so many shades, from bright emerald, olive, khaki, silvery turquoise and pale grey-green to bronze and subtle colours that defy written or spoken description.

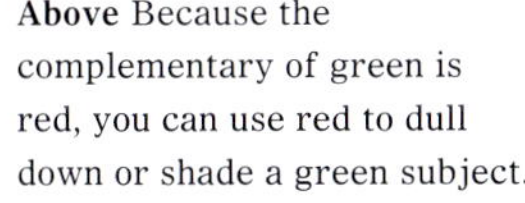

Black and grey

It may seem strange to discuss black in a chapter all about colour, but the fact is that the primary colours, and therefore the complementary colours, mix to a neutral black. Many painters choose to use a colour's complementary to produce dark shadows with a depth of colour and interest that are lacking from a ready-made black.

Subtle blacks and greys (diluted black) can be made by mixing a primary colour with its complementary. This is known as physical mixing and is done on the palette prior to painting.

Above Because the complementary of green is red, you can use red to dull down or shade a green subject.

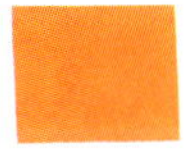

Orange (blue's complementary) and blue (primary) mixed to make black and grey.

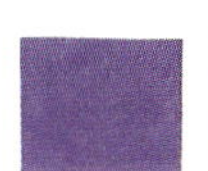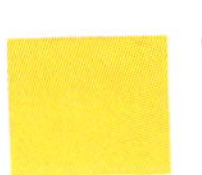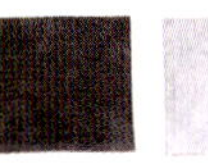

Purple (yellow's complementary) with yellow (primary) mixed to make black and grey.

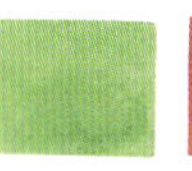

Green (red's complementary) with red (primary) mixed to make black and grey.

You can make many optical variations of greys and blacks by superimposing one colour over its complementary, or vice versa. This is known as optical mixing, and is done in layers, allowing the first colour to dry before adding the second.

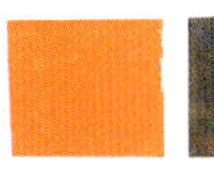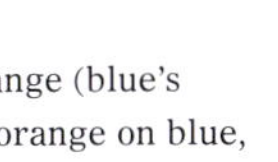

Blue (primary) on orange (blue's complementary) and orange on blue, with diluted colours below.

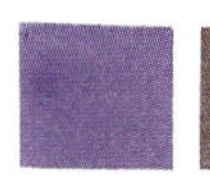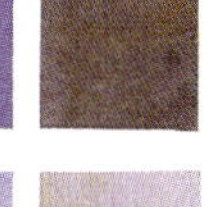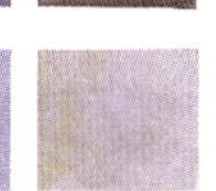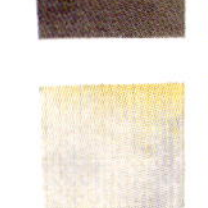

Yellow (primary) on purple (yellow's complementary) and purple on yellow, with diluted colours below.

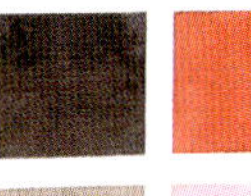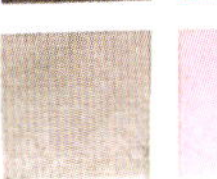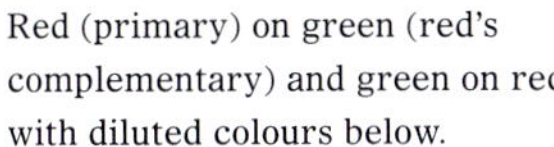

Red (primary) on green (red's complementary) and green on red, with diluted colours below.

Exercise: Mixing colours from a limited palette

This is an exercise using just six primary colours (cool and warm yellow, cool and warm red, cool and warm blue) plus three other useful colours: Winsor Violet, Opera Rose and Sap Green. Opera Rose, by Winsor & Newton, lends a wonderful resonance to paintings. The nearest alternatives are Permanent Rose (W&N) and Schminke Horadam's Brilliant Purple, but neither has its fluorescence.

With practice you will find that you can make virtually every colour under the sun using two colours from this limited palette – and each of these mixes can always be subtly altered with the addition of small amounts of a third colour.

Chart 1

This chart shows some of the colours you can make by adding reds to a yellow base. The initial colour is in the left-hand column and the added colour in the right-hand column, each divided from the mixes between them by a bold line. Rows 1–4 start with a cool yellow (Lemon Yellow). Increasing amounts of warm red (Scarlet Lake) are added in row 1, with a diluted version in row 2. Row 3 adds a cool red (Alizarin Crimson) to the cool yellow, and is diluted in row 4.

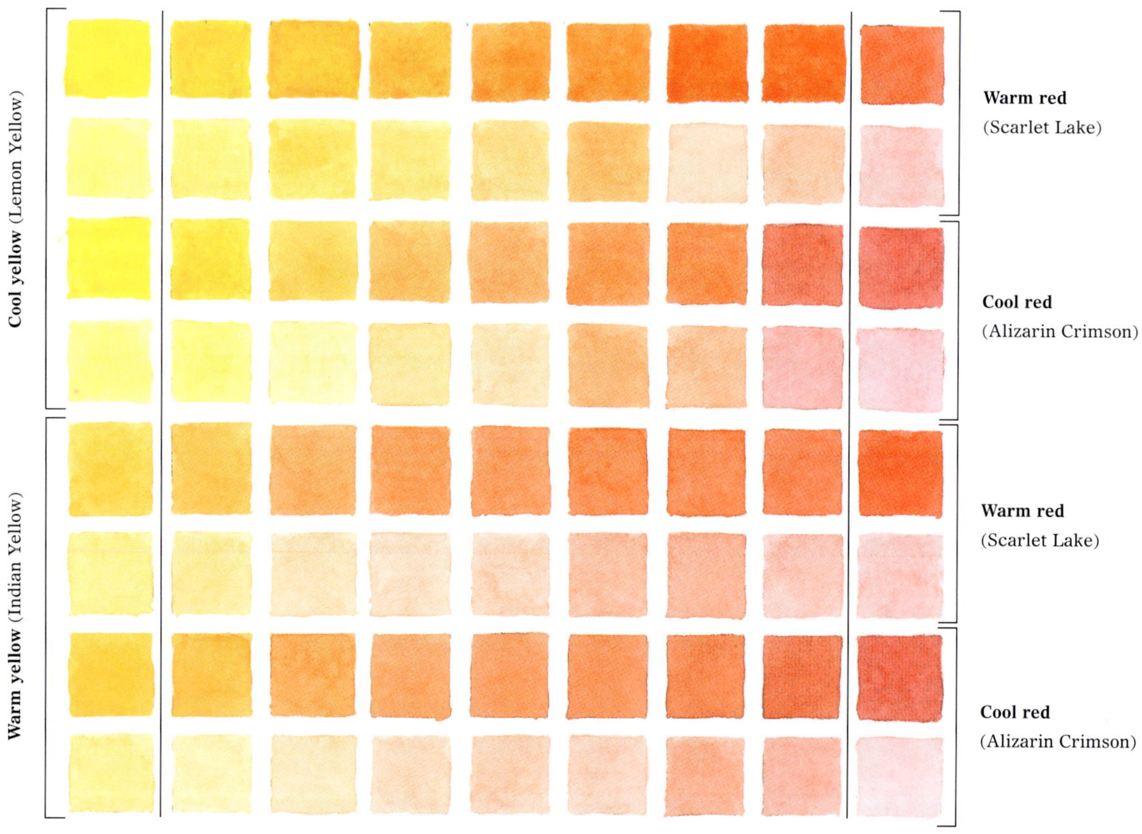

Rows 5-8 use a warm yellow base (Indian Yellow), with the addition of warm red (Scarlet Lake) in rows 5 and 6, and cool red (Alizarin Crimson) in rows 7 and 8.

Making your own chart will teach you a lot more than just studying the one shown here, and you can pin it up to refer to. Using good HP watercolour paper, either draw ruled squares to fill in or make freestyle blocks of colour across the paper from left to right.

Chart 2

The same yellows are used again, this time with warm blue (French Ultramarine) and cool blue (Prussian Blue). Note the different greens that result, depending on whether the colours in the mix are warm/warm, cool/cool or warm/cool.

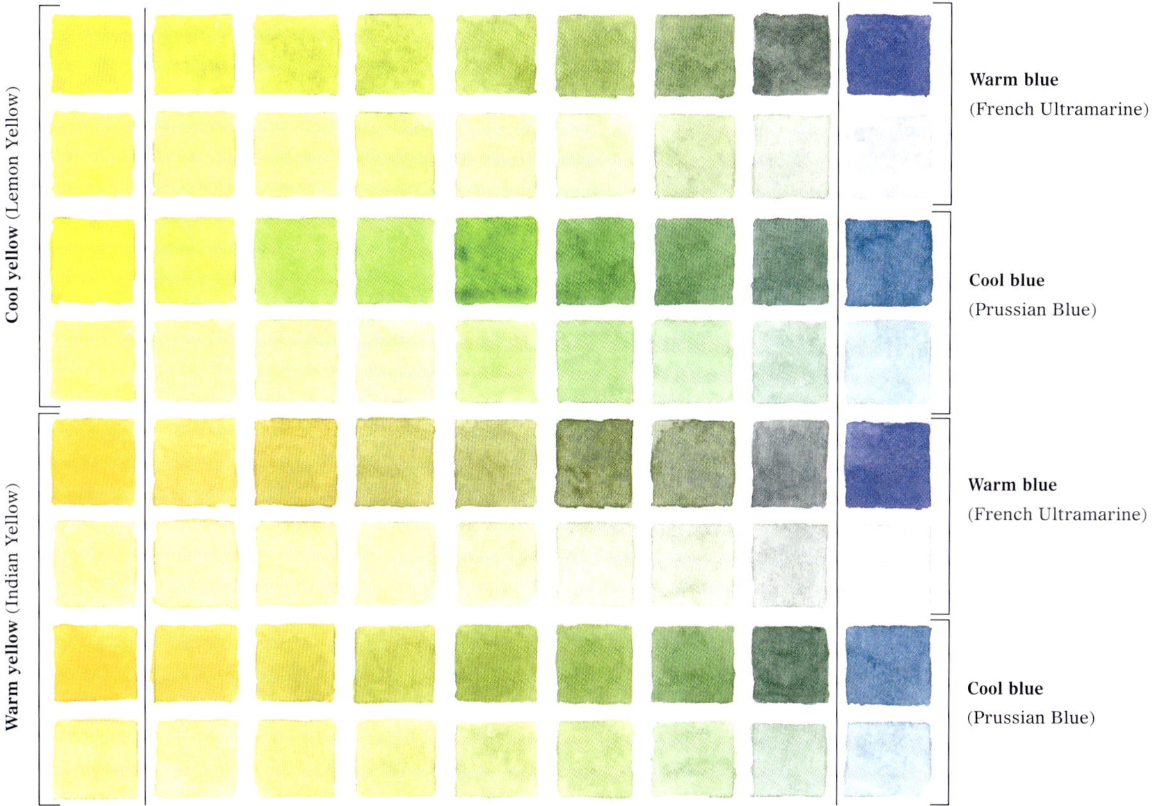

Chart 3

This time the yellows are mixed with Opera Rose and Winsor Violet. Some glorious oranges, khakis and greys are the result, because you are mixing complementary colours.

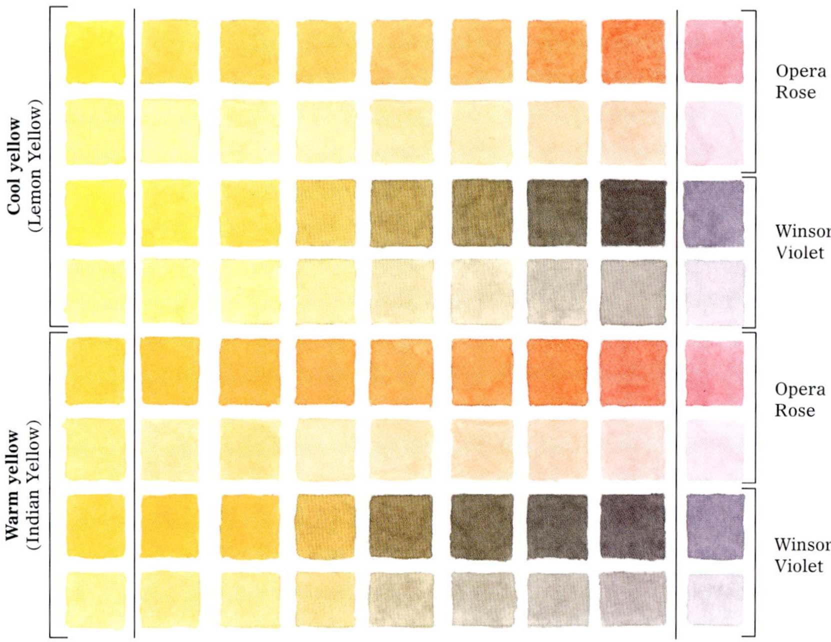

Chart 4

Here two reds – warm (Scarlet Lake) and cool (Alizarin Crimson) – are mixed with warm blue (French Ultramarine) and cool blue (Prussian Blue). Notice how a mix of red and blue sometimes gives a rich purple and at other times a brown, depending on whether the mix is warm/warm, cool/cool or warm/cool.

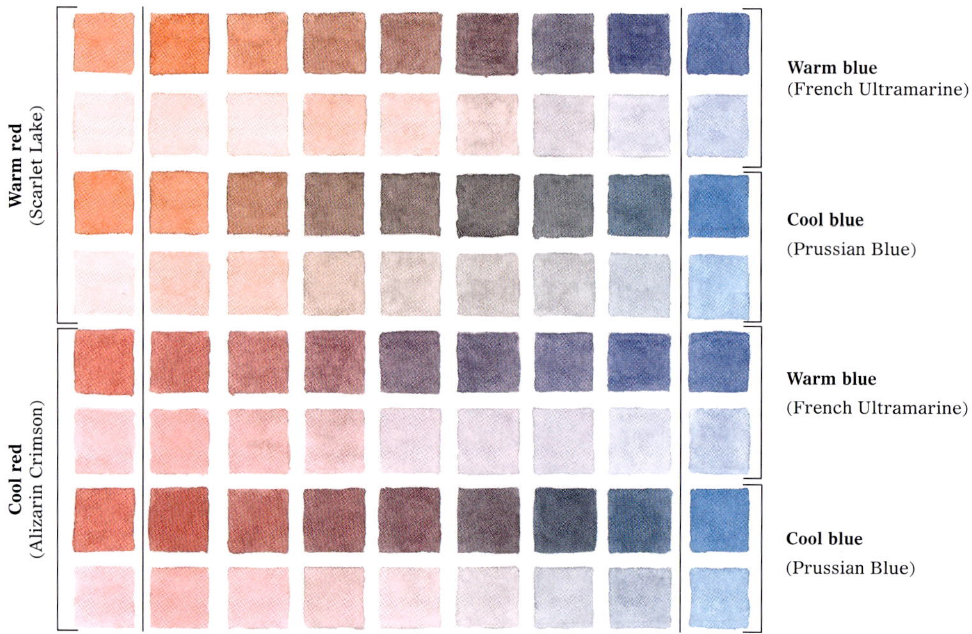

Charts 5 and 6

These two charts use Opera Rose and Winsor Violet as the initial colours, mixed with the two reds – Scarlet Lake (warm) and Alizarin Crimson (cool) and the two blues – French Ultramarine (warm) and Prussian Blue (cool).

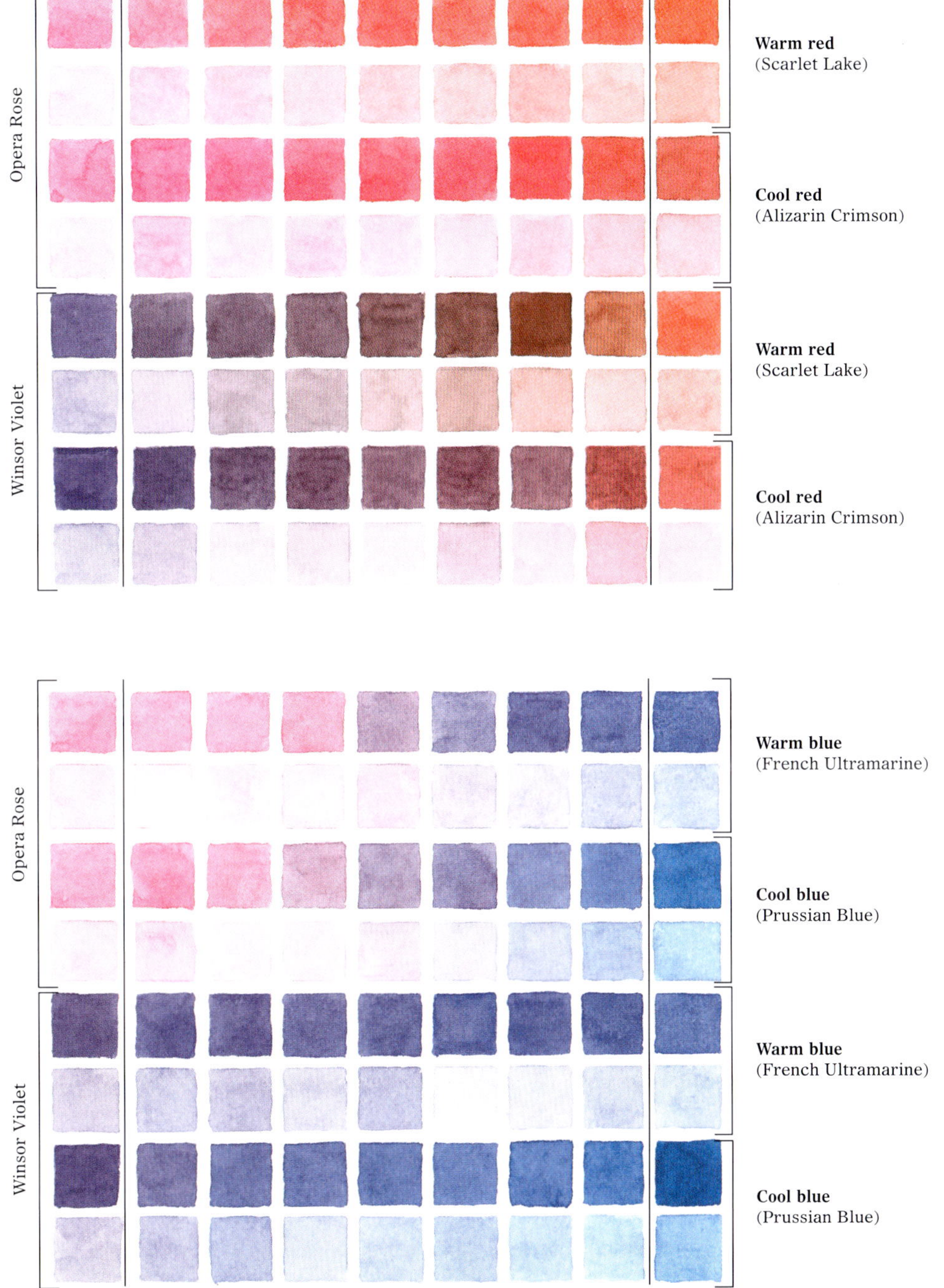

Using Sap Green

Sap Green is the only ready-made green we would recommend you to use. However, it's never advisable to use a bought green straight from the tube because it will rarely be the right colour. This chart shows Sap Green mixed with each of the other colours, resulting not only in some interesting greens, but also in some rich browns, greys and aquamarines.

When you have completed all your mixing charts, keep them in a safe place as a colour reference for the future, to show what you can achieve with the limited colours in your paintbox.

Exercise: **Colour-matching**

Some plants are so brilliantly or strangely coloured that it can be hard to decide which paints to mix to achieve an exact hue. Using the charts on pages 58–61, see if you can find the approximate colours that you might use for the deep reddish-violet of the *Curcuma*, the brilliant blue of the *Cerinthe* bracts and soft blue-green of the leaves, and the pale mauve fungus *Laccaria amethystea* or amethyst deceiver. Then try mixing them yourself, using the initial colour and the added colour as shown in each chart.

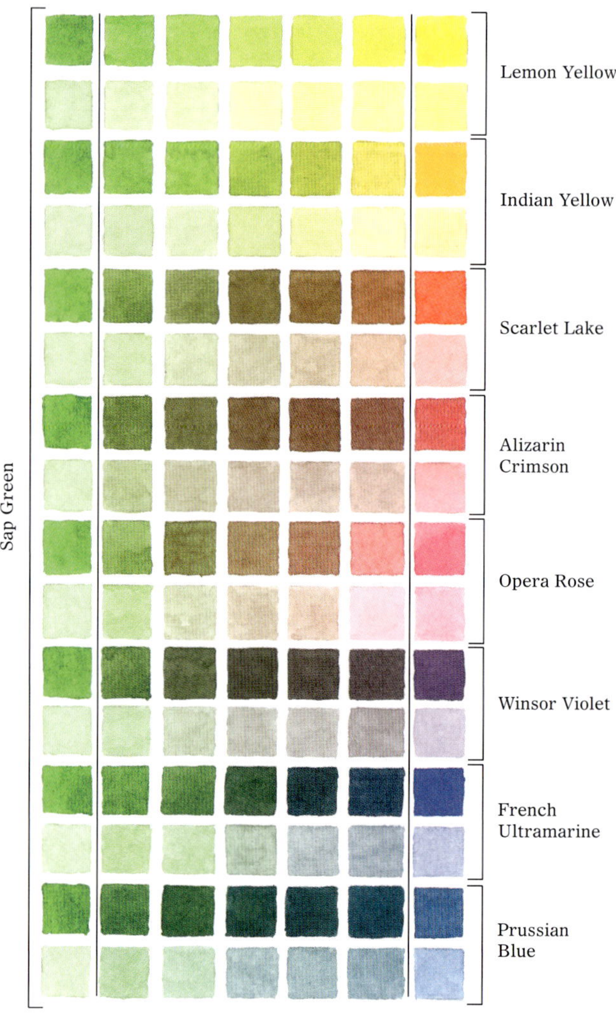

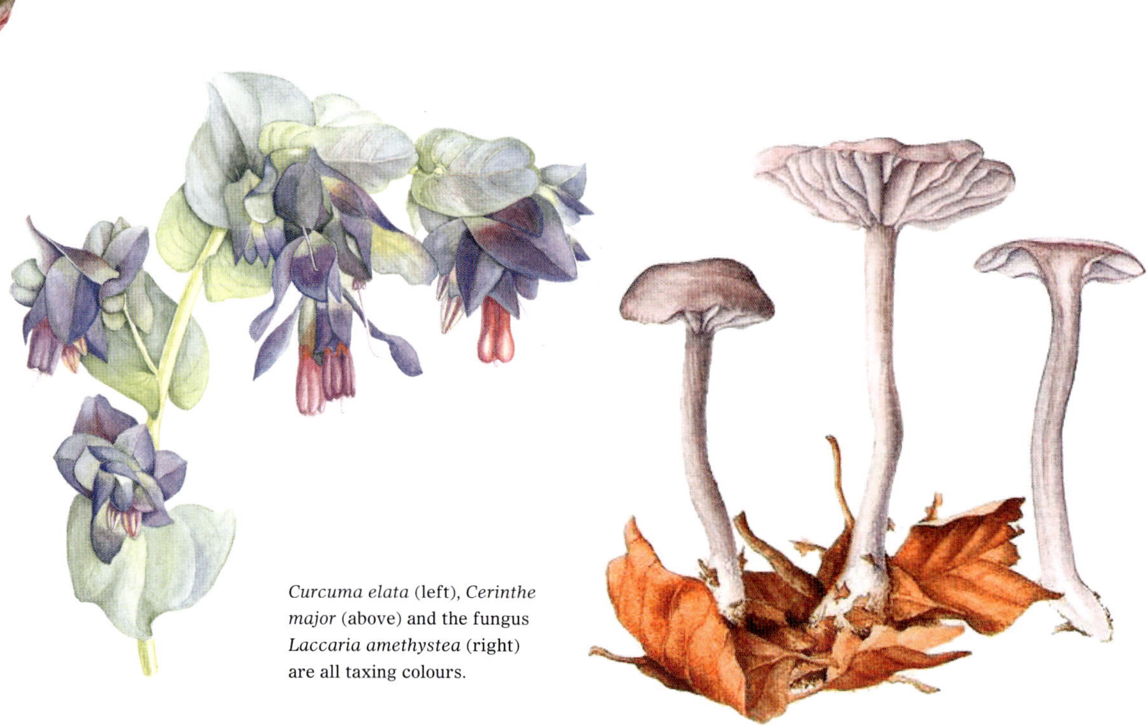

Curcuma elata (left), *Cerinthe major* (above) and the fungus *Laccaria amethystea* (right) are all taxing colours.

Exercise: Tertiary mixes and the role of complementaries

The next six exercises on greens, purples and oranges are arguably the most important for the botanical artist, because they clearly explain how complementary colours work.

Green

A green made from tertiary colours greeny-yellow and greeny-blue will be vibrant and bright because no red (green's complementary) is present (right). Look again at the colour wheel on page 54 and note that the greeny-yellow is a green leaning towards primary yellow and the greeny-blue is a blue leaning towards primary yellow.

In contrast, if you mix tertiaries orangey-yellow and purply-blue you will get a muddy green (right). Looking at the 12-hue colour wheel, you will see that both the orangey-yellow and purply-blue lean towards primary red. This therefore suggests that obtaining a bright green is impossible when the colours used both contain red.

Purple

The same rule applies when mixing purple. You can make a bright purple by mixing purply-blue with purply-red, both of which are tertiary colours and lean towards primary red (right). A bright purple results because there is no yellow (purple's complementary) present.

However, if you want a muddy brown-purple, use the tertiary colours greeny-blue and orangey-red, both of which lean towards primary yellow (right). The red and blue used both contain yellow and, as shown on the 12-hue colour wheel, yellow is the complementary of purple.

Orange

Primary red and primary yellow make orange. To make a bright and vivid orange, it naturally follows that you would choose tertiaries orangey-yellow and orangey-red (right).

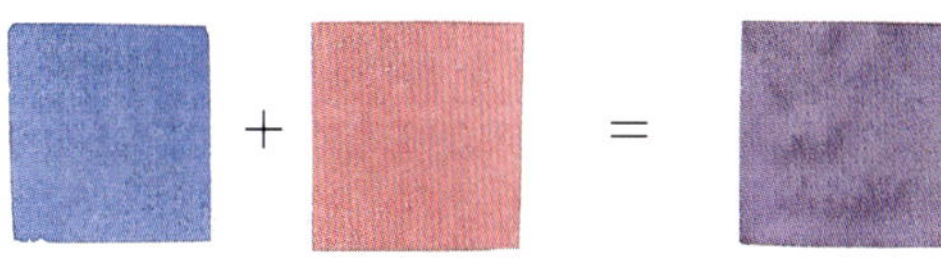

If, however, you were to mix a greeny-yellow (leaning towards blue on the colour circle) with a purple-red (also leaning towards blue) then you have blue present in both the greeny-yellow and the purple-red. Blue, as we know, is the complementary of orange and will therefore produce a much more muted, almost bronze, brown-orange (right).

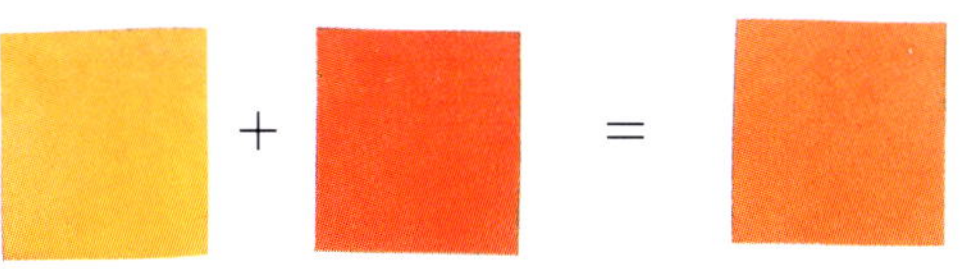

Try mixing other tertiary colours together and see what effects you can achieve. Always note which colours you have used so that your test pieces become a useful colour reference swatch for the future.

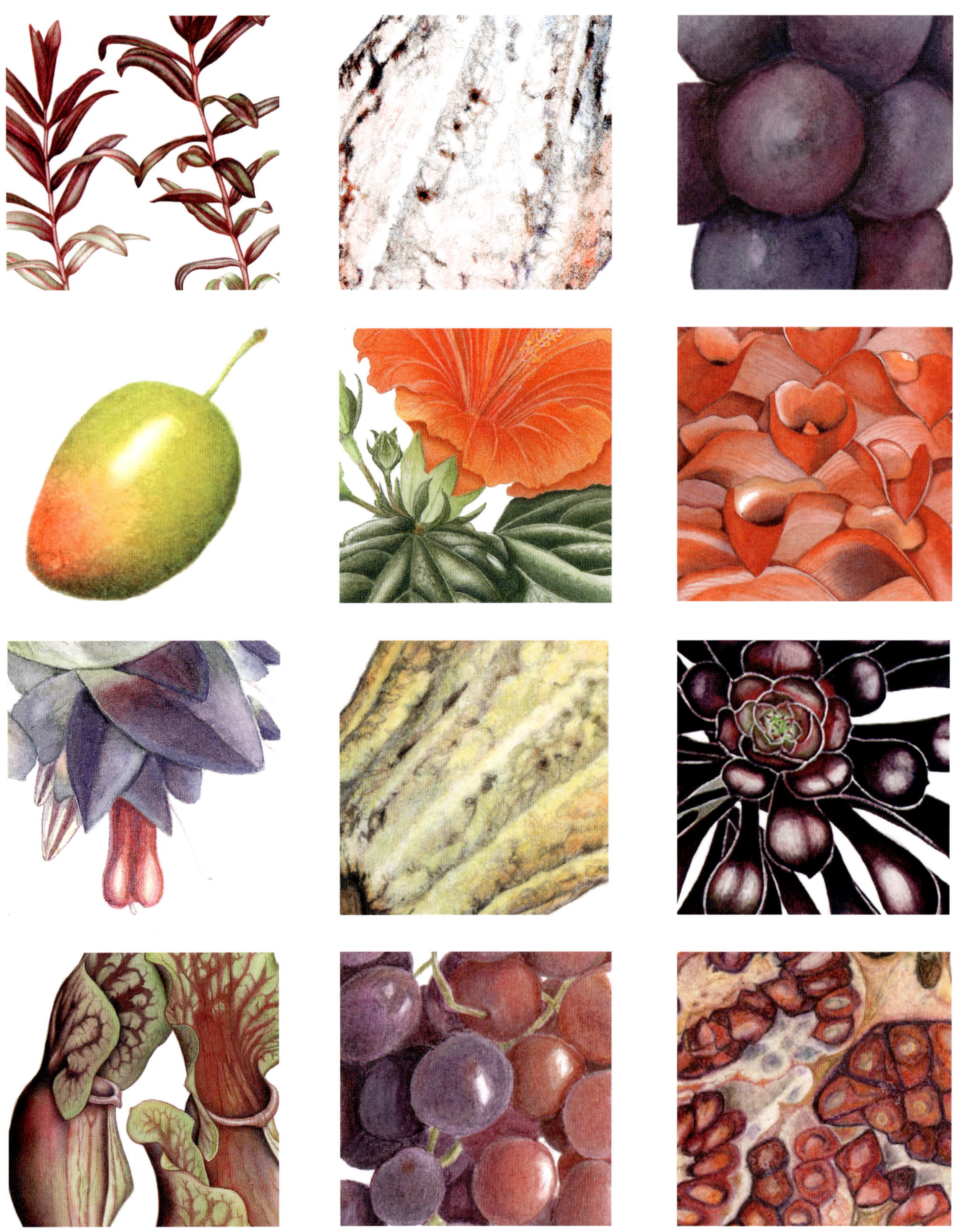

Physical and optical mixing

There are two ways of mixing colours: physical mixing, where paint colours are mixed on the palette before being applied to the paper or other support, and optical mixing, where colours are achieved through an understanding of how our eye perceives colours that overlay or juxtapose one another. Glazing or layering paint is a commonly used technique of optical mixing, although stippling one colour on top of another also works. In all cases, the first layer or layers must be completely dry before adding another.

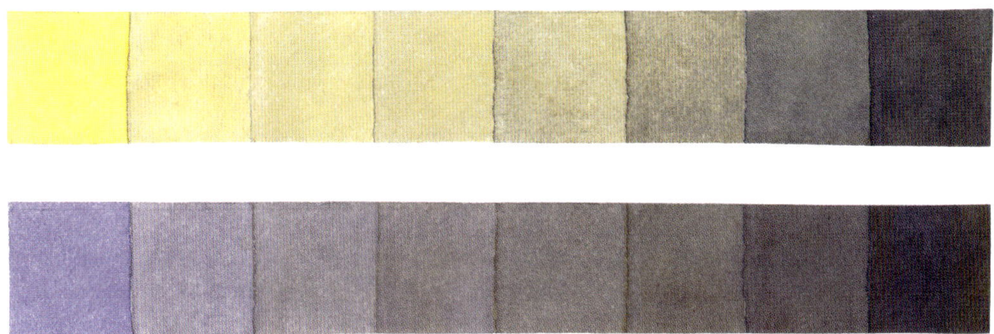

This enlarged, unfinished painting of the jelly bean plant (*Sedum rubrotinctum*) (below) shows how the initial washes have been augmented with colour, details and surface bloom.

Optical mixing is said to produce richer and more resonant colours than physical mixing, although this is open to debate. When you have completed the exercises in this section you should be able to draw your own conclusions.

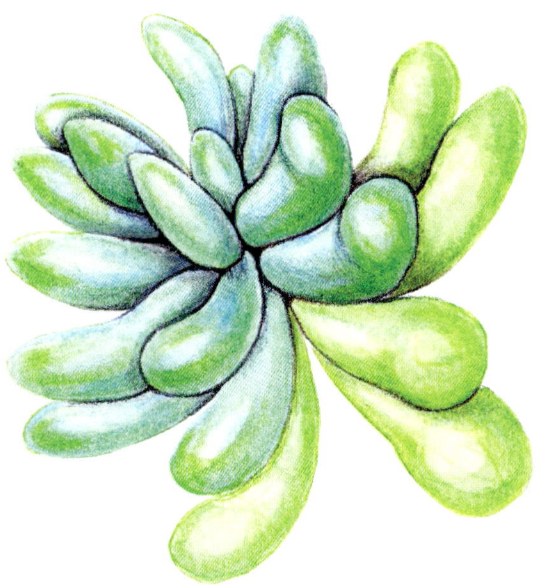

Left These are all examples of optical mixing, where layers of colours are superimposed one on another to give rich and resonant results.

Key to physical and optical mixes

These two groups of coloured squares show the same mixes: full strength in the group at the top, diluted underneath. Each row uses the named colours, first as a physical mix (left) then as an optical mix (centre and right). The colours in the left columns are secondaries mixed from the warm and cool primaries to their left and right. Note how two warm colours produce a warm, subdued mix, whereas two cool colours produce a cool, bright mix.

warm green

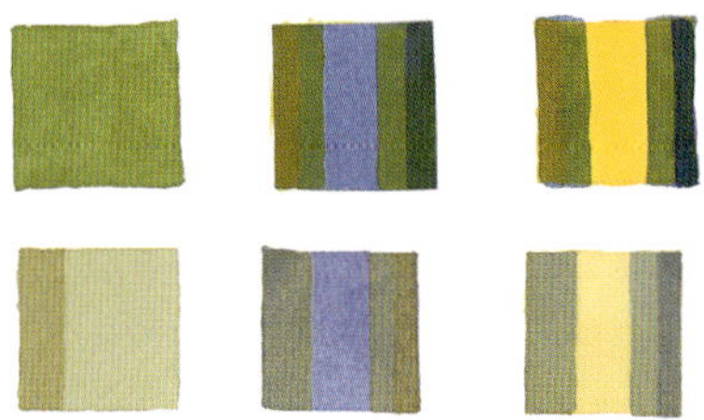

Left: French Ultramarine + Indian Yellow (both colours lean to red)
Centre: Optical mix – French Ultramarine with Indian Yellow superimposed on top, then a strip of French Ultramarine
Right: Optical mix – Indian Yellow with French Ultramarine superimposed on top, then a strip of Indian Yellow

cool green

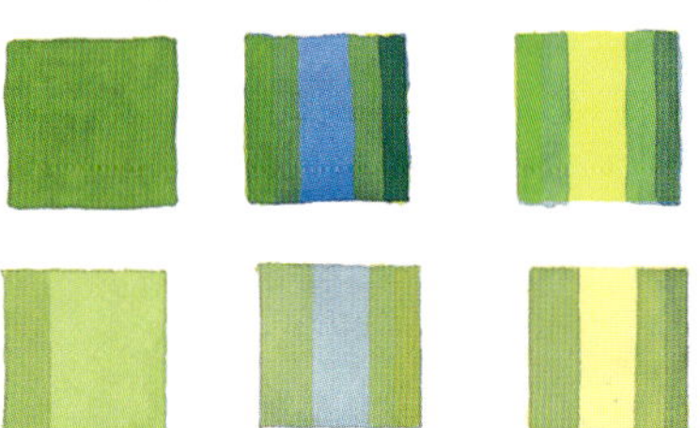

Left: Winsor Blue (Green Shade) + Lemon Yellow (both colours lean to yellow)
Centre: Optical mix – Winsor Blue (Green Shade) with Lemon Yellow superimposed on top, then a strip of Winsor Blue (Green Shade)
Right: Optical mix – Lemon Yellow with Winsor Blue (Green Shade) superimposed on top, then a strip of Lemon Yellow

warm purple

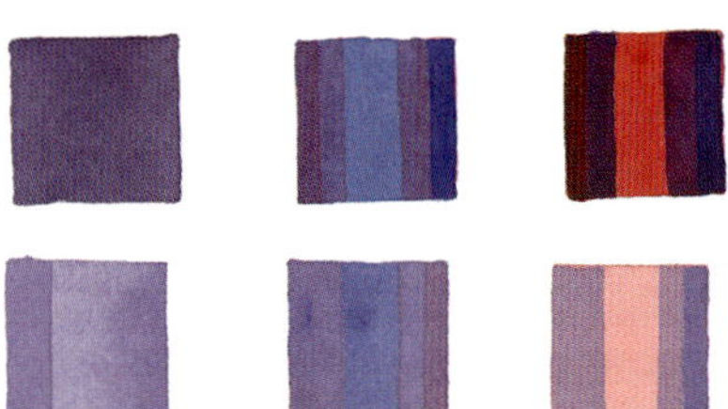

Left: Winsor Blue (Green Shade) + Scarlet Lake (both colours lean to yellow)
Centre: Optical mix – Winsor Blue (Green Shade) with Scarlet Lake superimposed on top, then a strip of Winsor Blue (Green Shade)
Right: Optical mix – Scarlet Lake with Winsor Blue (Green Shade) superimposed on top, then a strip of Scarlet Lake

cool purple

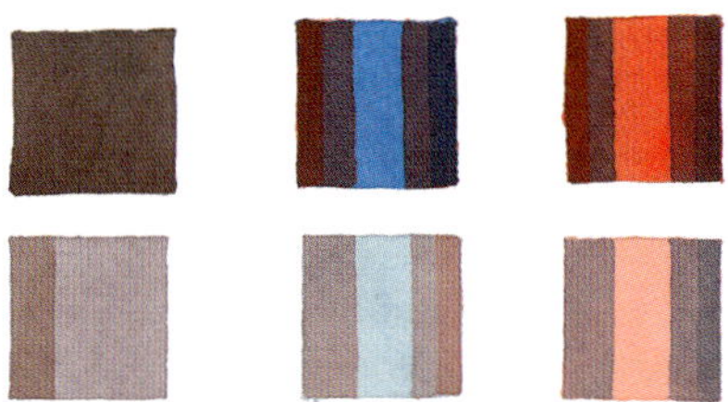

Left: French Ultramarine + Alizarin Crimson (both colours lean to purple/blue)
Centre: Optical mix – French Ultramarine with Alizarin Crimson superimposed on top, then a strip of French Ultramarine
Right: Optical mix – Alizarin Crimson with French Ultramarine superimposed on top, then a strip of Alizarin Crimson

warm orange

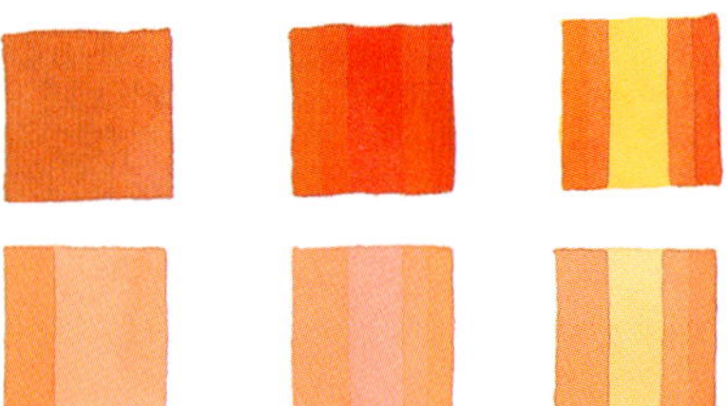

Left: Scarlet Lake + Indian Yellow (both colours lean to red)
Centre: Optical mix – Scarlet Lake with Indian Yellow superimposed on top, then a strip of Scarlet Lake
Right: Optical mix – Indian Yellow with Scarlet Lake superimposed on top, then a strip of Indian Yellow

cool orange

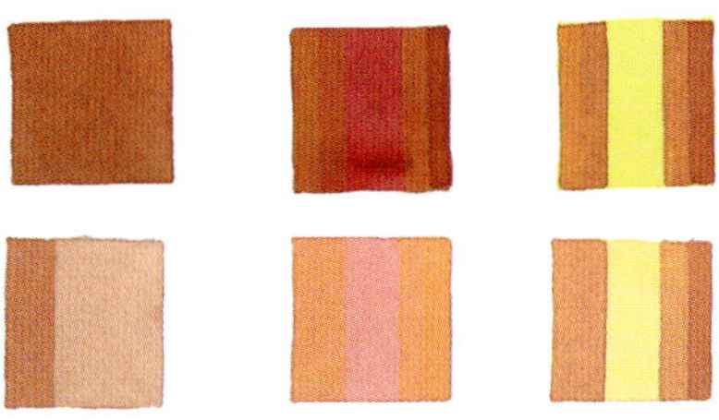

Left: Alizarin Crimson + Lemon Yellow (both colours lean to blue)
Centre: Optical mix – Alizarin Crimson with Lemon Yellow superimposed on top, then a strip of Alizarin Crimson
Right: Optical mix – Lemon Yellow with Alizarin Crimson superimposed on top, then a strip of Lemon Yellow

Do you know which colour to start with, and what you should add to it to achieve the correct mix? In this exercise, you will be matching as many natural colours as possible, using the six primary colours.

- Collect small plant bits from the garden or hedgerow, beach or moor. Separate them into blocks of similar colour, and divide the blocks into cool and warm (see the examples on the following pages).

- Mix the paint for each individual specimen, making a note of which colours you use. You can refer to them as 'cool' and 'warm' or give them the manufacturer's name, for instance Winsor Lemon. Do not use any bought greens.

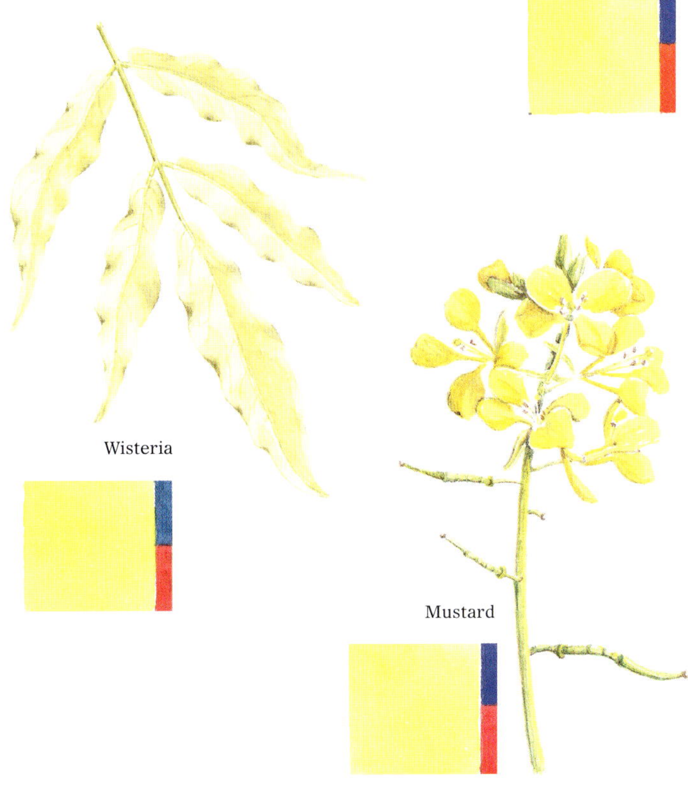

Privet

Cool yellows

Each of the examples shown right started with a cool yellow (for example Lemon Yellow); the privet used warm blue (French Ultramarine) and warm red (Scarlet Lake); the wisteria had the addition of cool blue (Prussian Blue) and cool red (Alizarin Crimson) and the mustard had the addition of warm blue (French Ultramarine) and cool red (Alizarin Crimson): No bought green was used.

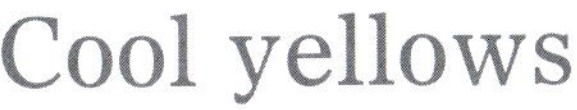

Wisteria

Mustard

Warm yellows

Both examples below, the oak leaf and the dandelion flower head, used mainly warm yellow but with the addition of cool yellow (Lemon Yellow), warm red (Scarlet Lake) and warm blue (French Ultramarine).

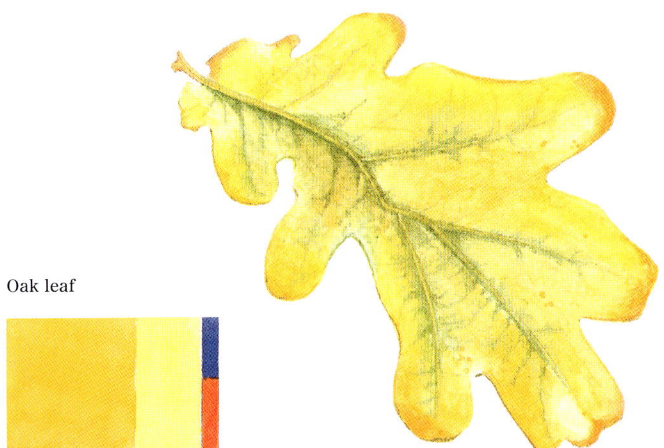

Oak leaf

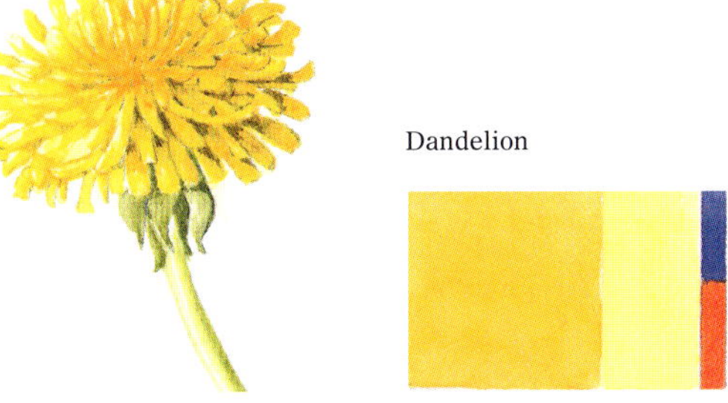

Dandelion

Cool blues

Most blues in nature are warm rather than cool. However, the hydrangea flower (below) and the delphinium (right) are good examples of plants that are based on a cool blue (for example Prussian Blue). In both cases small amounts of warm blue (French Ultramarine) were added. In addition, the hydrangea had some small amounts of cool red (Alizarin Crimson) and warm yellow (Indian Yellow). The delphinium had the addition of a cool yellow (Lemon Yellow) and some Opera Rose.

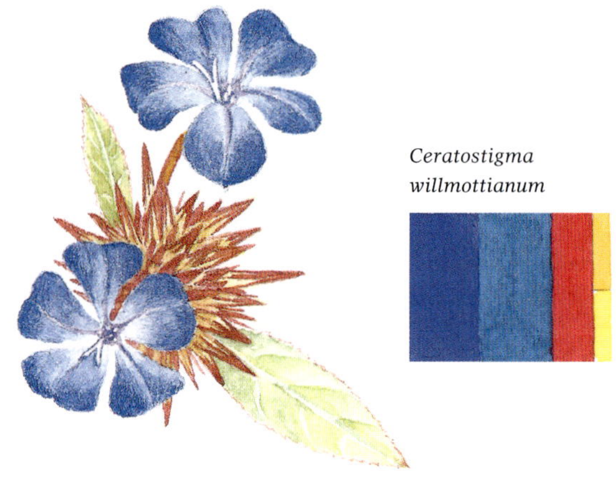

Delphinium

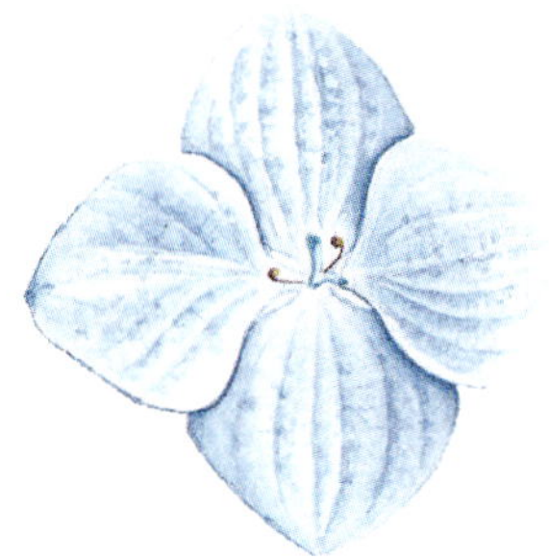

Hydrangea

Warm blues

The agapanthus floret (below right) used warm blue (French Ultramarine) with small amounts of Opera Rose and warm yellow (Indian Yellow).

Both blues were used for the *Ceratostigma willmottianum* (right) and the brunnera (below left) but with the emphasis on the warm blue (French Ultramarine). The *Ceratostigma* also had cool red (Alizarin Crimson), warm yellow (Indian Yellow) and cool yellow (Lemon Yellow), but the major use of these extra colours was in the stems and developing buds. The brunnera also used Opera Rose and cool red (Alizarin Crimson) which was the dominant colour in the stems.

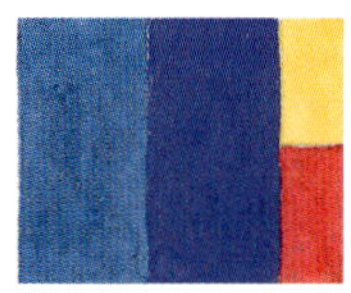

*Ceratostigma
willmottianum*

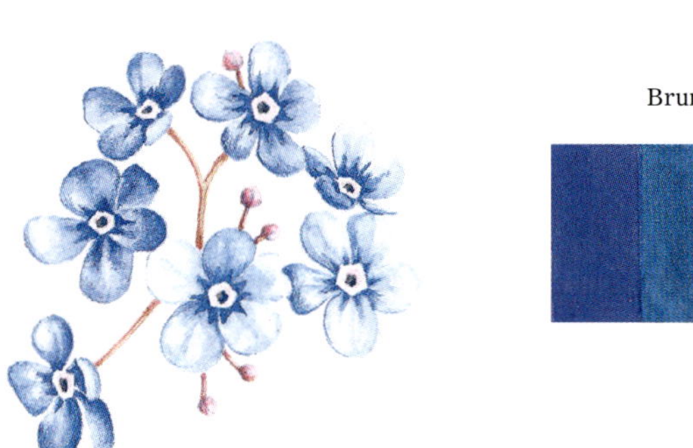

Brunnera

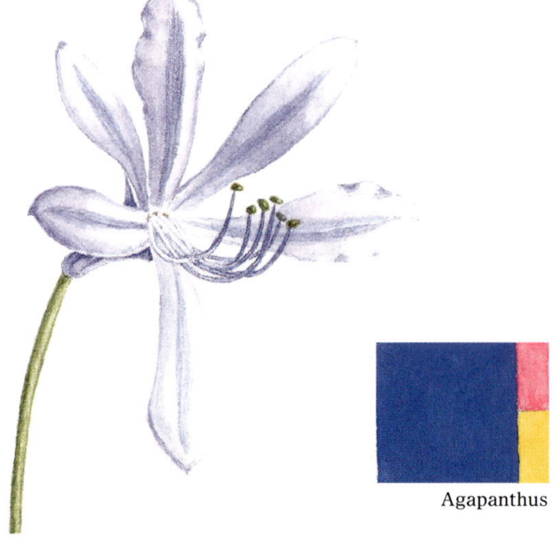

Agapanthus

Cool reds

There are relatively few cool reds in nature, although some leaves or berries tend to get a blueish look when they are 'going over'.

The honeysuckle berries (above right) use mainly cool red (Alizarin Crimson) with quite a bit of warm red (Scarlet Lake) and touches of both yellows and some warm blue (French Ultramarine). The green mix for the stem and leaves had some cool red (Alizarin Crimson) added to dull it down.

The photinia leaf (right) is made up mainly from a cool red (Alizarin Crimson) with the addition of warm red (Scarlet Lake) and some warm blue (French Ultramarine).

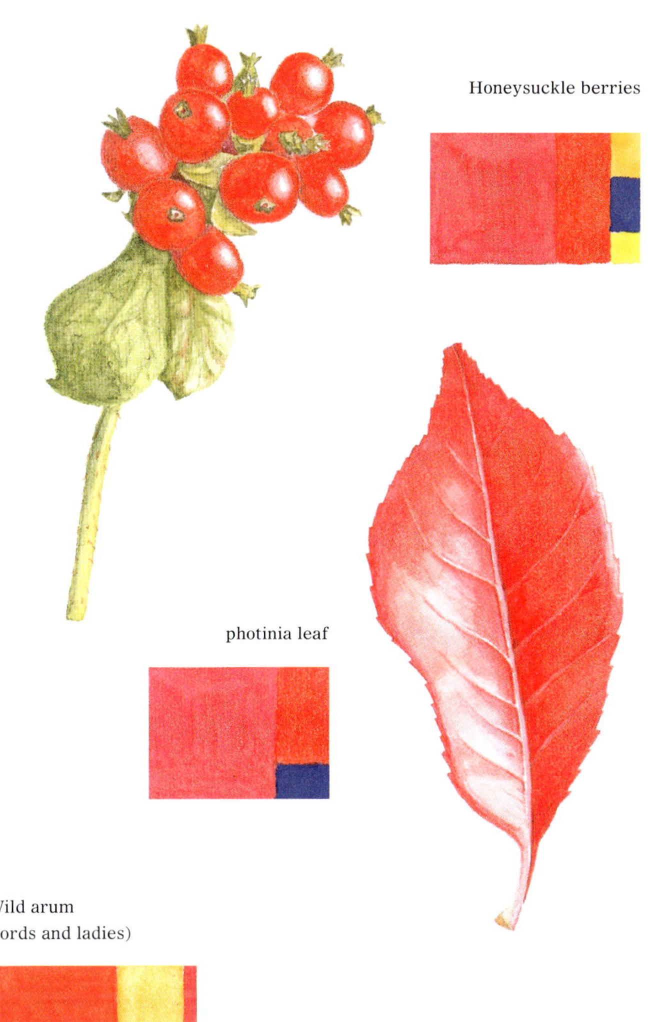

Honeysuckle berries

photinia leaf

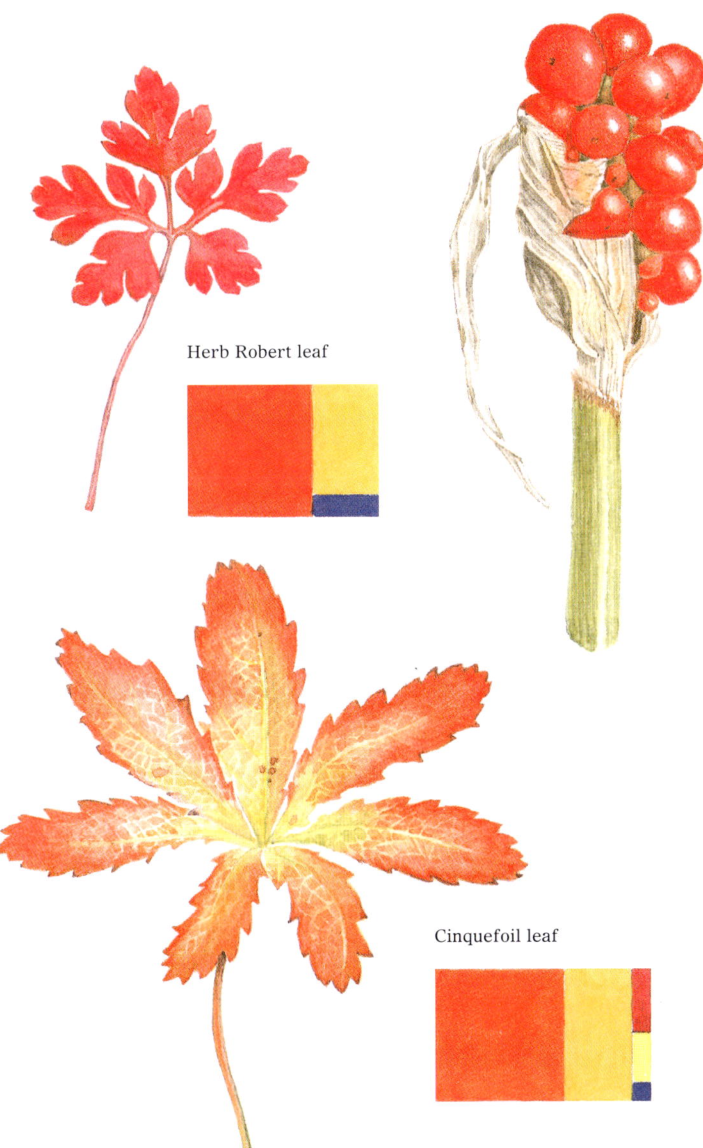

Herb Robert leaf

Wild arum
(lords and ladies)

Cinquefoil leaf

Warm reds

The herb Robert leaf (far left) used predominantly warm red (Scarlet Lake) with a little warm yellow (Indian Yellow) and warm blue (French Ultramarine).

The berries of the wild arum, lords and ladies, (above) are painted with warm red (Scarlet Lake) with warm yellow (Indian Yellow), cool red (Alizarin Crimson) and touches of warm blue (French Ultramarine). These colours were also used in varying proportions for the dry, papery calyx and the shiny stem.

The cinquefoil leaf (left) again started with warm red (Scarlet Lake), with the addition of some warm yellow (Indian Yellow), cool red (Alizarin Crimson), cool yellow (Lemon Yellow) and just a little bit of warm blue (French Ultramarine).

Difficult colours

The main colour of the hibiscus flower shown right is Winsor Violet, with additions of Opera Rose and touches of cool red (Alizarin Crimson) in the flashes at the base of the petals.

The red hydrangea (below left) used mainly warm red (Scarlet Lake), with Opera Rose, cool red (Alizarin Crimson), cool yellow (Lemon Yellow) and warm blue (French Ultramarine).

The geranium (below centre) started with Winsor Violet mixed with Opera Rose, adding tiny amounts of cool yellow (Lemon Yellow) and cool blue (Prussian Blue). Notice how the pink has been allowed to shine through in places.

The fuchsia flower (shown right) divides into four distinct colour sections. The colours used are warm red (Scarlet Lake) with Opera Rose, Winsor Violet, Lemon Yellow and some cool blue (Prussian Blue).

Hibiscus

Fuchsia

Geranium

Hydrangea

Snow-in-summer
(*Cerastium
tomentosum*)

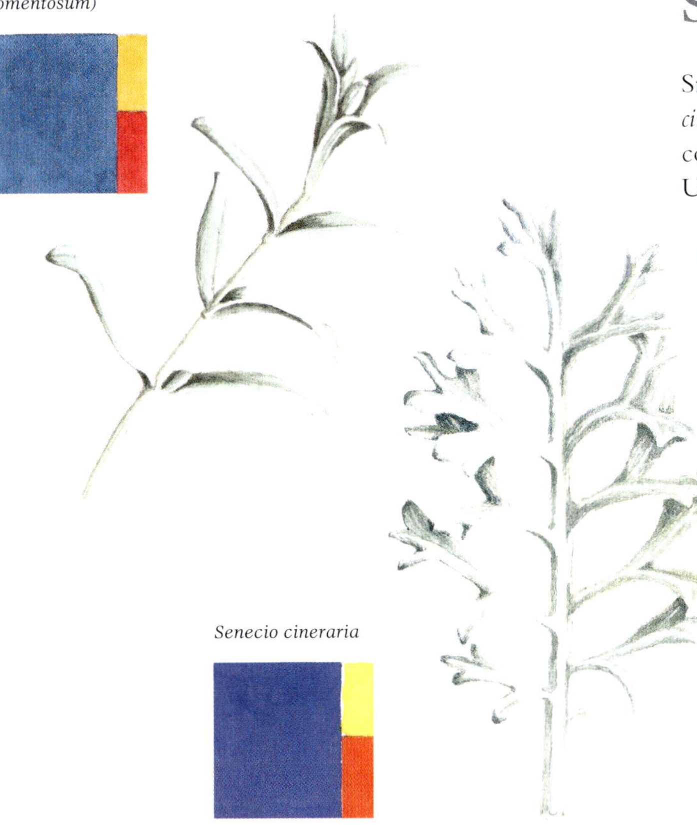

Senecio cineraria

Silvery-greens

Snow-in-summer (*Cerastium tomentosum*) (left) and *Senecio cineraria* (below left) are both examples of silvery-greens, a colour that many students find extremely difficult to mix. Using very diluted colour will help you here.

For the snow-in-summer, mix a small amount of cool blue (Prussian Blue), warm yellow (Indian Yellow) and cool red (Alizarin Crimson), then add clean water to some of it until it is the pale bluey-green you require. Use the stronger mix for darker areas.

The *Senecio cineraria*, on the other hand, uses French Ultramarine, Lemon Yellow and Scarlet Lake.

Try both mixes and see how they differ – and how similar you can make them.

Almost black

There are lots of examples of 'black' flowers and leaves in nature, but if you look closely at them you will see that they are not black at all. The leaf of *Sambucus nigra* (right), for instance, has flashes of pale blue where it catches the light, together with some areas that are more pink than any other colour.

Practise mixing 'black' colours using both blues, both reds and both yellows. Look carefully at your subject to determine whether it is a blue-black, a red-black or a yellow-black. See how you can alter the character of the paint mix by adding a little more of one colour – in effect, see how many different blacks you can make. Keep a note of which colours you use, and which one dominates, as this will be a very useful reference for future paintings.

It's interesting to note that the colours used for the dark *Sambucus nigra* are the same as were used for the white orchid on page 114. In the case of the orchid, the paint was well diluted to give pale blue-greys, pink-greys and yellow-greys.

If you can understand and develop clever control and use of colour, it will greatly enhance your work, giving it strength and vitality as well as subtlety and harmony.

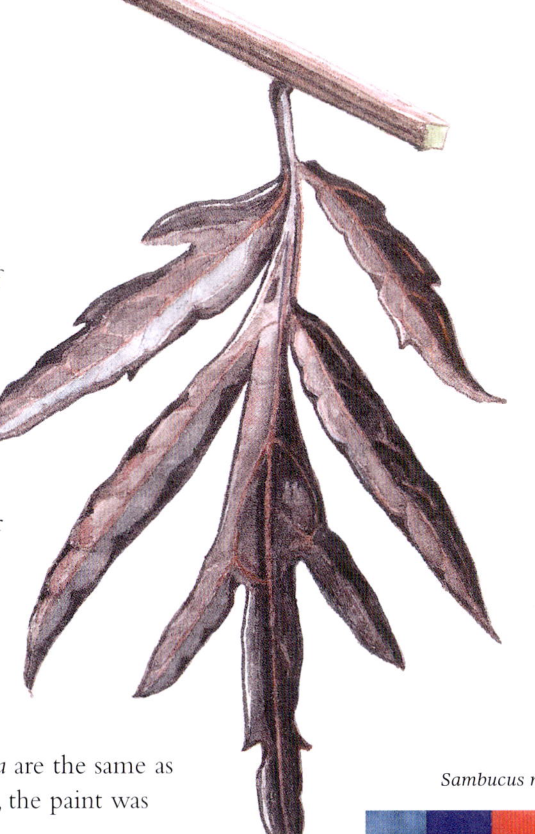

Sambucus nigra

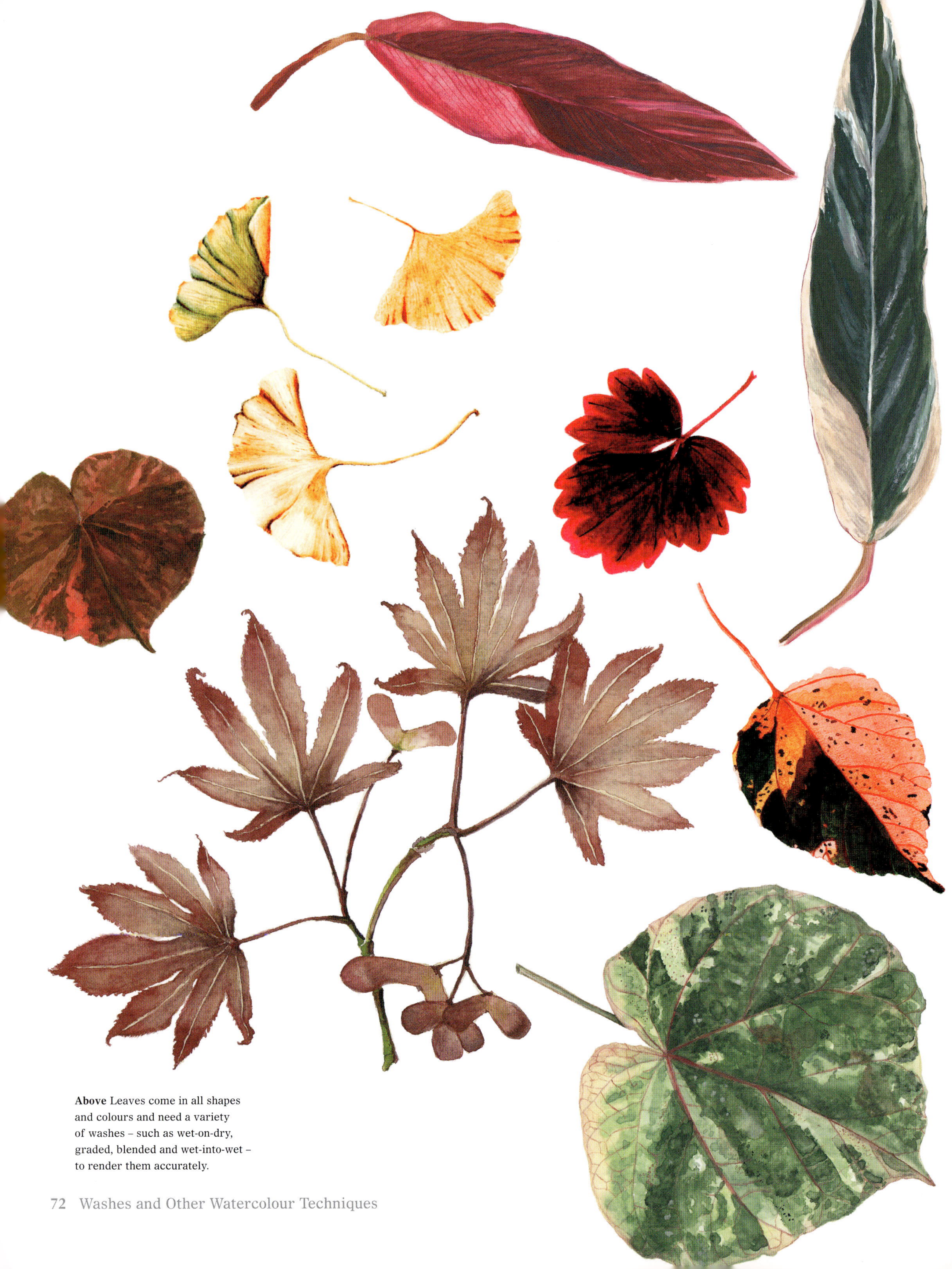

Above Leaves come in all shapes
and colours and need a variety
of washes – such as wet-on-dry,
graded, blended and wet-into-wet –
to render them accurately.

Washes and Other Watercolour Techniques

Before you start to paint a subject, you need to understand the stages of painting and how you can apply these to any given specimen.

The watercolour artist uses the white of the paper to shine through and lighten colours. This means that, unlike the process of oil painting, the light colours are usually worked first, and depth of tone is built up in stages. An example of this is shown below, where you can see the trial sheet for the dried nepenthes pitcher (right). You can also see a trials page and a finished portrait of a live nepenthes on page 122. The main techniques are washes – flat, wet-on-dry, graded, blended and wet-into-wet.

If you are about to tackle a new effect, trial sheets are vitally important. It's best to make your trials on the same watercolour paper that you will use for your finished painting, but offcuts left over from earlier work will save you starting a new sheet.

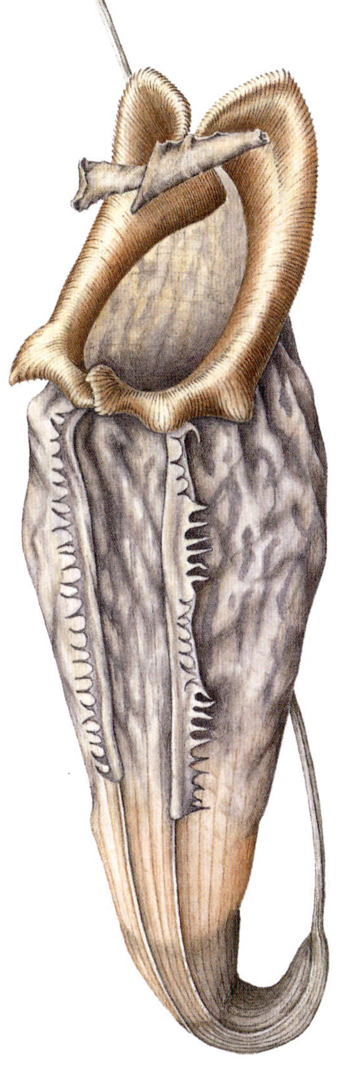

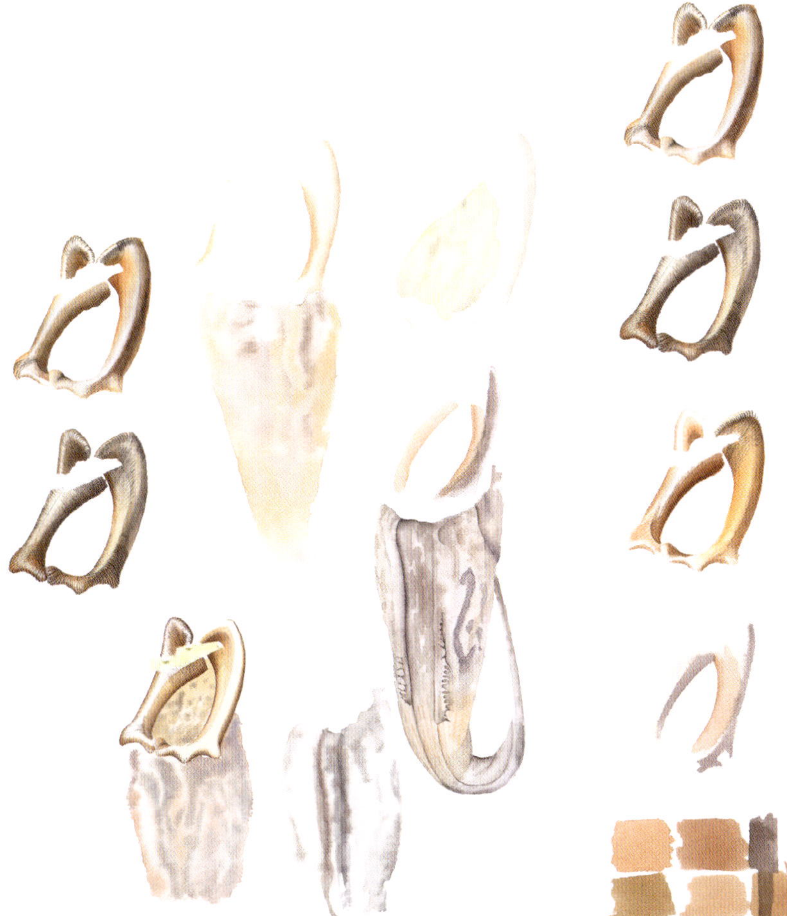

Above and left Work light colours first, building up depth of tone in stages.

Some initial washes

Wet-on-dry

A pale wash applied directly on to dry
paper. Paint should be fluid so that it
flows on to the paper easily and
smoothly.

Graded wet-on-dry

Paint on to dry paper, starting with a
fairly strong colour and gradually
dilute it with clean water as you work
down the page.

Blended wet-on-dry

Paint on to dry paper with one colour
blending into another smoothly and
evenly.

Wet-into-wet

Wet the paper thoroughly, and when
its 'shine' becomes a 'sheen' drop strong
paint on to it. If the paper is too wet
you will have no control over where
the paint stays.

Superimposed colour

Paint two or more colours over one
another once the previous layers are
dry (see page 65).

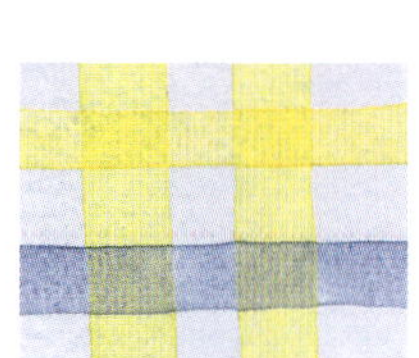

Building up tones

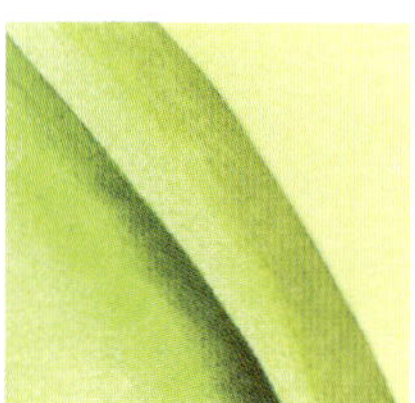

There are two basic techniques used
here for a three-dimensional effect:

1) Apply stronger or deeper paint on
to the dry initial wash and then blend
it smoothly and evenly into the background using a damp
brush. Allow to dry. Repeat until previous paint layers start
to lift.

2) At this stage, change to stippling, applying tiny strokes or
dots of paint with a fine brush, laid side by side or on top of
one another to produce a smooth and even tonal change
from light to dark.

Highlights

You can leave out highlights altogether
by applying paint up to the highlighted
area and blending the edges with a
damp brush. If you find the highlights
are too stark when your painting is
finished, lay a very pale wash of French
Ultramarine over them.

Lowlights

Lowlights are not as definite as
highlights. They can be lifted off when
the wash is dry, using a damp brush.
When the paint is lifted it leaves a
little hazy colour.

Lifting paint

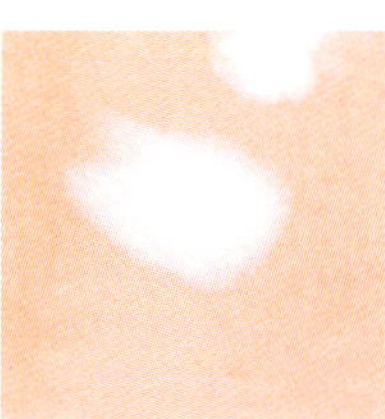

You can also lift paint for highlights
and lowlights by flooding the area with
clean water and blotting with absorbent
paper. Don't scrub as this will roughen
the surface of the paper and might
compromise future applications of paint.

Good and bad washes

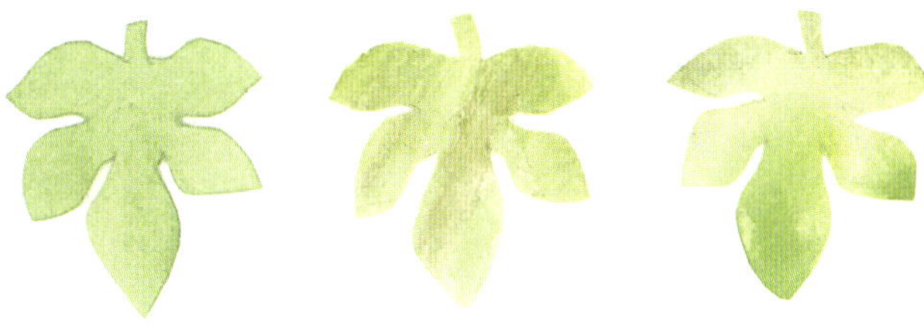

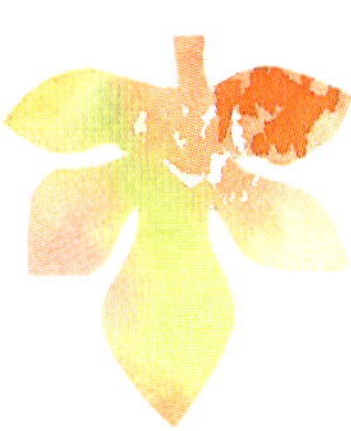

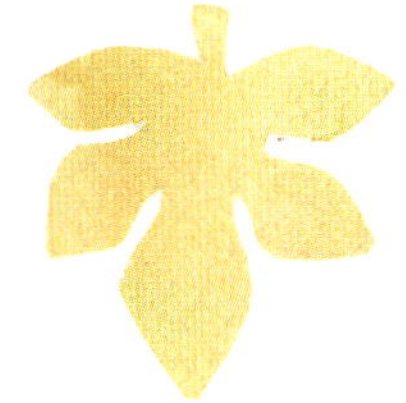

Flat wet-on-dry washes: good (left), too dry (centre) and too wet (right)

Blended wet-on-dry washes: good (left), too dry (centre) and too wet (right)

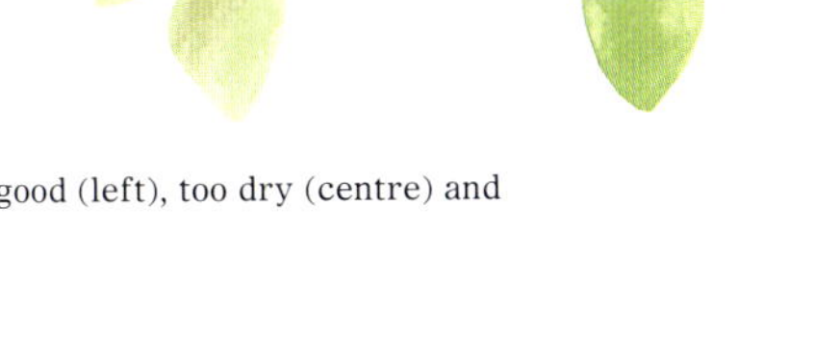

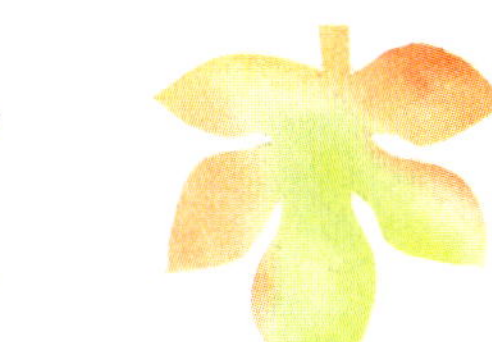

Graded wet-on-dry washes: good (left), too dry (centre) and too wet (right)

Paint dropped into clear water: good (left), too dry (centre) and too wet (right)

Exercise: Stages of painting

Try painting the parts of a generic flower, building up layers of paint with washes and stippling. This simple exercise shows the basic steps for painting a subject, using a generic plant.

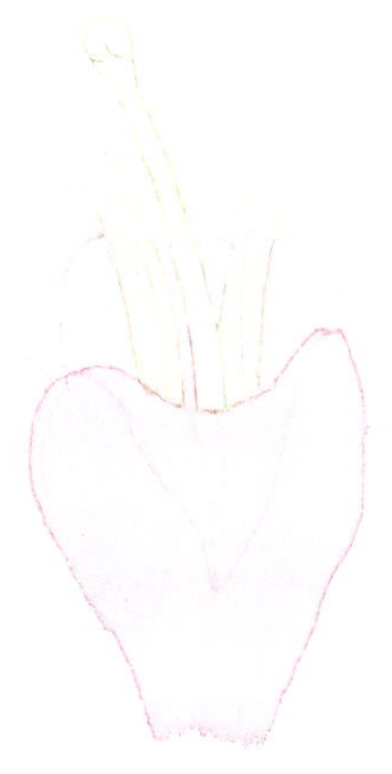

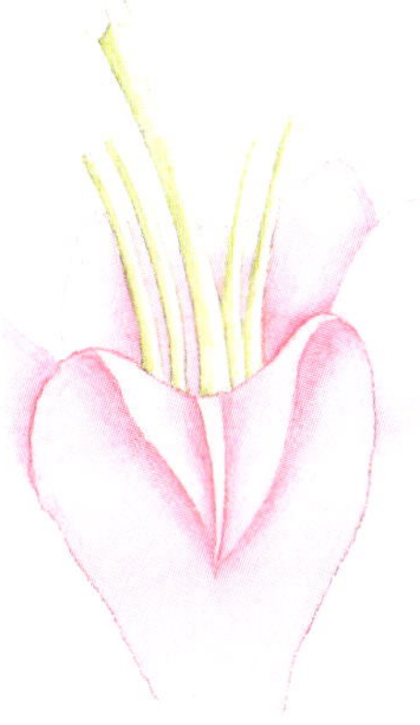

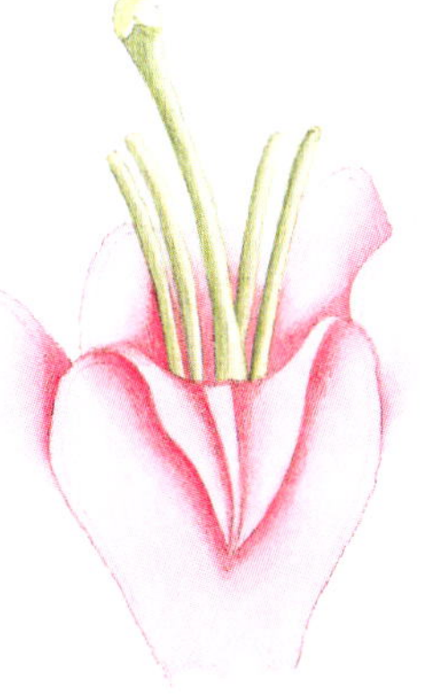

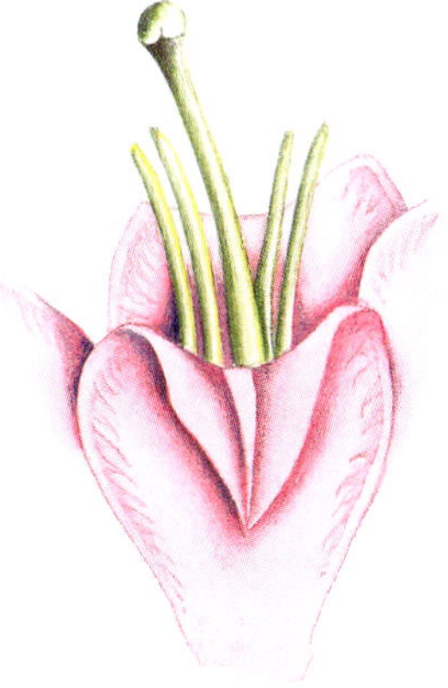

Step 1
Make a wet–on–dry initial wash to paint the individual plant parts.

Step 2
Now start building up tones by applying a slightly deeper shade of the same pink in places where shadow is required, then blending the paint with a damp brush.

Step 3
Increase the tonal build-up of the petals and between the stamens using Permanent Rose with a small amount of Winsor Blue (Green Shade). Add a deeper shade of Sap Green along the edge of stamens and blend carefully.

Step 4
Using a strong mix of Permanent Rose with small amounts of French Ultramarine and Winsor Blue (Green Shade), stipple on top of the previous layers. Add the markings with a fine brush, using the some pink-and-blue mix.

Exercise: Hebe 'Wild Romance'

Optical mixing has been described in detail on page 65–66, and here you might like to have a go at using it for a small subject such as the hebe (right). Take a look also at the hebe on page 6, which is another good example of optical mixing.

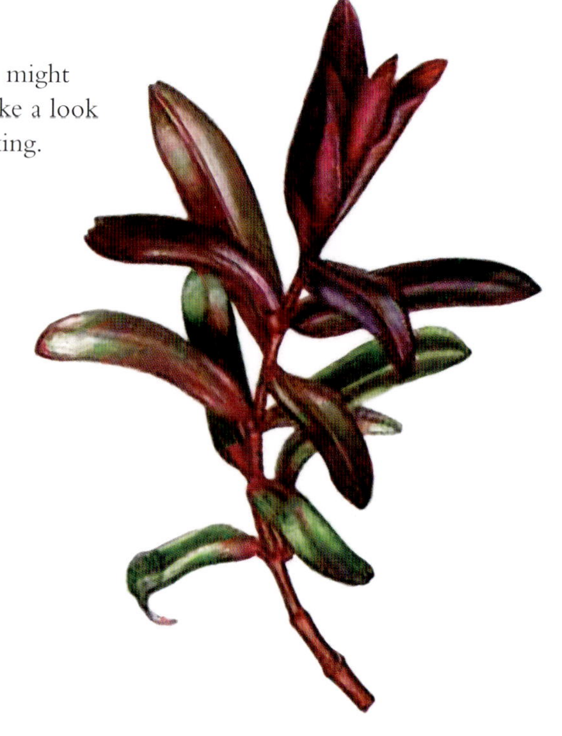

Step 1

On your worksheet, start by layering a selection of different colour washes one over the other. Try Alizarin Crimson, Sap Green, violet made from Alizarin Crimson and French Ultramarine, Opera Rose, Ultramarine Blue and a mixed blue-green. Layer each of these colours, using both glazing and stipple techniques, in different orders to achieve different final colours. You will probably find that the Alizarin Crimson/Sap Green/violet mix (shown at the end) is the right one for the painting.

  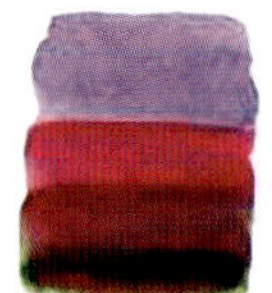 

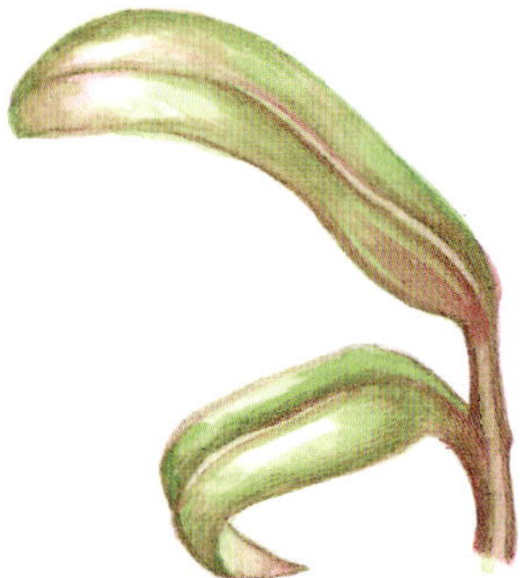

Step 2

After drawing the picture with a 2H pencil, begin painting the leaves with very small, light washes of Sap Green. Use paler Sap Green on the leaves at the top. When they are dry, stipple layers of Alizarin Crimson, adding the details of the veining and the way the leaf joins the stem. Be careful to leave the highlights on the leaves.

Above This sprig of hebe is a good example of layering and stippling successively dark colours to give depth and vitality.

Step 4

As you work up the stem, introduce a layer of the Alizarin Crimson and French Ultramarine mix where the colour of the leaves becomes bronze and darkens to nearly black. At the top of the plant use predominantly Alizarin Crimson and the violet mix, darkening it with Sap Green. The stem is a layer of Alizarin Crimson with a layer of Sap Green over the top.

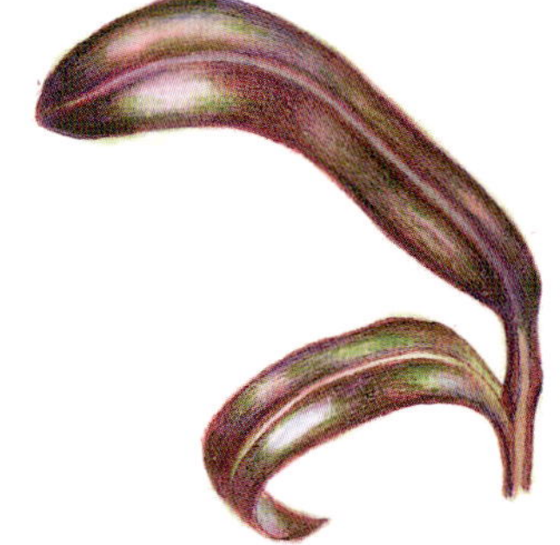

Step 3

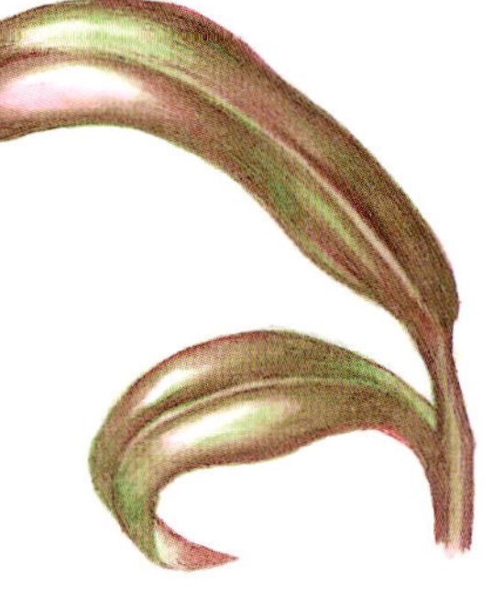

Repeat the layers, using the two colours until you achieve the required depth of tone.

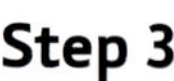

Bloom

Using watercolour to paint bloom is shown here. As it's the lightest colour on the subject, you may either establish it with your first wash or leave the paper unpainted in those areas and wash it in at the very end.

The mahonia berries (right) are painted with cool blue (Prussian Blue), a little Winsor Violet, Lemon Yellow and Indian Yellow, plus some cool red (Alizarin Crimson). The stems are a mix of the last three colours.

The sloe (blackthorn) fruits (below left) are again predominantly cool blue (Prussian Blue), with warm yellow (Indian Yellow) and cool red (Alizarin Crimson). You can use all three colours mixed together in different proportions for the woody, greyish-brown branches – for example, using more red and yellow will make a browny-grey.

The bloom on the fig (below right) was put on at the end, using Permanent White watercolour or Permanent Chinese White gouache. You could also use Titanium White Opaque, possibly mixed with a little blue. Bloom can look like a white coating on fruit and therefore it works well to replicate the effect with white paint over the otherwise finished watercolour painting.

You may also add bloom to a watercolour painting by using a white pencil (see page 94).

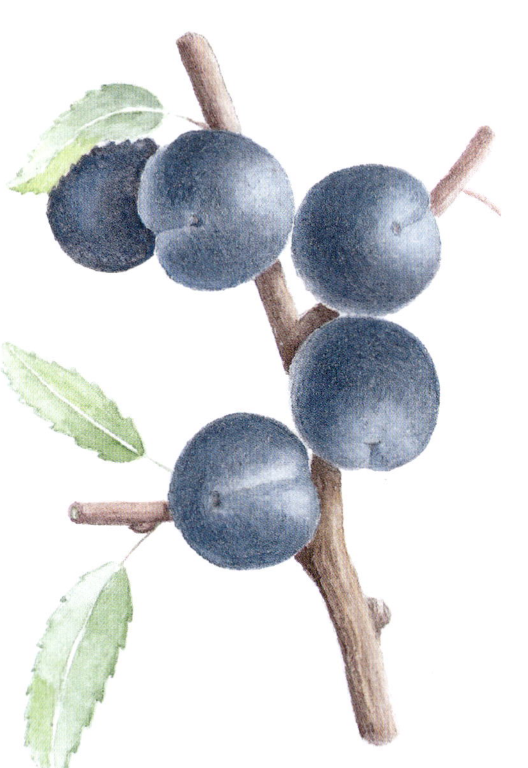

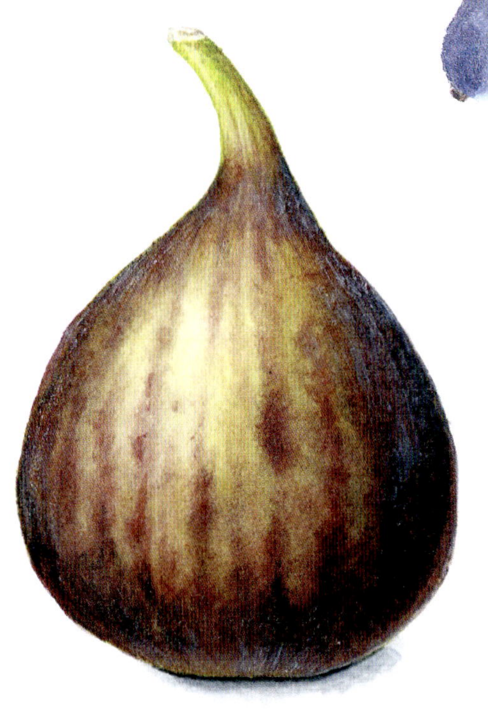

Above and left Bloom can be established with your first wash (as above), or added at the end with white paint or white pencil (as on the fig, left).

Exercise: Using washes to paint a leaf

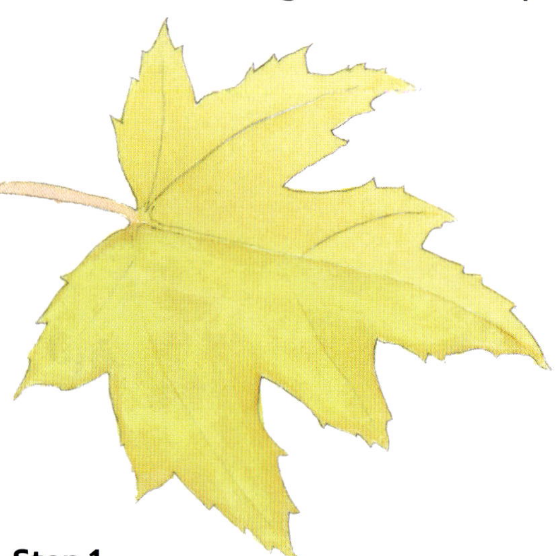

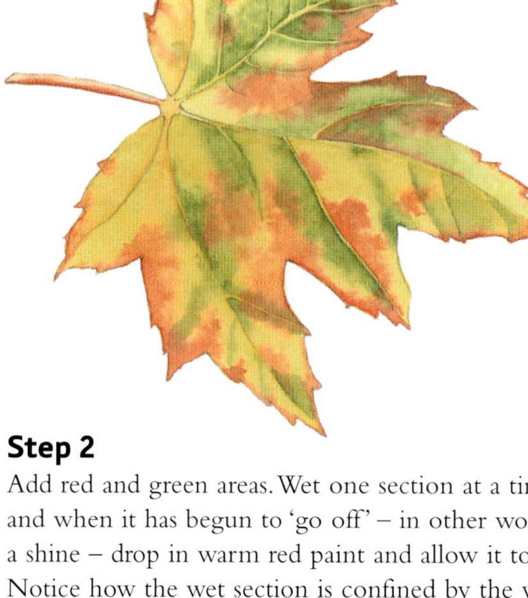

Step 1

Draw the leaf, taking care to make the lines exact. Mix a pool of Lemon Yellow and Indian Yellow, and lay down the first wash over the whole leaf.

Step 2

Add red and green areas. Wet one section at a time with clean water, and when it has begun to 'go off' – in other words, it has a sheen, not a shine – drop in warm red paint and allow it to find its own space. Notice how the wet section is confined by the veins in some places, allowing the colour to go up to the vein but no further. Treat each section individually, allowing the paint to dry each time. Do the same with a mix of green using warm yellow and cool blue.

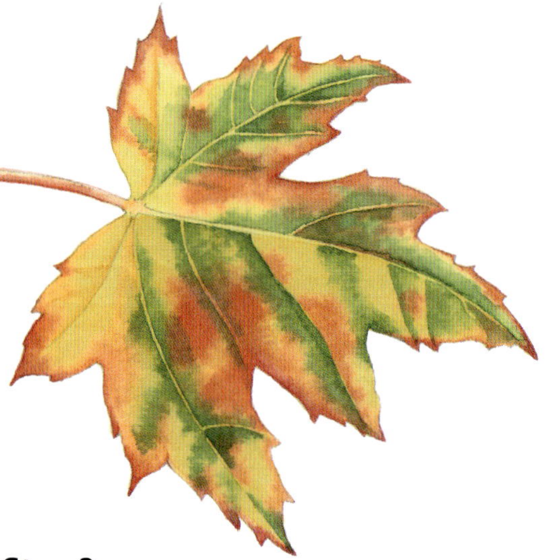

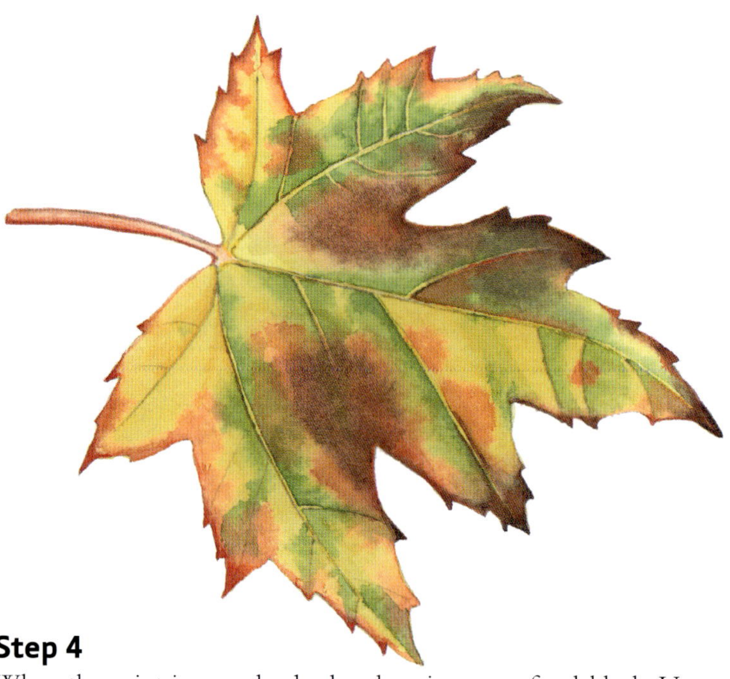

Step 3

Make a darker red mix by adding some cool blue and accentuate some of the leaf tips, using a fine brush. You can do this either wet-into-wet, as before, or use a graded wash, placing the paint on the darkest areas and blending it out with a small brush and clear water.

Step 4

When the paint is completely dry, drop in areas of red-black. Use wet-into-wet or the blending technique to show where the leaf has begun to decompose. Treat some of the leaf tips in the same way.

Stippling

Towards the end of your painting you may want to add fine details, in which case you could use stippling. This means applying small amounts of paint with a fine, almost dry brush, making tiny dots or small parallel lines to accentuate darker areas. Some artists like to use a 'miniature' brush for this.

Stippling has been used on the directional markings of *Canna* 'Picasso' (right), and to deepen the shadowed areas. Notice how stippling has been used around the veins of the leaves of the hibiscus (below left) to give extra depth.

The colour and form of the little cherry plum (below centre) were built up with washes of yellow, red and a blue-green, the final darker colours being stippled on with a fine, almost dry brush to give a smooth, shiny, unblemished appearance.

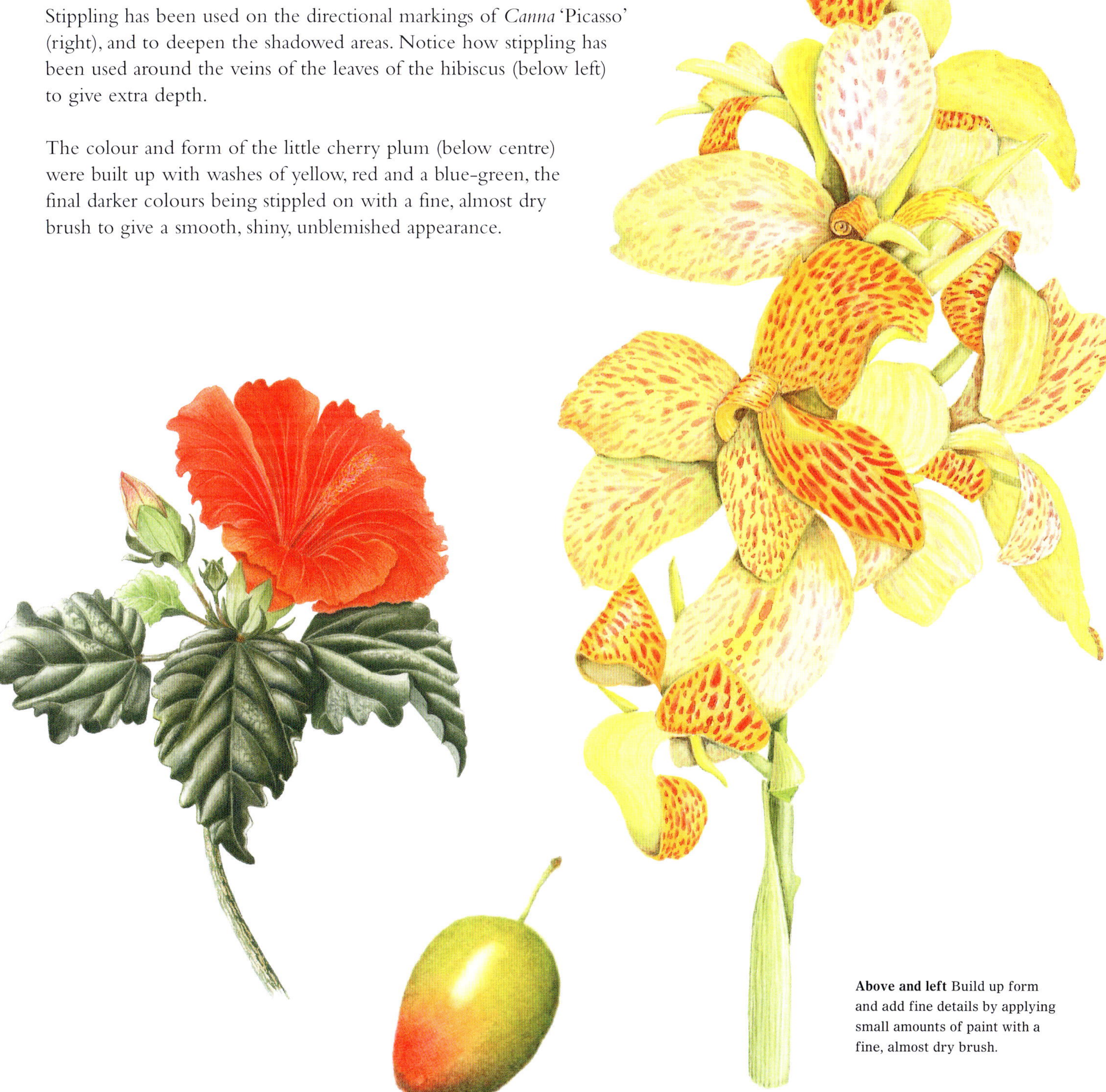

Above and left Build up form and add fine details by applying small amounts of paint with a fine, almost dry brush.

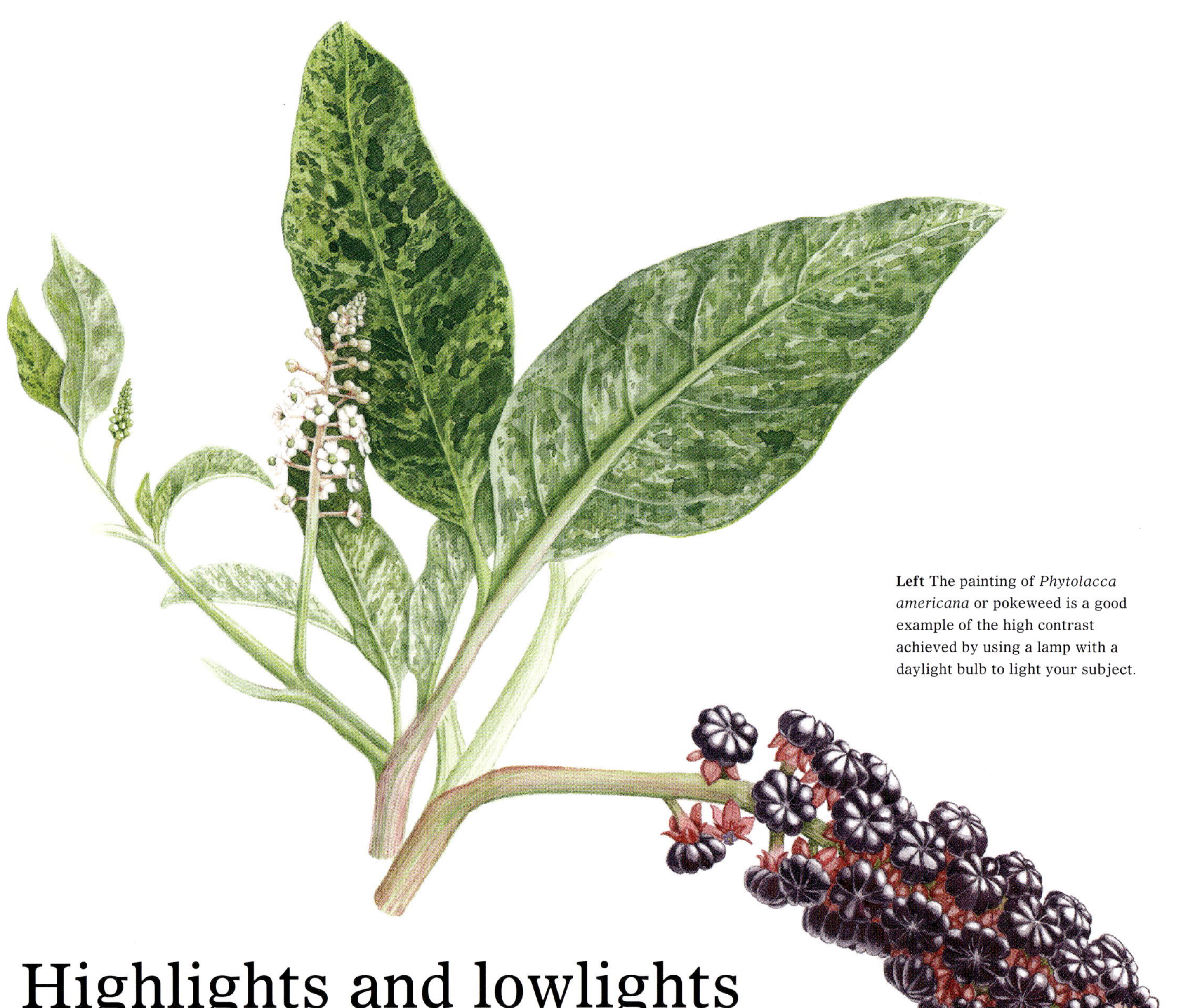

Highlights and lowlights

The function of highlights and lowlights is to indicate the direction of light and to help give the subject form, so you need to establish the light source at the beginning of the work. If you have more than one source (two windows, for instance), you must decide which is the dominant highlight and ignore the other. In the case of natural light, unless you have a north-facing window, the direction of light will change as the day wears on, but you will need to adhere to your initial plan as to where your highlights are.

Some people choose to light their subject artificially, as this gives good contrast. The *Phytolacca* (above), is a good example of the high contrast achieved on an extremely shiny subject by using a lamp with a daylight bulb. The leaves exemplify the building up greens, layering or glazing several different ones on top of each other.

It sometimes helps to indicate highlights or lowlights with a fine dotted pencil line to remind you to leave that area untouched when applying washes. The pencil marks can be erased at the end, as long as you have not painted over them. Allow the white of the paper to shine through and, right at the end, if you feel it is too garish, you can add a wash of very pale colour.

To indicate a lowlight, you might find it preferable to lift off some paint. This can be done with a dry brush while the paint is still wet, or, once the paint is dry, you can lift it off by gently touching it with a brush dipped in clean water and then blotting it with absorbent paper. You might have to repeat this several times. Do not scrub at the paint, as this will alter the surface of the paper and may compromise any further additions of paint.

The painting of black maize (right) displays extremes of tonal contrast and colour. The shades used in the maize kernels are exaggerated versions of the real thing; the old adage for art students to 'find the colours at their maximum' inspired the very colourful example here. The subject was brightly lit with a spotlight from the side to intensify the contrast, which ranges from extreme light to dark, on both the cob and the dry bracts. Every kernel was painted individually and each highlight had to be carefully worked around, even if it appeared in shadow.

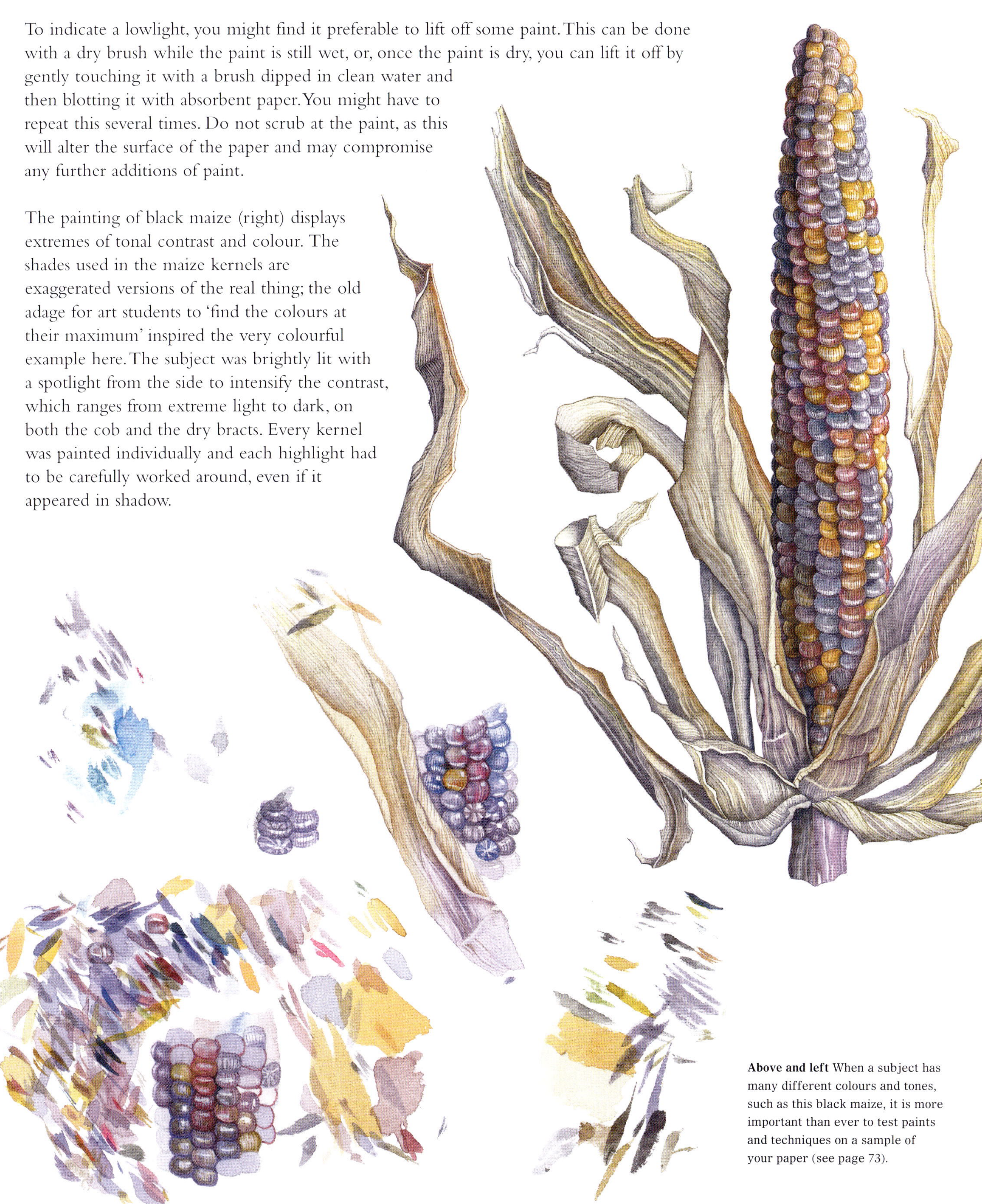

Above and left When a subject has many different colours and tones, such as this black maize, it is more important than ever to test paints and techniques on a sample of your paper (see page 73).

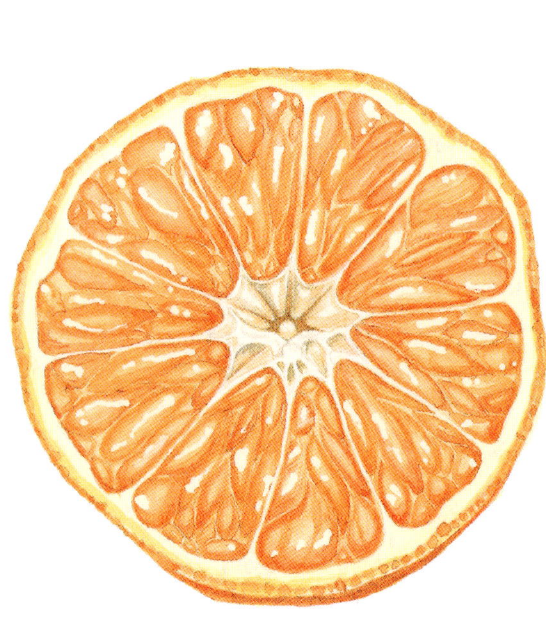

Above The highlights are so pronounced in the orange segment that it really does look juicy. The best way to achieve this is to allow the white paper to shine through, painting around it with increasing strengths of colour and using a fine brush.

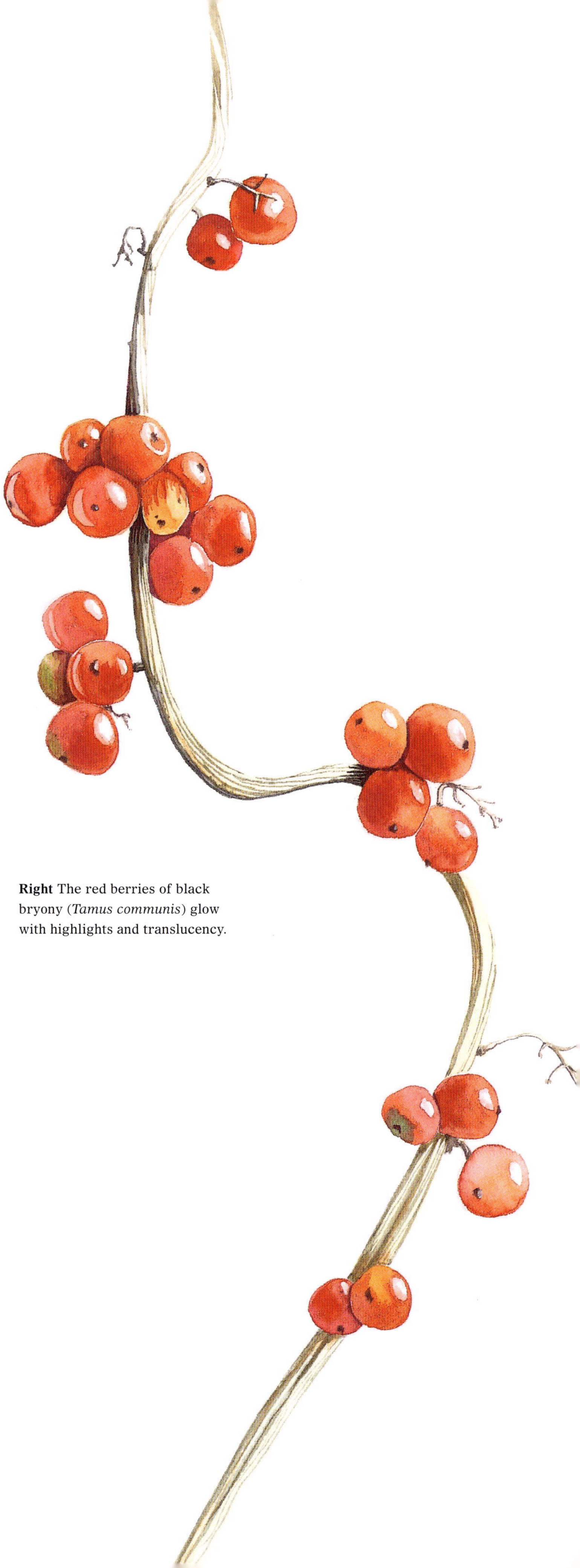

Below Because of their wrinkly shape, the shiny areas on dates are fine, long and narrow. You can achieve this by using masking fluid, by painting carefully round these fine slivers, or possibly by using white watercolour or gouache at the end to give a concentrated, sharp shine. Try out the options before deciding which one to use.

Right The red berries of black bryony (*Tamus communis*) glow with highlights and translucency.

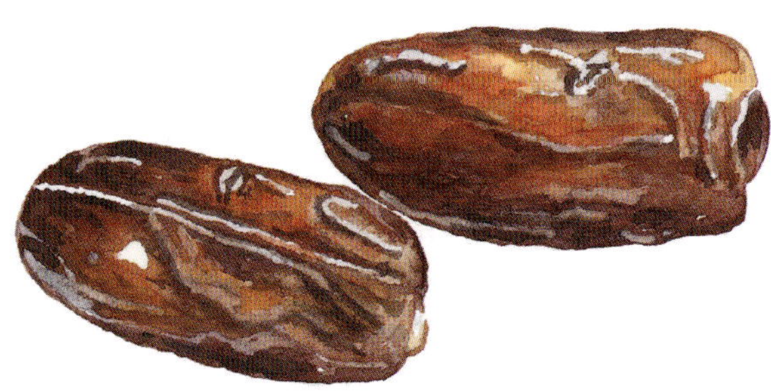

Exercise: *Aeonium* 'Zwartkop'

Step 1

First draw the aeonium and then begin the painting process by using light washes of Alizarin Crimson, followed by Sap Green, then by a mix of Alizarin Crimson and French Ultramarine to make a violet. Leave highlights and white edges for fine hairs.

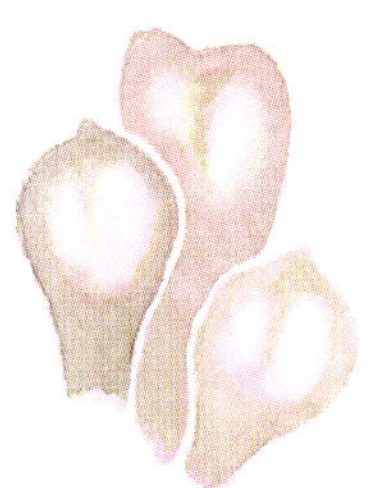

Step 2

Using a light black made from Alizarin Crimson, Sap Green and mixed violet (see stage 1), wash and blend over the darker areas of the leaves. Continue until depth of colour is reached.

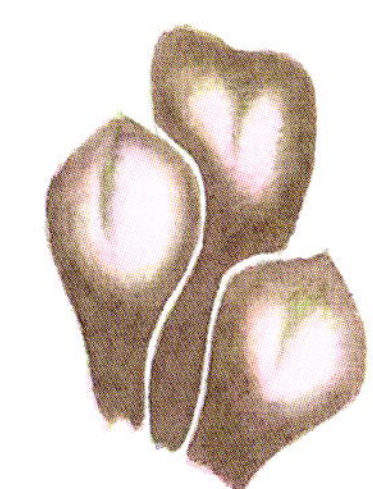

Step 3

If your painting is still too light, stipple a red-black and a green-black in layers over the leaves. Continue until a deep red-purple-bronze colour is reached.

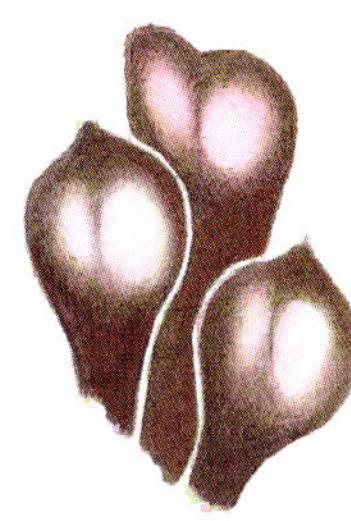

Step 4

Stipple layers of French Ultramarine and Prussian Blue in places to give the dense black that occurs in this plant. If the overall appearance of the plant is too red, add a pale wash of French Ultramarine over the highlights. This will give the leaves a blue-black appearance. Paint in between the white areas around the leaves using a very small brush with mixed black. Finally, using your small brush, neaten all edges.

Above The finished *Aeonium* 'Zwartkop'. If your leaves look too red, add a wash of diluted French Ultramarine highlights to darken the effect.

Exercise: Painting grapes

Spend some time studying a bunch of grapes and decide how to place it on the paper to its best advantage. Your drawing will be made easier by the amount of observation you have done beforehand – anything up to an hour's contemplation before you even pick up your pencil is normal.

One hazard of painting perishable subjects is that they can dry out or change position. It is a good idea to make sketches or take photographs to use as references later. Once you start to mix paints it's also wise to make a few colour swatches or samples in case the colours change as the fruit matures.

First make a simple drawing on layout paper, using a medium-weight pencil such as HB. Using layout paper allows you to refine the drawing, erasing any parts that don't work.

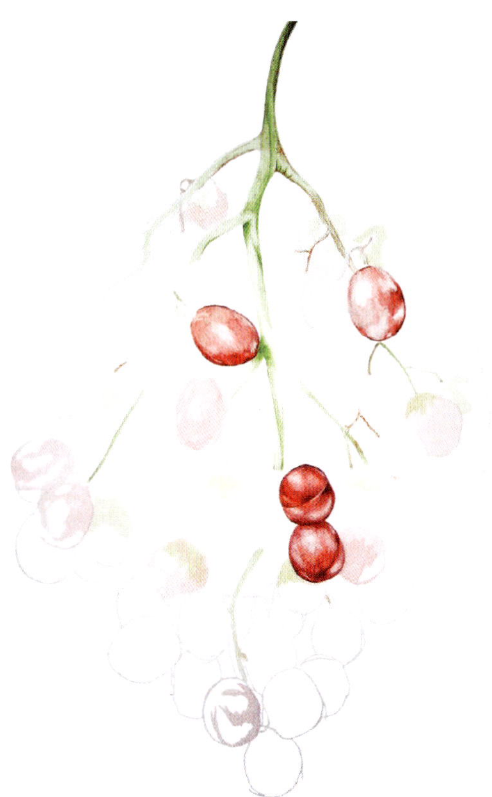

When you are happy with your drawing, trace it on to HP watercolour paper. From this point onwards you need to protect the watercolour paper from splashes, smudging and your skin by having a sheet of paper or acetate under your hand while you work. The painting can be worked up area by area without mishap. Check the progress of the whole painting periodically.

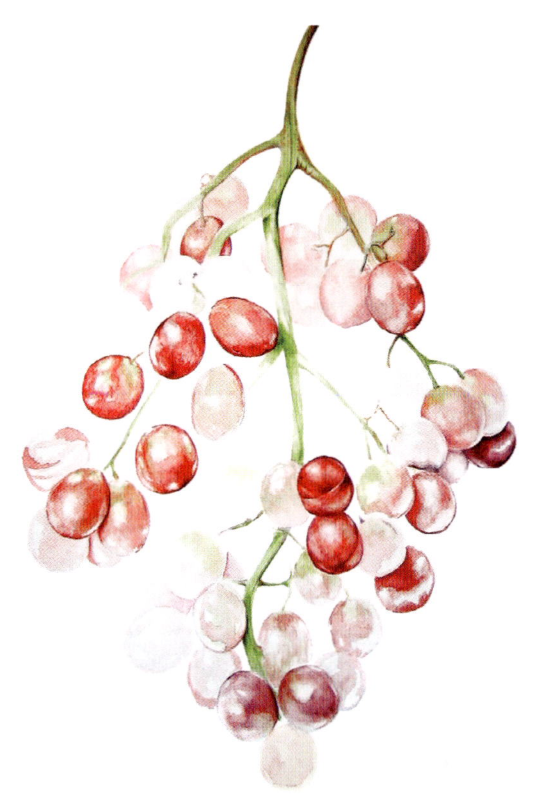

Step 1

Your first wash will be the lightest shade you can see in the grapes – in this case it is a very light pink. Don't forget to leave unpainted any areas where you can see highlights. As was done here, you might like to paint two grapes until they are almost finished. This gives you an idea of what the final painting will look like and also helps you to work out how to set about the rest of the painting.

Step 2

Carry on adding washes to deepen the colour, adding a little yellow for some of the fruit. You may find that a wet-into-wet wash is the one to use here. Try it out on watercolour paper first.

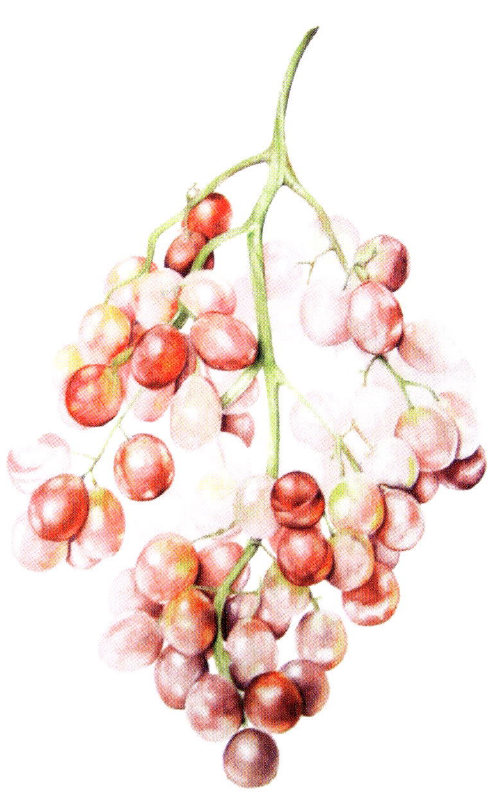

Step 3

Notice how the grapes are not all exactly the same colour, and alter your paint mix accordingly. Remember to avoid painting the highlighted areas. If the paint becomes dark around the edges of the highlights, use an almost dry brush and gently worry the paint to spread it infinitesimally, blurring the paint line into the white paper of the highlight.

The general rule in botanical painting is that the further away a part of the subject is, the lighter it is. So ensure that the grapes in the foreground are darker than those towards the back of the bunch.

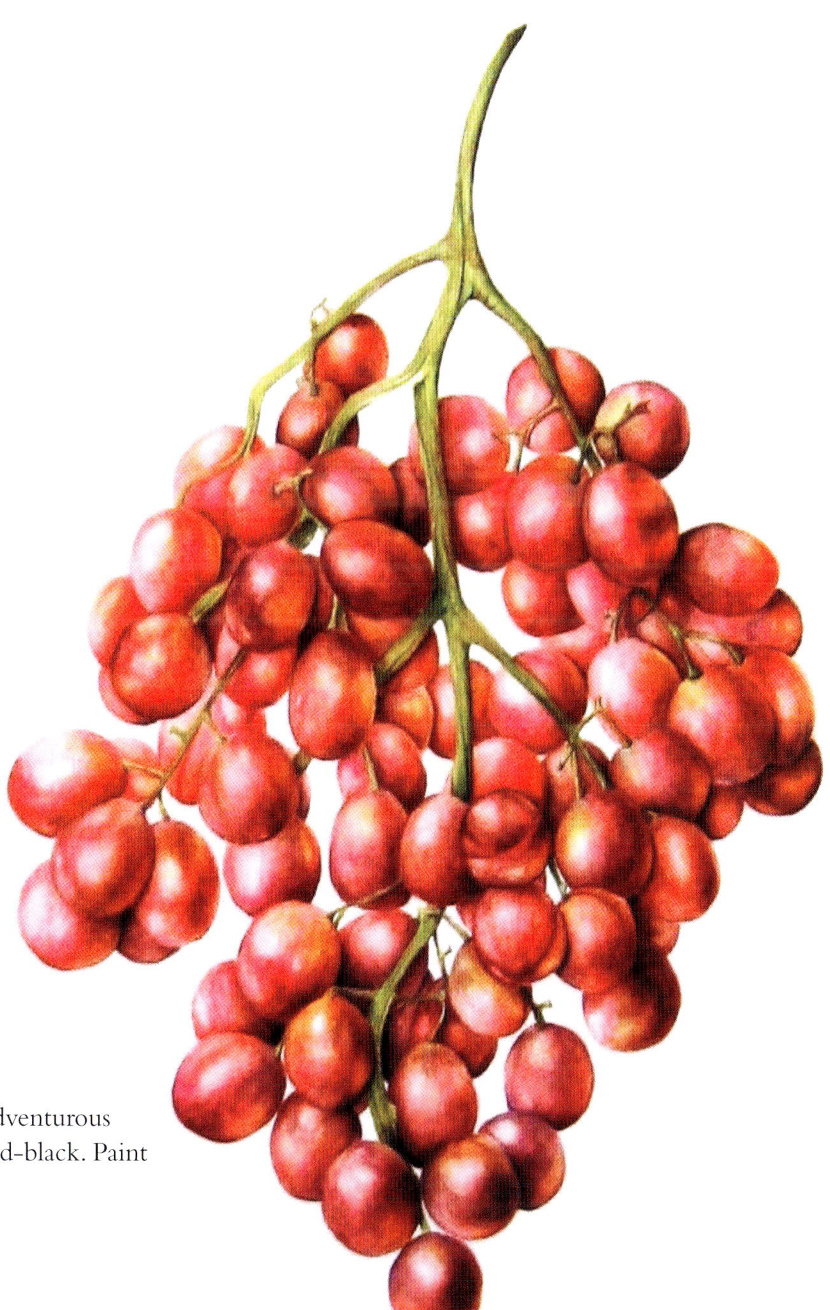

Step 4

Look for veins on the fruit and paint them accordingly with a fine brush. Try to capture the translucency of the grapes. Look carefully at not only how the light falls on them, but also how it travels through the fruit and what effect it has. In this case the darker highlight (on the other side of the fruit) has been painted a yellow-green, suggesting the colour of the flesh inside.

Check your colours, and add some darker, more adventurous washes – blues, purples, bright orange and some red-black. Paint the stems carefully.

Watercolour over pencil

If you are happier using a pencil than a brush but don't want to use coloured pencils, you might like to try the technique called watercolour over pencil, shown in the example of a little agave (below), and the portrait of a clivia (page 103). You shade all the tonal areas from light to dark using a graphite pencil, following this with a watercolour wash layered over the top. You might need to increase the depth of colour in some places, but there is nowhere near the amount of brushwork needed as in laying down washes in the traditional way.

The tonal pencil work needs to be applied very carefully and smoothly, using non-directional shading (see page 47), giving the essential three-dimensional look. You may wish to use different grades of pencil, depending on the tones of the subject, but make sure that they are fairly hard – softer (B) pencils can leave traces of loose graphite on the paper, which will muddy the effect when you add the watercolour wash. Understand what your pencils can do at the outset, and do a lot of experimentation until you are happy with this skill.

Above Apply tonal pencil, working very carefully and smoothly, and using non-directional shading.

Below Layer one or more watercolour washes over your pencil study, increasing the depth of colour in places.

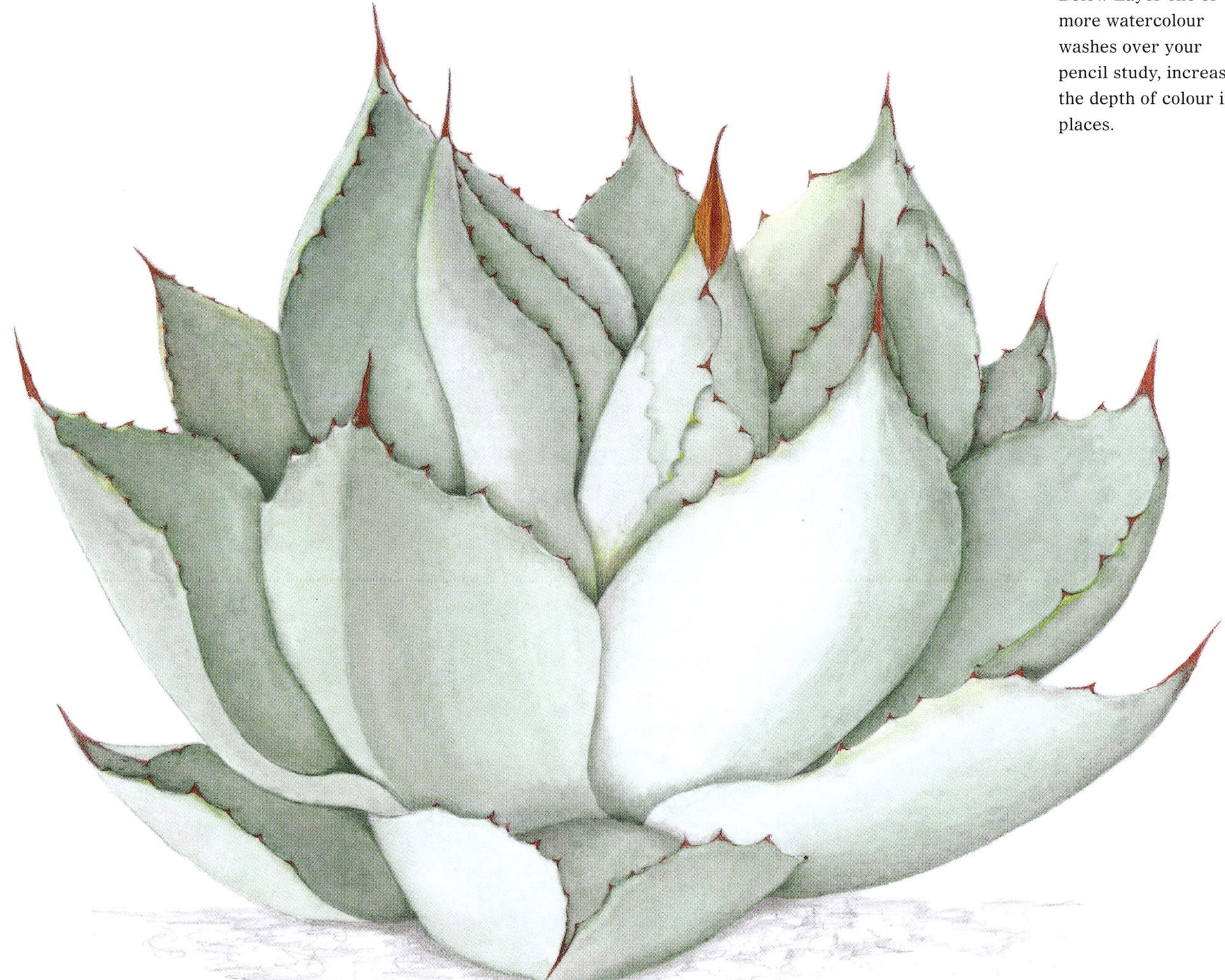

Pattern and texture

Two of the most testing textures to paint are surfaces that look like velvet or satin. The seedpod of the deciduous tree *Sterculia mexicana* gives a fine example of both (below). The fruits are tough and leathery, with hard, blue, pea- or grape-sized seeds attached to the margins. Although the husks appear velvety, they are very hard. Their outer surface is pleated – yet another texture – and they have ginger hairs around the edge. The linings of the husks look like creased satin, the seeds have bloom and the stalk is deeply serrated. All in all, this is a very interesting subject, offering many different textures.

When fresh, the outer surface of the husks is a deep, intense, velvety scarlet, which dries to a reddish-brown, as shown in the illustration. You may find the seeds the most challenging part to tackle. Where the light falls on them they are almost white, darkening to a deep blue in the shaded areas. They have intense bloom, which you could achieve by a series of washes, becoming increasingly intense away from the light. The seedhead shown here was lit strongly from the left, but notice how there is reflected light from the right on some of the seeds. Some of the blue colour of the seeds is also reflected in the interior of the pod.

You will need three main colours to paint this subject: cool red (Alizarin Crimson), warm blue (French Ultramarine) and warm yellow (Indian Yellow). To avoid the pale areas on the lining of the pod becoming too pink, add a light wash of Indian Yellow and a little Scarlet Lake. You will also need to mix a bit of purply-grey for the darker areas of the seeds.

Below The dry seedpods of *Sterculia mexicana* offer a challenge with their different surfaces – velvety outer surface, linings like creased satin and seeds with intense bloom.

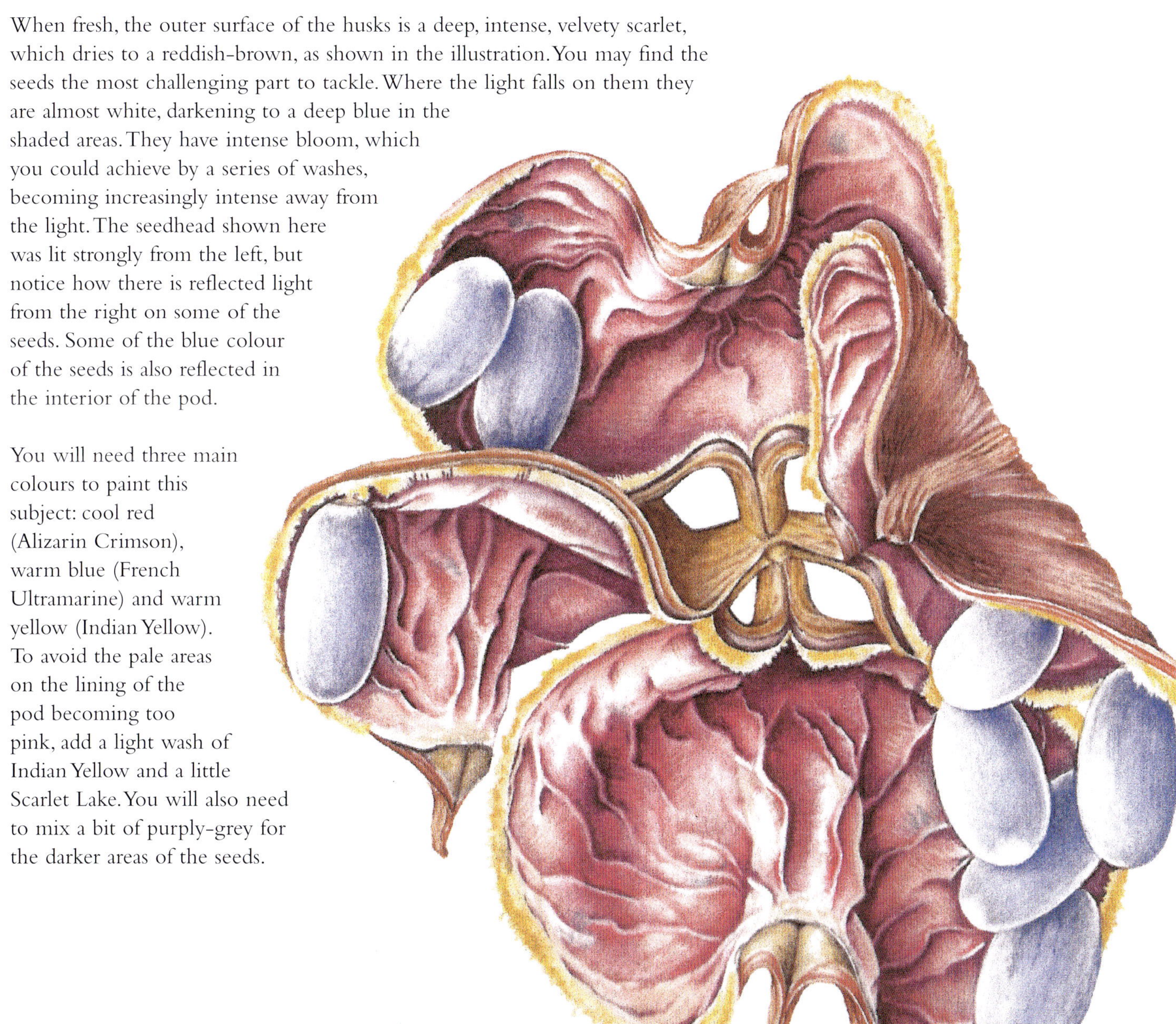

Cacti

Cacti are a very testing subject because of all the spines, small hairs and occasionally spots or other patterning. These little studies of small cacti are good examples of simple pattern and texture.

If you look at each cactus carefully, you will see that the seven little cacti have very different characters. *Astrophytum ornatum* has eight segments, and there are more thorns towards the top than the bottom. *Notocactus warasii* has twelve segments with very fine, slightly golden hairs in small clusters, while *Euphorbia submammillaris* has eight segments on each section, branching out from the main stem. The different sections of *Pilosocereus glaucochrous* each have six segments. They are all at different heights, and it is useful to mark these on your worksheet with horizontal lines so that you get the proportions correct. There are alternating clusters of very fine, straight thorns, about five to a cluster, and each segment is topped with white fluff. The *Aloe peglerae* is bluish and fleshy, with sharp red-tipped spines mainly along the edges, with some on the central ridge. *Gymnocalycium riograndense* has smooth, pebble-shaped lumps with long spines, and *Haworthia pumila* is dark green with white pimples, mainly on the outer sides.

Laying a wash around pale fine hairs is almost impossible, so you might like to put them in afterwards, using a tiny brush and white gouache (see page 15). This could be tinted with a little colour, depending on what is needed. You could try using masking fluid, but would probably find that you are not able to get fine enough lines with it.

If you are going to paint the hairs last, treat the cactus as a solid, smooth surface and lay washes so that the tones graduate smoothly from one area to another.

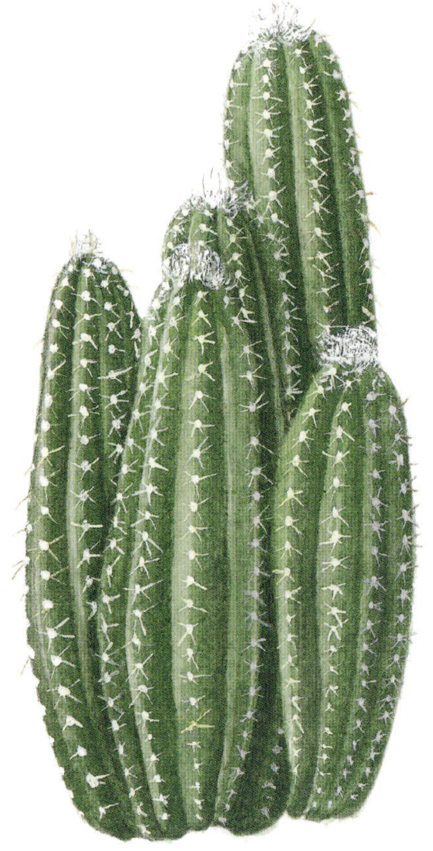

Pilosocereus glaucochrous

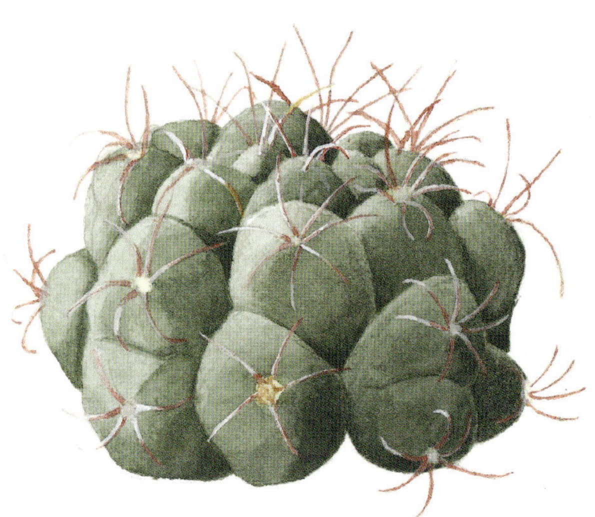

Gymnocalycium riograndense

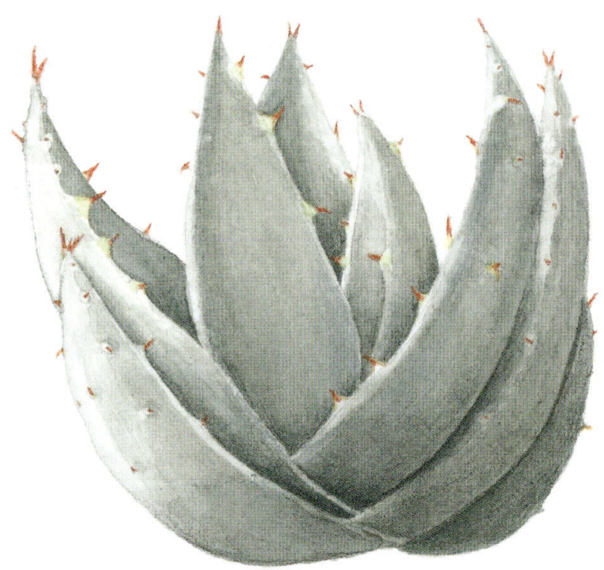

Aloe peglerae

Practising with different textures

Pattern and texture are endlessly fascinating, and if you confine yourself to small examples of each, working on them is not particularly time-consuming. Make your own page of small studies of pattern and texture, using both pencil and watercolour (see page 53 for some skilful examples in pencil). Use whatever you can find in the way of subject matter – it doesn't have to be botanical.

Look at the patterns in a scrap of woven material, the texture of cat's fur, knitting, a stone, the sole of a shoe, a piece of wood, some embroidery, bark, a butterfly's wing. The choices are endless, and you will learn so much from looking at, drawing, and painting a wide range of different subjects.

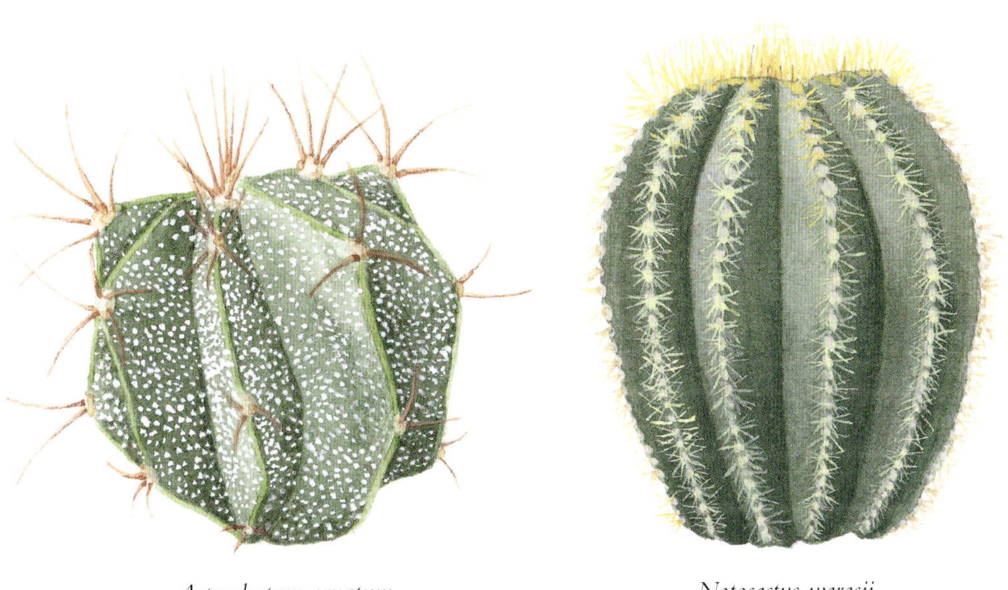

Astrophytum ornatum

Notocactus warasii

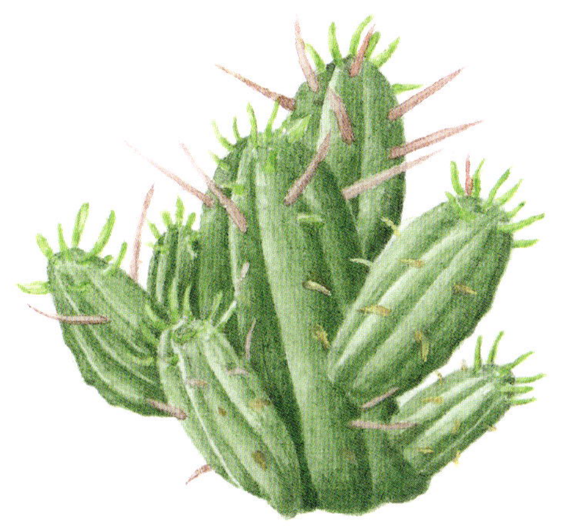

Euphorbia submammillaris

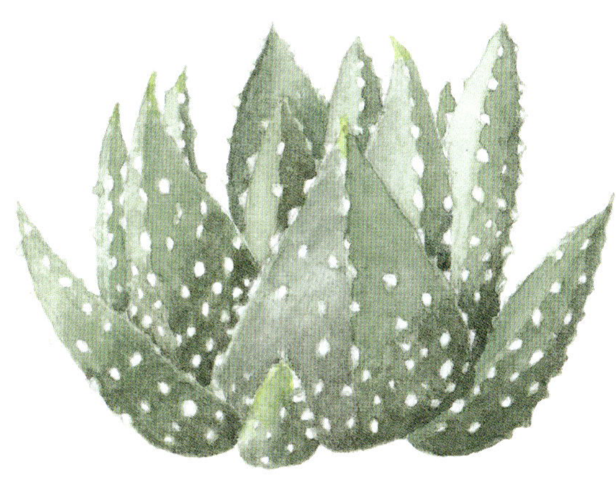

Haworthia pumila

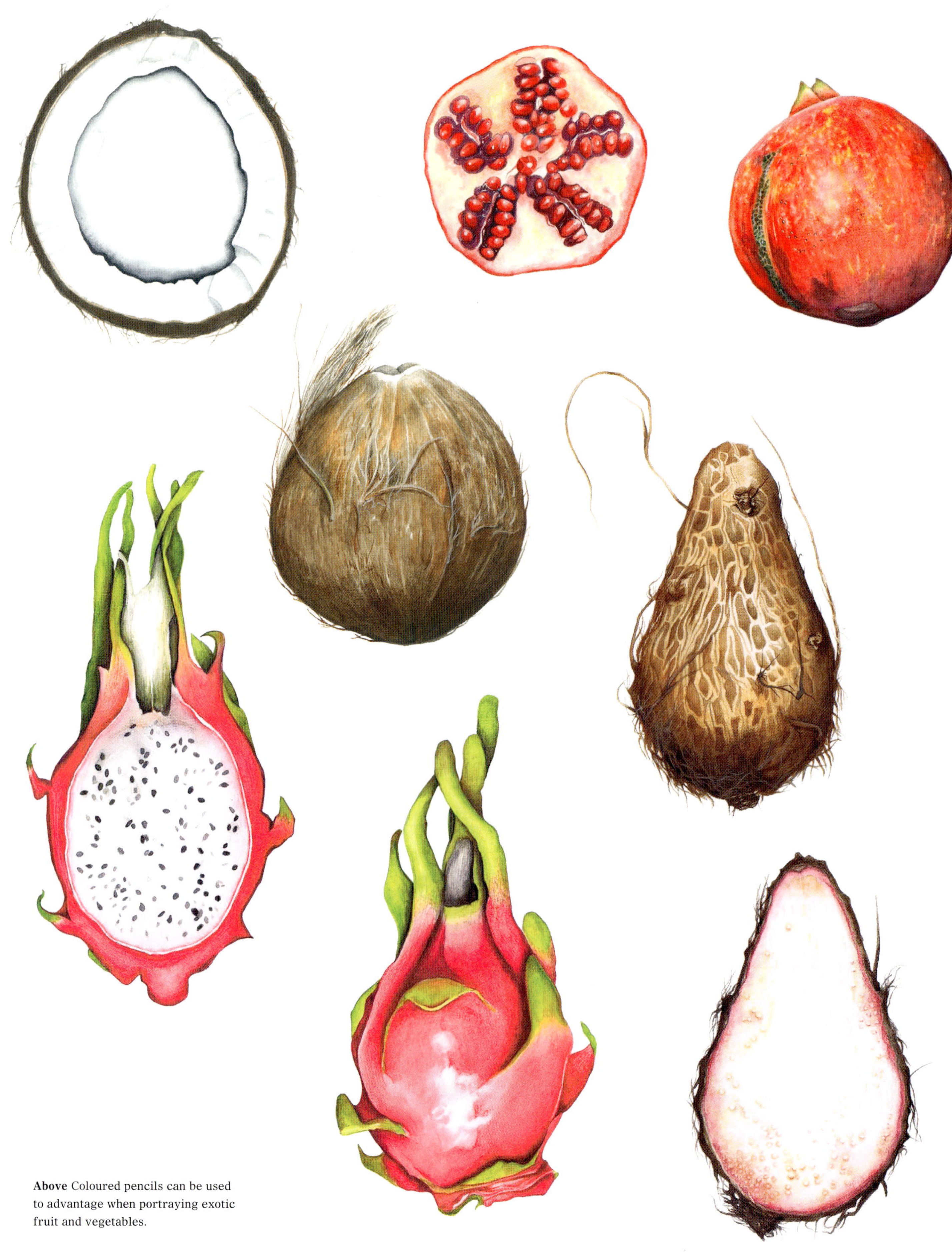

Above Coloured pencils can be used to advantage when portraying exotic fruit and vegetables.

Using Coloured Pencils

You may be one of the many botanical artists who find paint and paintbrushes unfriendly and prefer to use pencils, or perhaps you want to work on a subject that's unfamiliar to you and feel that you need to develop a new approach in order to show unusual textures or features. If so, coloured pencils may be your way forward. They are extremely versatile, there's a huge range of colours to choose from, and they also have the advantage of being easier to transport than paints and a jar of water. However, they aren't an easy option and can be just as time-consuming as the more traditional wet-paint methods.

Some artists use coloured pencils in conjunction with watercolour; this could mean laying down washes in watercolour and putting in fine details and finishing touches with pencils, or doing the body of the work in coloured pencils and then putting in final details with watercolour. This chapter discusses using coloured pencils on their own or alongside conventional watercolour techniques to solve some of the problems encountered when faced with unusual and exotic plants.

Paper

Normal HP watercolour paper is suitable for coloured-pencil work; the paper should be 300gsm (140lb) or heavier. HP paper is smooth, but still has a bit of 'tooth', which will hold the pigment. Other options are a good-quality, smooth, heavy cartridge paper of about 220gsm (100lb) or Bristol board, which many artists like to use.

Coloured pencils

Above This bunch of grapes illustrates how many different shades of purple and red can be found in the same bunch. The different colours also help to strengthen the tonal variations that identify the direction of the light.

Recent developments in the manufacture of coloured pencils have elevated them from the simple children's crayon to a serious tool in the professional artist's weaponry. Technical advances have improved pigmentation and lightfastness and they can now take their place alongside artists' quality watercolour paints in terms of quality and permanence.

While most manufacturers produce some beautiful boxed sets, a large number of the chosen colours are not very useful for botanical work. You may find it best to buy a limited number of individual pencils that you feel will be the most useful. Start with a couple of dozen pencils in a range of colours from white through yellow, red, blue, green, brown and grey.

Accessories

With all coloured pencils, it's essential to keep the point very sharp at all times. There are a number of ways to achieve this. A **scalpel blade** is very effective and enables you to control the length of the exposed pigment very accurately, but it does take practice to produce a consistent point.

The best type of **mechanical pencil sharpener** has a spiral metal sharpening core that is cranked by hand. These are not only very efficient but will accommodate any thickness of pencil. Two good makes are Rapesco and Helix. The small metal sharpeners that are widely available are adequate but the moment the blade starts to chew up the wooden casing of the pencil, renew it. They cost only a few pence, but be prepared to use four or five in a typical botanical portrait.

You will also need a **hard white eraser**. Cut a small piece off the corner of the eraser for detailed work. Colour can also be lifted off by pressing lightly with a pencil through a piece of sticky-back plastic. An **erasing shield** can be useful, allowing you to select with greater accuracy the area to be erased.

Blender pencils allow you to mix two or more colours by pushing them together and into the grain of the paper. You can also use white or ivory or one of the lighter pencils in the picture.

Solvents dissolve the pigment into the paper, making a mark that you can then work over. This gives the same effect as a preliminary wash with watercolour, but is more permanent.

Finally, a small selection of embossing tools will allow you to portray fine hairs and other tiny details by pressing lines or dots into the paper before applying the pencil (see page 95).

Below These colours were used for the olive branch, shown opposite.

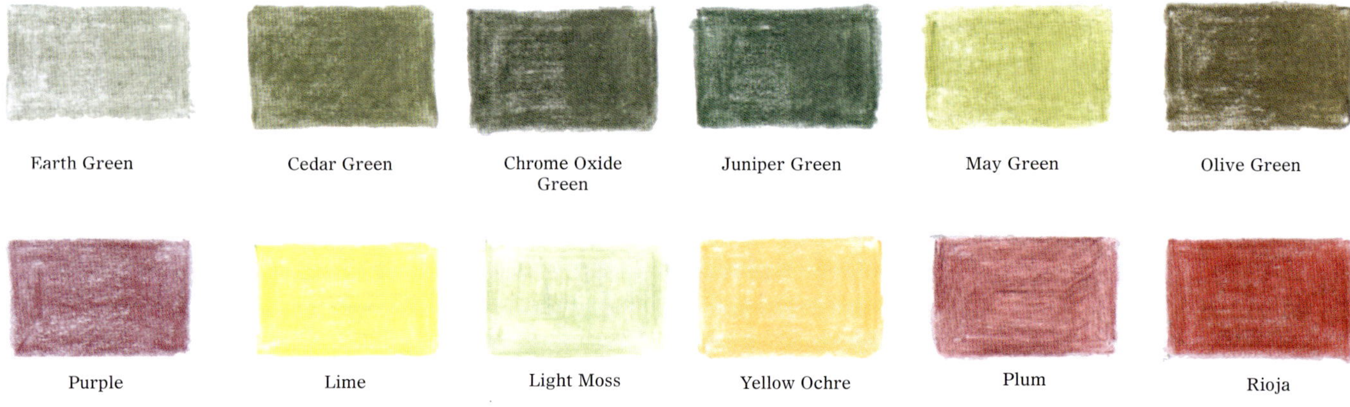

Using coloured pencils

If they are worked carefully, it can be difficult to tell the difference
between coloured pencils and pure watercolour. The basic principles
are the same: colour is built up gradually in layers from light to dark.
Single colour is intensified by layering, taking care to change the direction
of the pencil stroke continually to avoid lines. A common technique is to
apply the colour by using small circular motions of the pencil. Different
colours may be applied on top of each other to build up a complex blend
of hue and tone, with all the underlying colours shining through
and influencing the overall effect.

Once the colours have been built up to a high
density they will normally need to be burnished by
rubbing over the colours with either a colourless burnishing pencil or a
white or champagne-coloured pencil. This pushes the colours together,
smoothing them and producing a more paint-like finish.

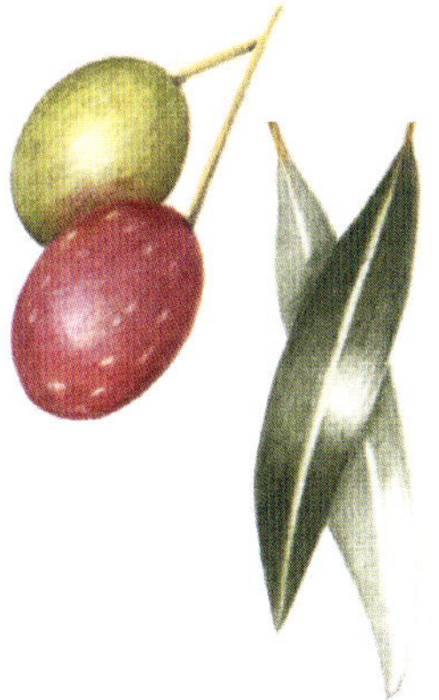

Above If coloured
pencils are worked
carefully, it is difficult
to tell the difference
between them and pure
watercolour.

Exercise: **Olive branch**

The olive branch was rendered using just coloured pencils.

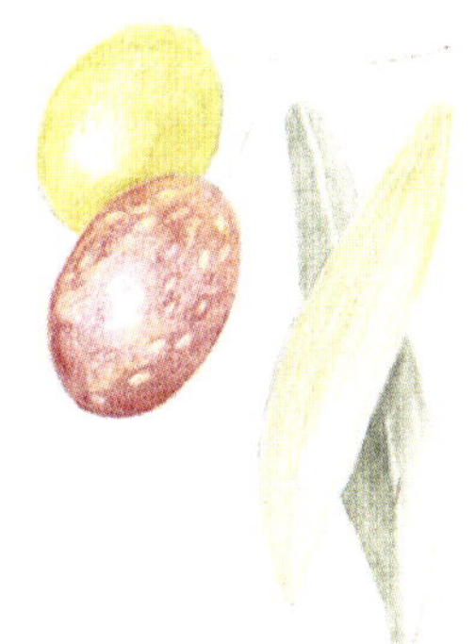

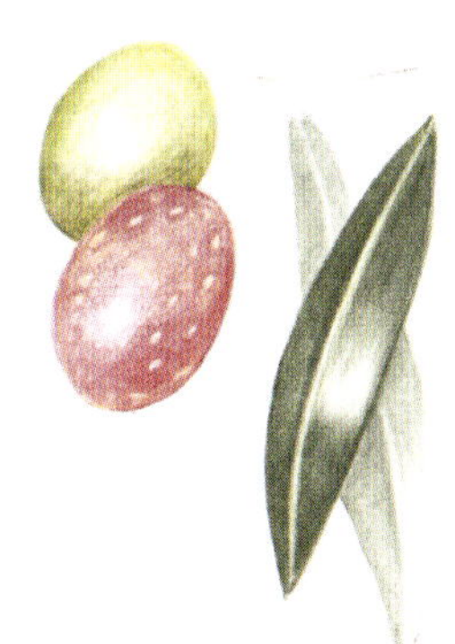

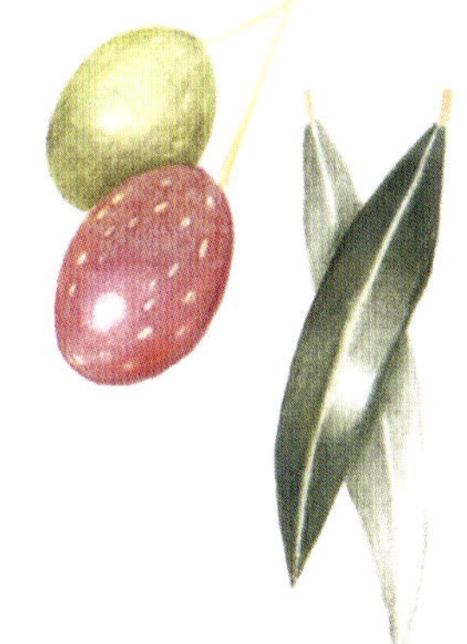

Step 1
Apply a very light
layer of the base
colour, leaving
white paper for the
highlighted areas.

Step 2
Intensify the base
colours and start to
introduce further
colours, taking care to
retain the luminosity
from the underlying
layers.

Step 3
Continue building
up colour and adding
details such as
markings and
shadows.

Step 4
When you are satisfied
that the colour is deep
enough, burnish
the image with a
burnishing tool or
pale-coloured pencil.
Rub until all the
pencil marks have
disappeared and the
surface is smooth.

Step 5
If necessary, apply
a final layer of
colour. Tidy up the
edges and complete
the final detailing.

Bloom and sheen

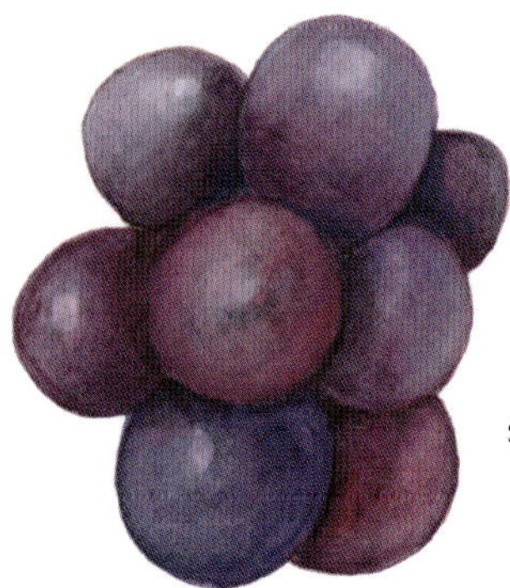

For fruit and vegetables that have a natural bloom or sheen, coloured pencils can provide a very effective solution to the problem of how to depict them in watercolour alone. Once you have established the colours with watercolour paint, use a white or silver-grey coloured pencil gently on the surface. Take care to maintain the three-dimensional effect of the subject by carefully observing how the highlights, although soft, still follow the contours and help to establish shape.

Cocoa pod and pomegranate

These are good examples of finely worked illustrations made with a simple range of colours on 220gsm (120lb) smooth, heavy cartridge paper. The pencils used were from an inexpensive box of 36 artists' pencils. This artist tends to use pencils with fairly blunt points, which she hones on a spare piece of paper to get a fine chiselled edge for working on small details. She burnishes her work with a polished stone from the beach.

The cocoa pod (right) shows how the shading was put in first, using a range of reds, light blue, brown, violet and purple. A very dark Indigo was also used. These colours were built up in density, using also a Lemon Yellow (below right). In all only six colours were used.

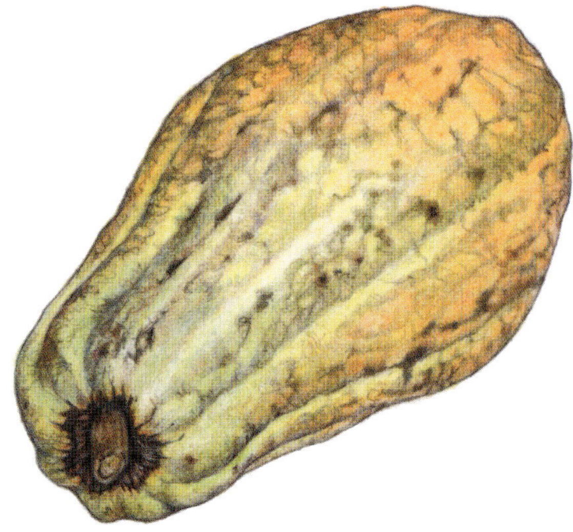

As with the cocoa pod, the pomegranate (left and below) uses superimposition, or optical mixing of colours. There is no white used and the textures of both the outer skin and the seeds have been built up layer upon layer.

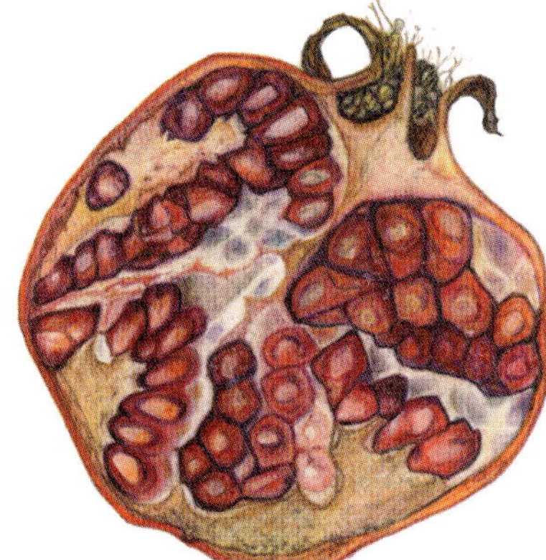

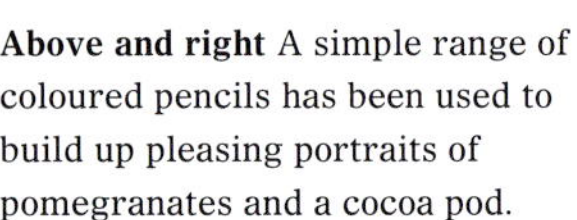

Above and right A simple range of coloured pencils has been used to build up pleasing portraits of pomegranates and a cocoa pod.

"

Exercise: Maize – pencil and watercolour

This exercise uses coloured pencil on top of a blended and graded watercolour wash.

Step 1

Draw the maize cob lightly in pencil, showing the shaded areas and suggesting the ridged texture of the bracts. It is worth drawing horizontal lines to remind yourself of particular characteristics, so that you get the proportions correct. Transfer your drawing to watercolour paper.

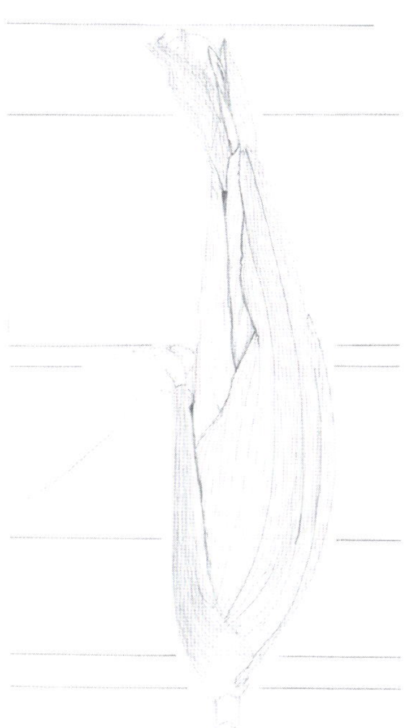

Step 2

Lay down an all-over watercolour wash of the lightest colour, in this case a pale cream. While it's still wet, drop a blueish-purple into the areas of deepest shade.

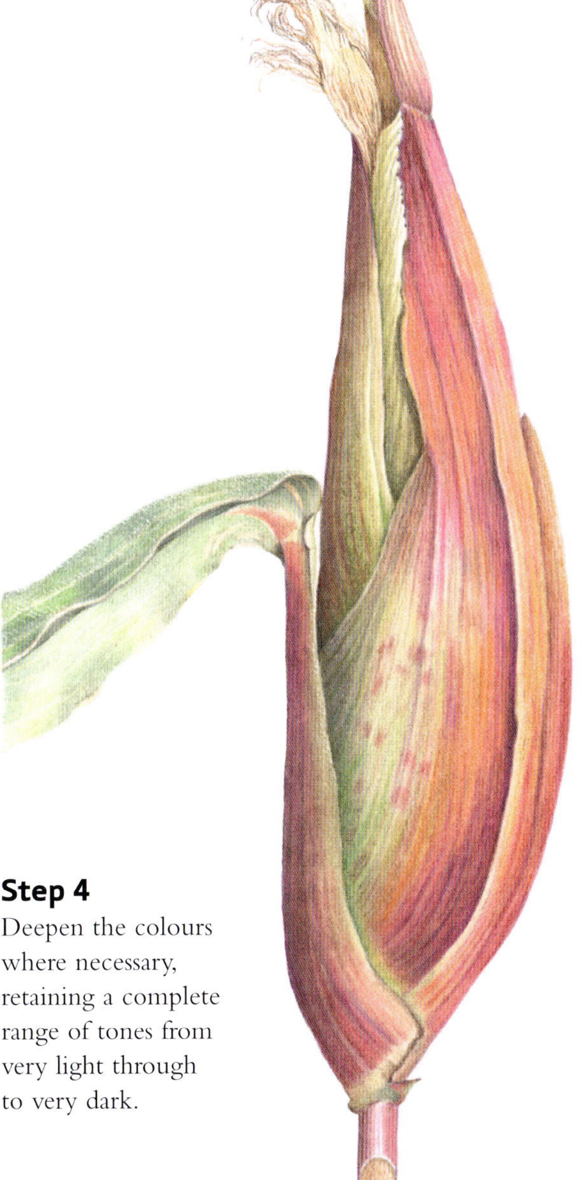

Step 3

Allow to dry thoroughly before working on the picture with coloured pencils. For the fine white hairs on the upper surface of the leaf, the paper was indented with an embossing tool, allowing those tiny areas to remain untouched by the pencils as they were worked over the top.

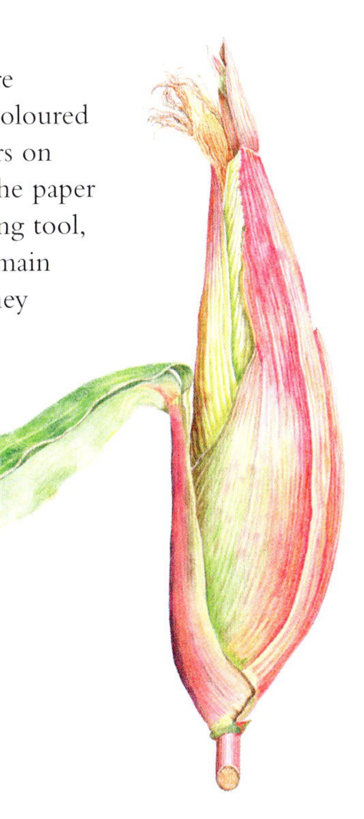

Step 4

Deepen the colours where necessary, retaining a complete range of tones from very light through to very dark.

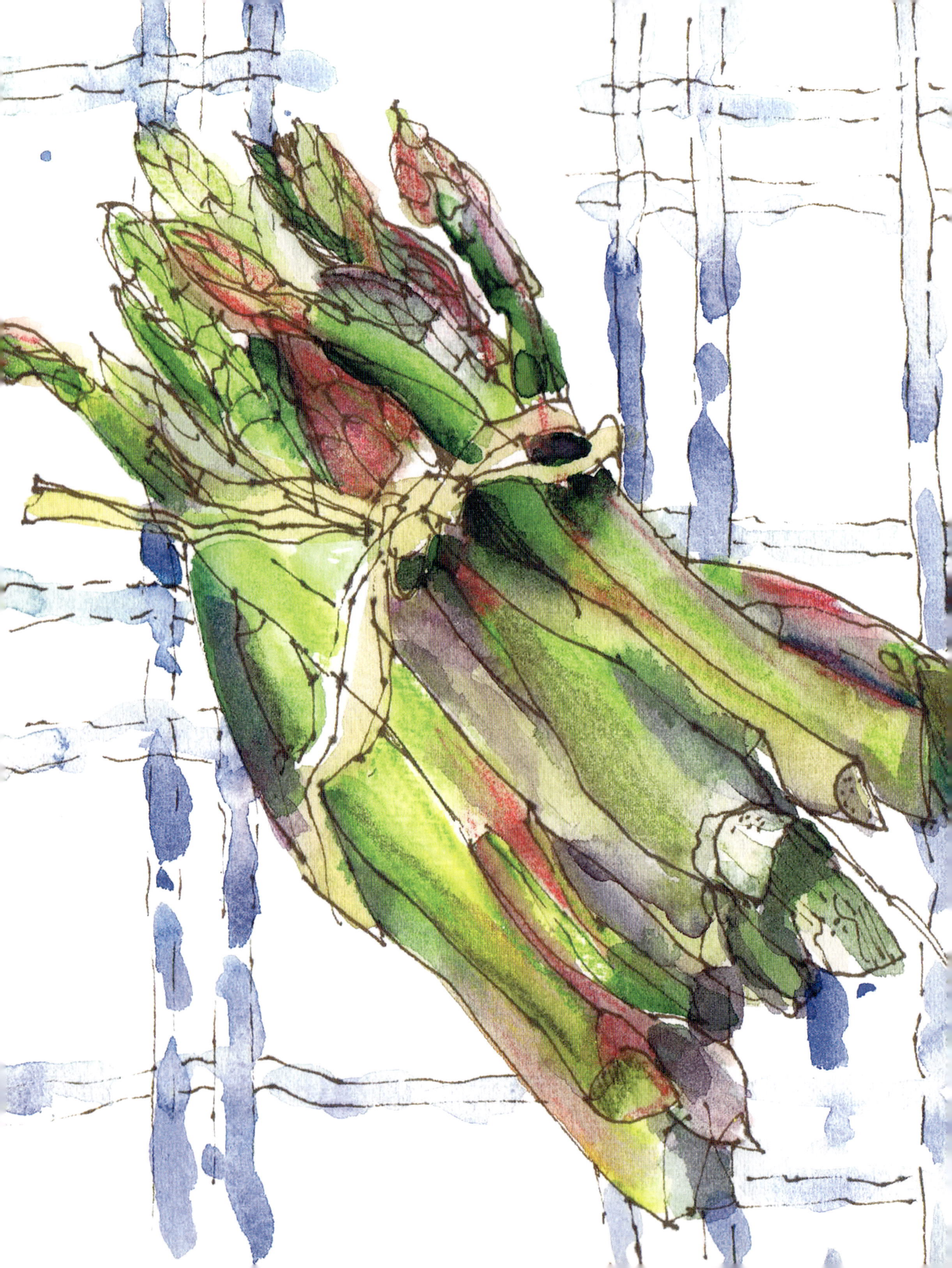

Your Sketchbook

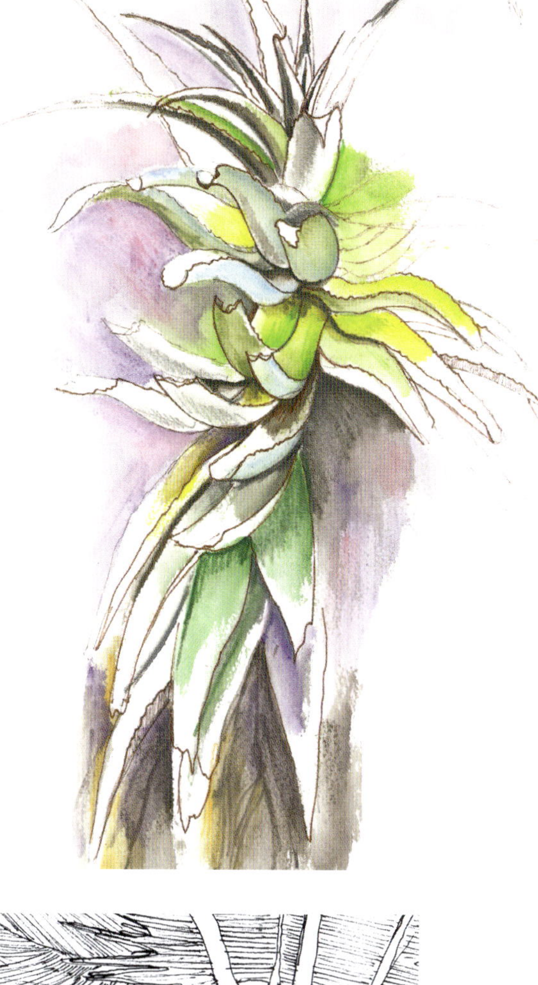

Botanical artists rarely have the luxury of unlimited time with their chosen specimen and, even if they do, the specimen is very likely to change in character: buds open, flowers wilt or turn with a changing light source, leaves wither. These problems can be magnified when dealing with exotic plants, so it's vitally important to record as much information about your specimen as possible.

If possible, do your homework first. Check reference books, look on the internet, and make sure that what you are proposing to paint is the best example of its kind that you can find. Consider its growth habit and structure and place yourself in the best position to record as much information as possible, even if this means lying on the ground or balancing precariously on a stepladder.

Now make sketches, picking out important details and sampling colours. Such sketches are not only invaluable references but they also provide opportunity for you to familiarize yourself with the specimen.

Photographs can be a great help (see pages 26–28) as long as your camera is used merely as an extension of your own understanding and vision. The camera cannot see the whole plant in the way that your eye can, so remember to take close-up shots from all angles of how the leaves join the stems, of a particular pattern on the petals, of the backs of flowers or the complicated nature of a bud or seedhead.

Left and top right A bit of background can add interest to your subject.

Right 'I knew I should have gone for groundcover plants.'

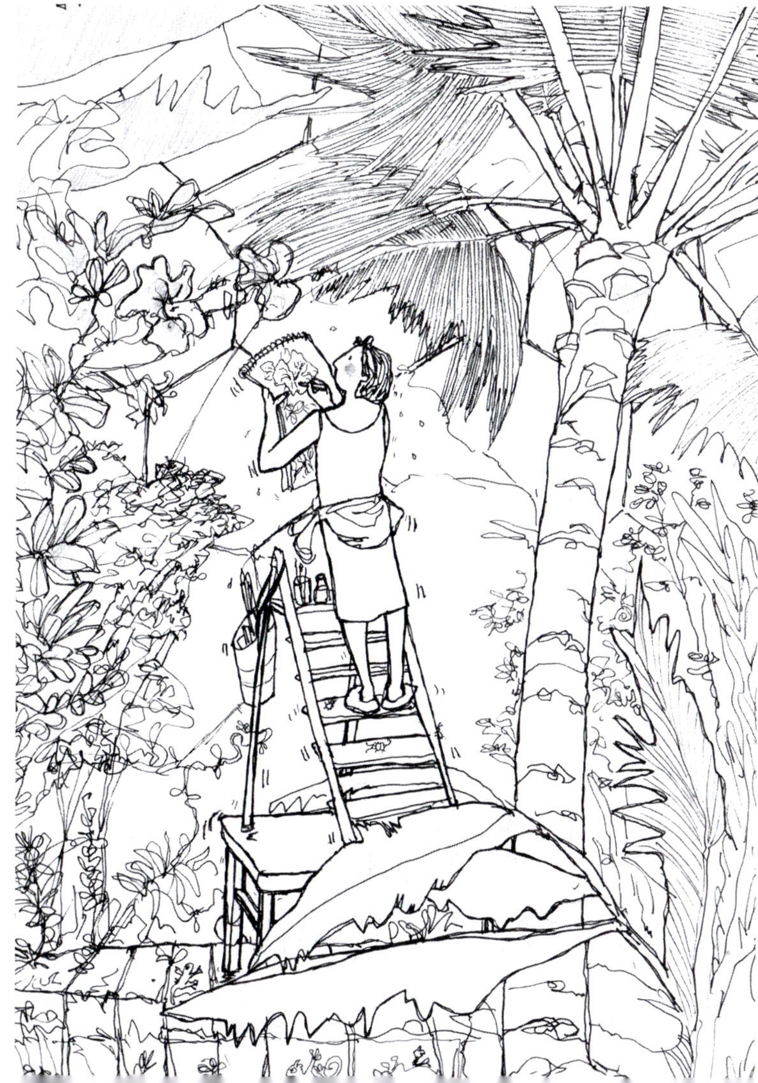

Out and about

You may wish to record the environment in which your plant grows. This could be with a quick pen drawing filled in with watercolour such as the Shell House (below right) or a small painting like the one of Neptune Steps (right), both in Tresco Abbey Gardens, Isles of Scilly. These quick watercolour sketches use the 'window effect' to draw the eye through the archway or between the palm trunks and up the steps to the feature at the top.

Give some thought to what you need to take with you, bearing in mind that you will have to carry it all. Pack only as much paper as you think you will need. If you take watercolours, select only those that you know you will use, rather than a large paintbox. You will also need a container of water and brushes, which will have to be protected in transit. Coloured pencils are preferred by many artists for outdoor work, as they are easy to carry and use when time is limited. Or you might prefer felt-tip pens – any colouring medium can be considered according to its suitability. Two sketchbooks will allow you to work in one while the other is drying. You might also want something to sit on, such as a folding stool or a sheet of waterproof material.

Your choice of materials is dictated by what you are most comfortable with, how portable they are and how suitable they are to the environment in which you will be using them. For instance, watercolour will dry in an instant if you are in desert conditions but will remain wet for a long time if you are in the humid atmosphere of a tropical jungle, or outside on a rainy day; it will also run or blotch if rain or snow fall on it. Waxy pencils could melt on a very hot day in a glasshouse or in the tropics.

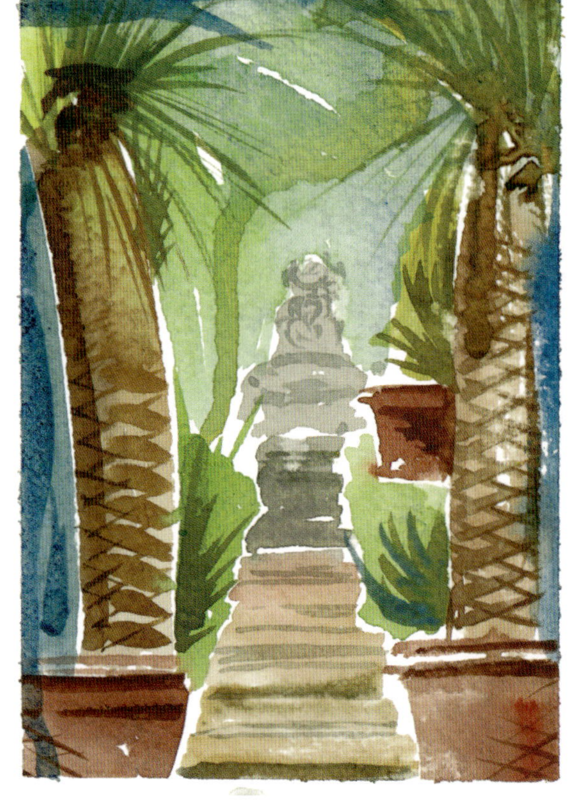

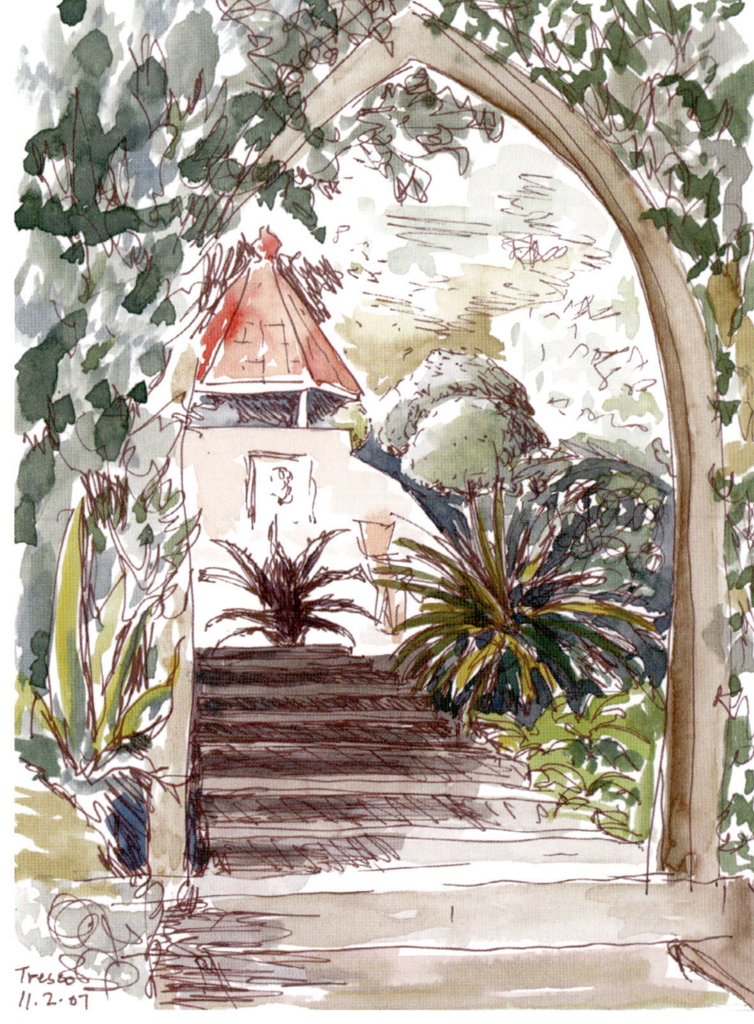

Right and above right Both of these watercolour sketches use the 'window effect' to draw the eye up the steps to the feature at the top.

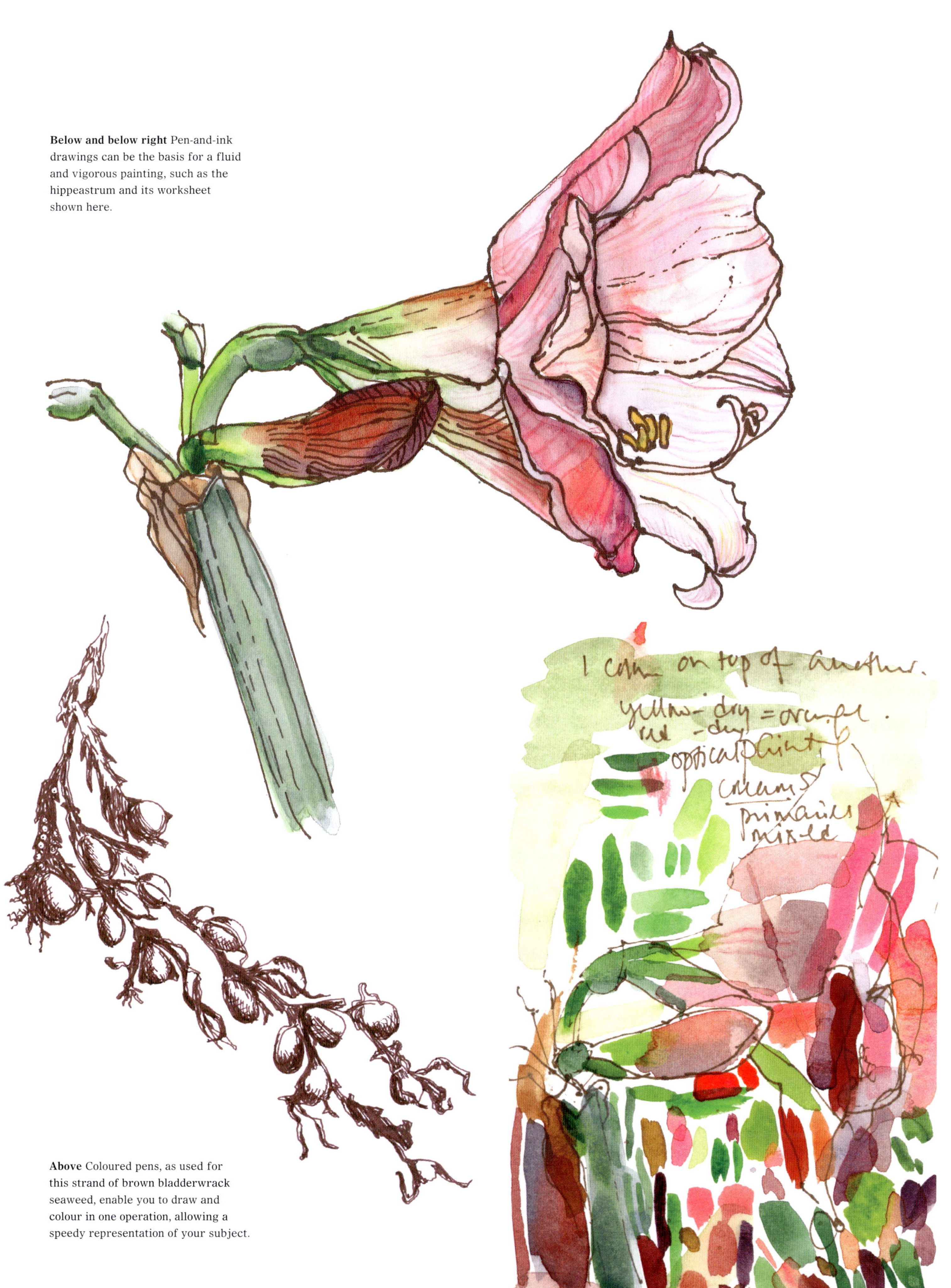

Below and below right Pen-and-ink drawings can be the basis for a fluid and vigorous painting, such as the hippeastrum and its worksheet shown here.

Above Coloured pens, as used for this strand of brown bladderwrack seaweed, enable you to draw and colour in one operation, allowing a speedy representation of your subject.

Familiarizing yourself with your plant

You do not need to produce a finished drawing to 'learn the botany' of your plant. This sketchbook page (right) is drawn in pencil to show all aspects of a hoya. Notes include: 'Leaf node – thick, waxy leaves, top with flecks. Underside plain, grey-green, dull'; 'very new leaves purple tinge, thinner and curled over'; 'spherical/open flowerhead'; 'thick cable-like shoots', and so on. The flowerhead is likened to an 'umbrella', with a bud referred to as a 'jewel clasp'.

With sketchbook work, speed is of the essence. You are making practical notes for yourself and recording as much of the plant as you can so that you can work on it later. You might like to make a series of quick pen-and-ink outline drawings and then fill some of them with colour (right and far right). These examples show hibiscus flowers and the colourful version has the added background interest of the hexagonal roof sections of the biome at the Eden Project in Cornwall, where they were growing.

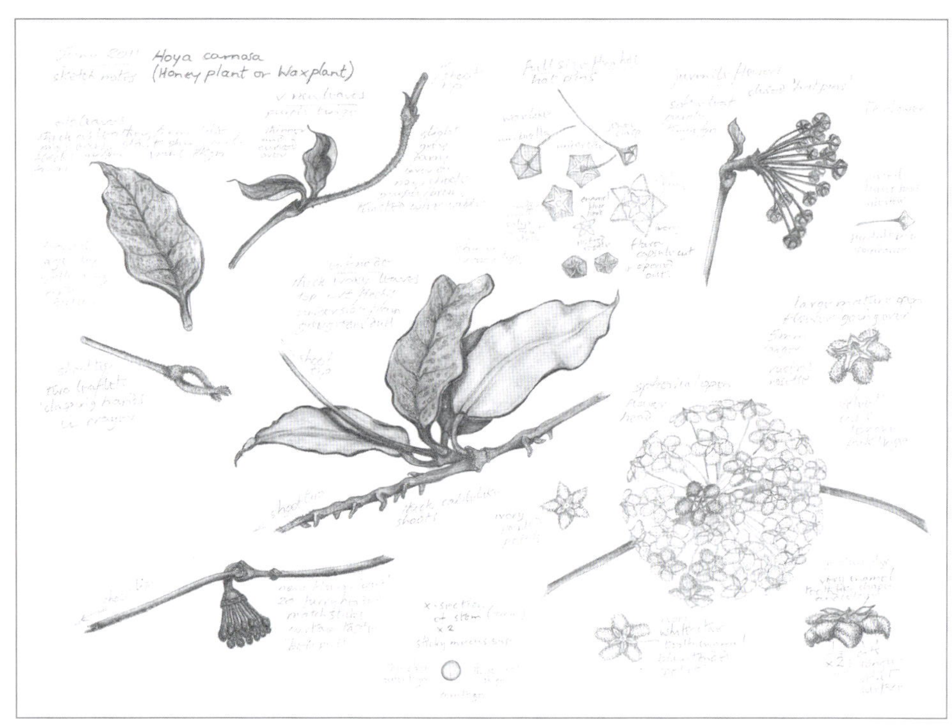

Top Make detailed drawings of parts of the plant, with notes, as with this *Hoya carnosa*, the honey plant or wax plant.

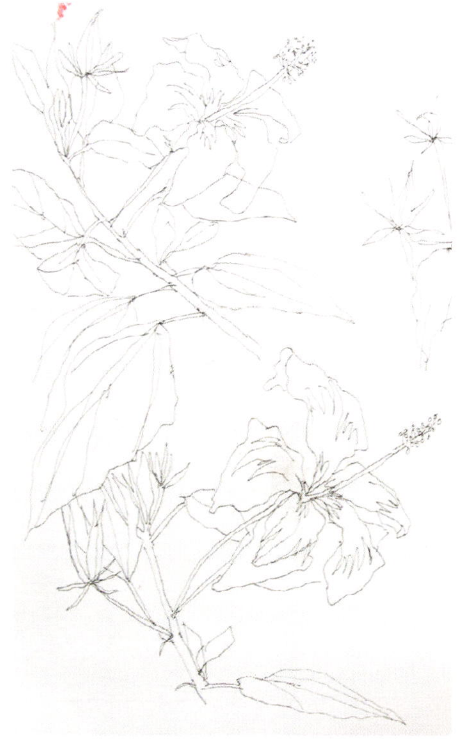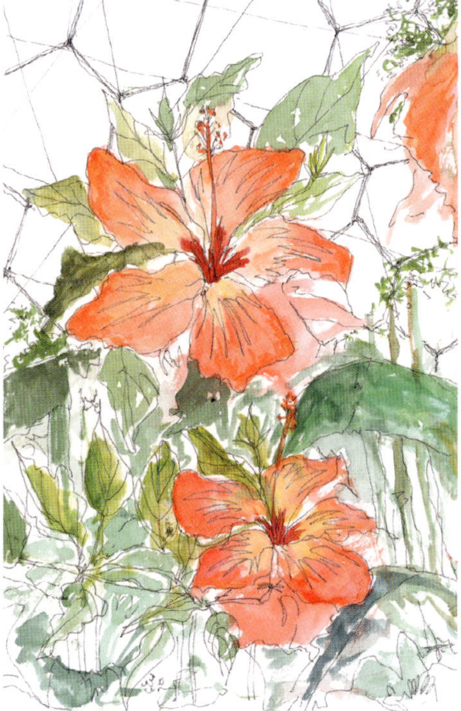

Right Quick pen-and-ink drawings can be filled with colour, as with these hibiscus flowers at the Eden Project in Cornwall.

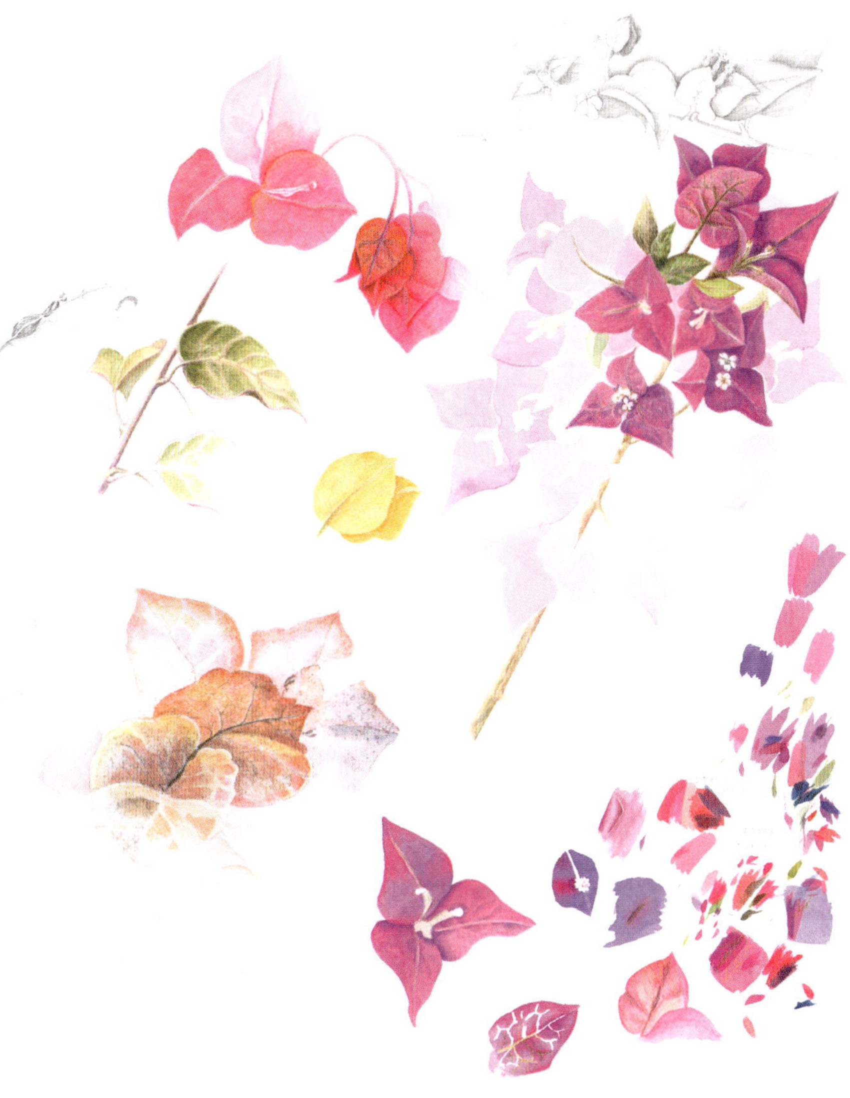

These examples were painted to serve as reminders for the future, but have a vitality and freshness that make them desirable studies in their own right.

Remember that the object of a sketchbook is to give yourself as much information as possible as quickly as possible. So record as much colour as you can, as demonstrated by the studies of bougainvillea (left).

Left The object of a sketchbook is to give yourself as much information as possible, as quickly as possible.

Below Two exotic and flamboyant treatments of magnolia seedheads, in pen-and-wash (top) and acrylic paint (bottom).

Magnolia seedheads

A traditional treatment of magnolia seedheads is shown on page 10, but the watercolour-and-pen drawing (right) suggests something far more flamboyant and exotic. The acrylic painting (below right) was derived from the initial pen-and-wash sketch and evokes high drama by way of its strong and resonant colours, bold directional composition and confident brushstrokes.

The colours have been over-emphasized in both renditions to maximize the effect. Notice how both use a limited colour range of reds, purples and blues, with the soft, creamy background echoing the warmth of the subject.

The primary purpose of your sketchbook work is to inform you when you come to paint your subject later on – but you may well find, as shown in some of the examples in this chapter, that the pages are also a beautiful record of where you were and what you were doing at the time, and you may wish to preserve them as such.

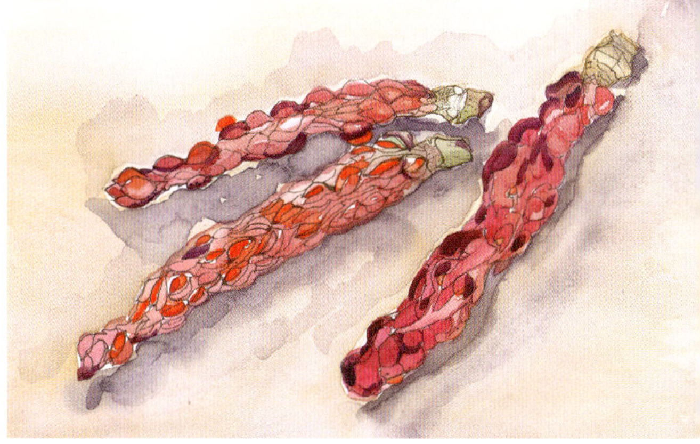

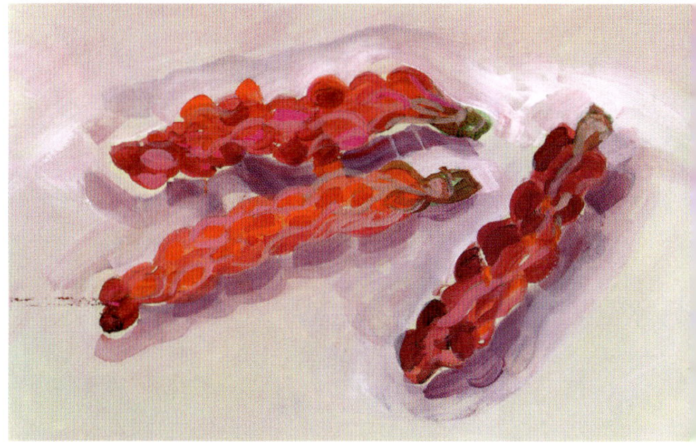

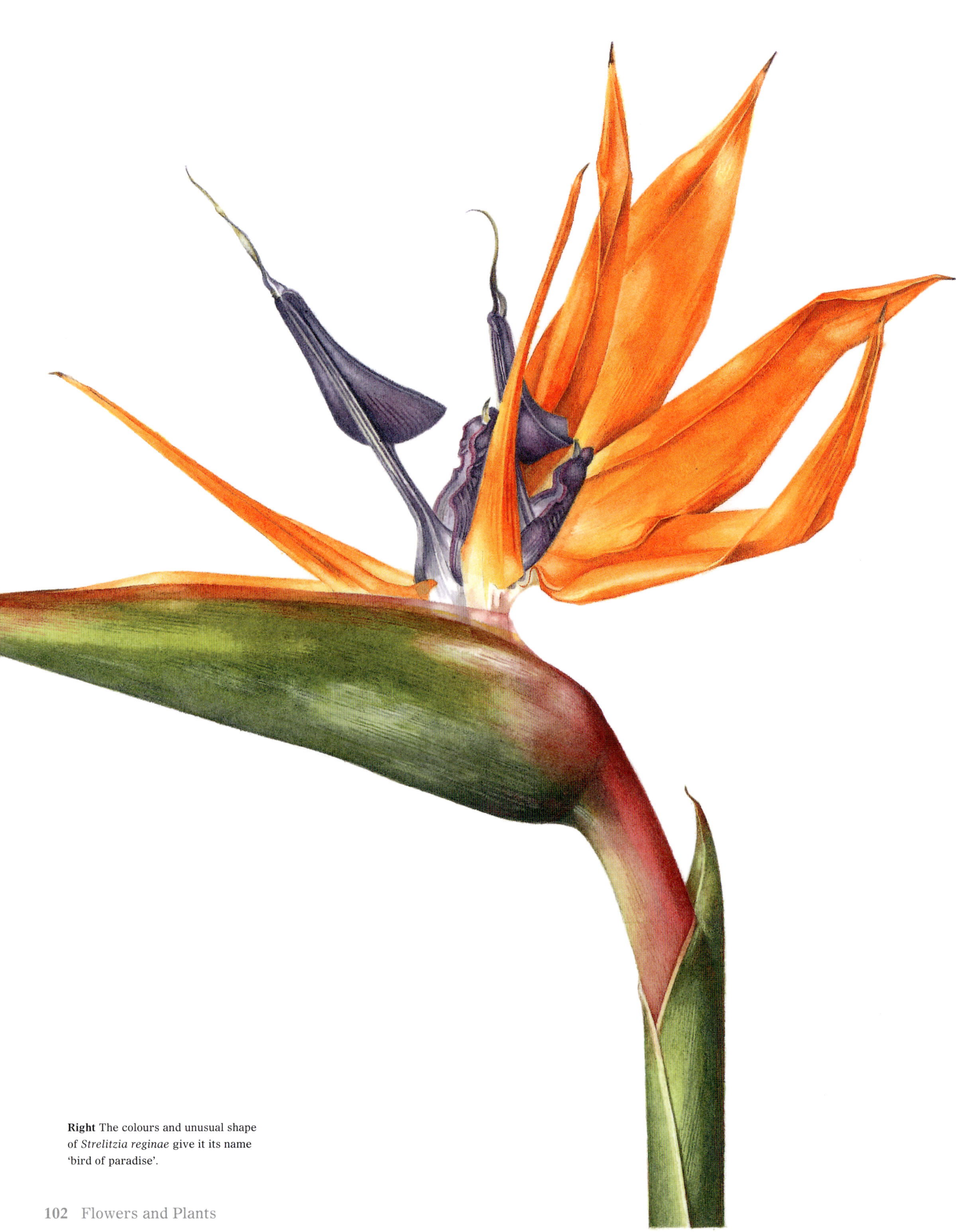

Right The colours and unusual shape of *Strelitzia reginae* give it its name 'bird of paradise'.

Flowers and Plants

The lure of the rare and bizarre, of jewel-coloured flowers and extraordinary leaves, is strong. Many botanical artists have an intense desire to paint such subjects. The colours, textures and unusual shapes are exciting, challenging and rewarding.

However beautiful your flower, the task is simplified if you start with the basics. Study your plant from all angles, choose the aspect that is the most pleasing and light it well to bring out its intense character.

Make sure you study the things that make it look out of the ordinary, such as the texture and pattern on the leaves, as well as the flowers. Check growth patterns as they too can often present unexpected positions. Some dangle, such as the eucalyptus (page 109); some throw up a spray, such as the agapanthus (page 108) and hippeastrums (page 106); some have sharp points, like the strelitzia (left).

Leaves, too, can be quite complex – for example those of the clivia (right), where you can see how the leaves overlap one another in sequence. It's interesting to note how the waxy flowers of the clivia connect with the equally heavy stem and leaves by means of a fine, dry, papery spathe.

The colour combinations of exotic plants can be flamboyant and often unusual, and it's important to record them accurately. One example is the strelitzia, one of the most sought-after plants when it comes to painting. Its combination of striking shapes and high-contrast colours have given it the name of 'bird of paradise'. *Strelitzia reginae* (left) contains two sets of complementary colours on the one flowerhead – the orange and blue of the florets, plus the red and green of the bract.

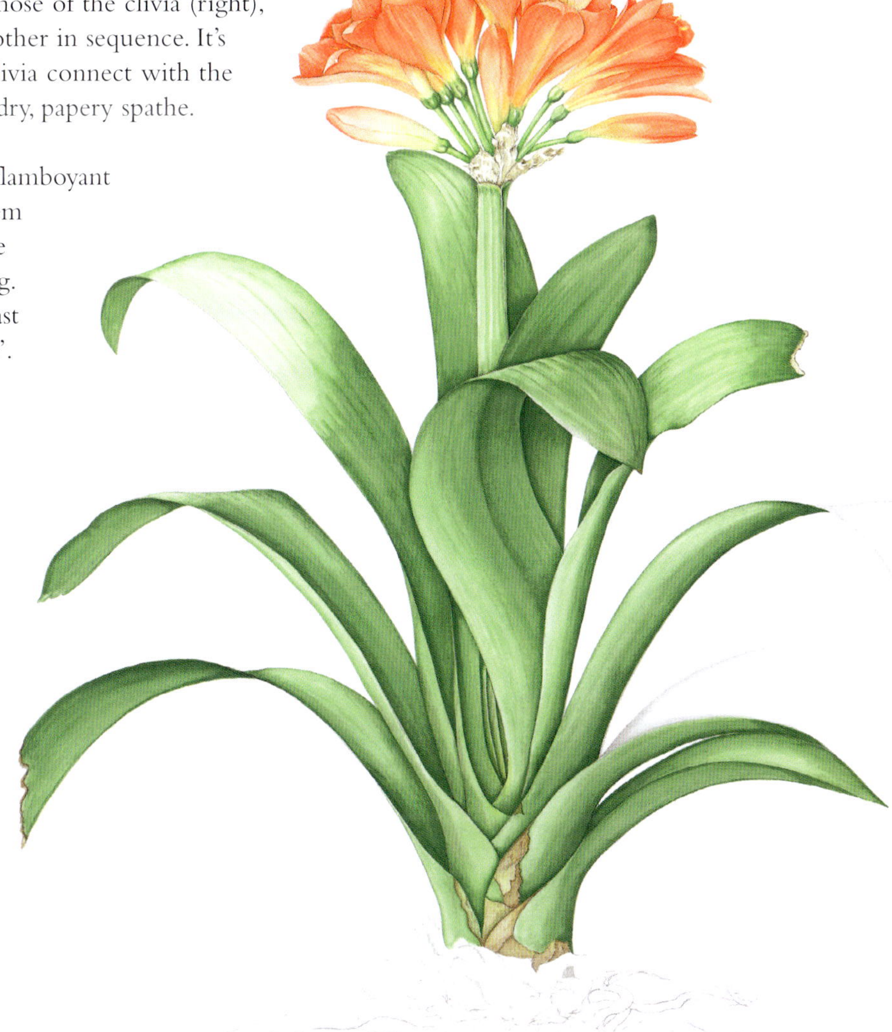

Right See how the clivia leaves overlap one another in sequence. This elegant painting was produced by making a tonal drawing and then adding watercolour (see page 86).

Exercise: *Anthurium* 'Fever'

This exercise in painting an exotic plant uses Sap Green. If you prefer to mix your own
version, use a mix of Winsor Blue (Green Shade), French Ultramarine and Indian Yellow,
varying the quantities until you have the correct colour.

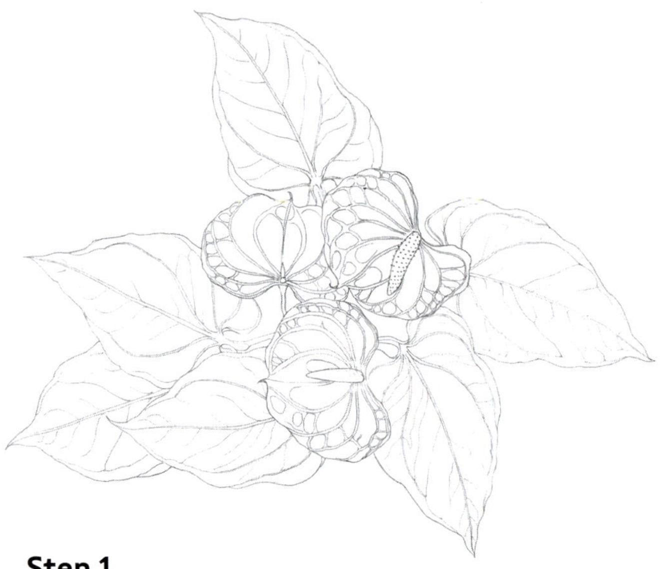

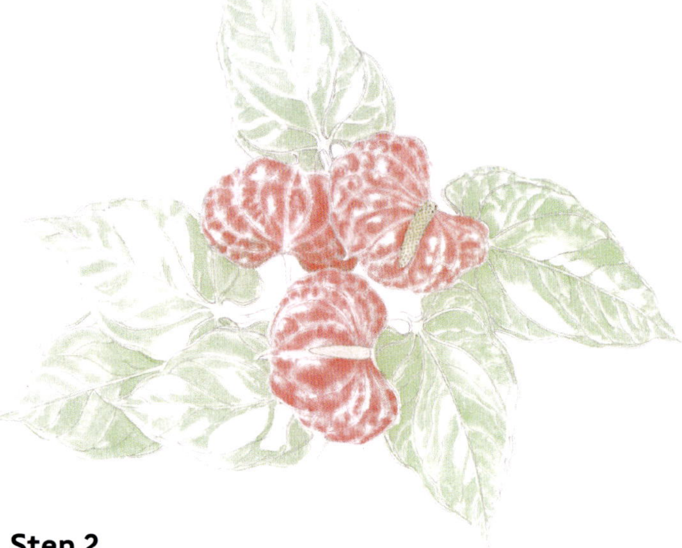

Step 1

You can make an interesting design by choosing an unusual
angle, as with this *Anthurium* 'Fever', where the viewpoint is
from above. Draw it carefully, marking in all the veins and
areas of the spathes that catch the light.

Step 2

Mask out the clusters of pollen on the larger spadix (flower
spike) as they are very pronounced and would be difficult
to paint around. Paint the spathes with a light wash of
Permanent Carmine and Scarlet Lake, reserving the
highlights. Follow this with a further wash of warm red
mixed with a small amount of Permanent Carmine in
selected areas. For the leaves, mix a creamy colour using
Indian Yellow and Winsor Violet, and use this well diluted.
This wash could be further diluted and used on the spadix.
Drop in Sap Green and Indian Yellow, wet-into-wet, again
leaving plenty of highlights.

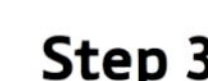

Step 3

Slowly build up the colours on the flowers using Permanent Carmine and
Scarlet Lake in several washes. Make sure that each layer is completely dry
before applying the next. Build up the intensity of the colour with a mix
of Opera Rose and Scarlet Lake by applying stronger colour, blending with
a damp brush and defining areas around the veins. Use a mix of Permanent
Carmine and Winsor Violet to build up the darker areas. When everything
is dry, use a well-diluted wash of Scarlet Lake with a touch of Lemon
Yellow over the whole area. Drop a combination of Sap Green and
Winsor Violet wet-into-wet on to the leaves.

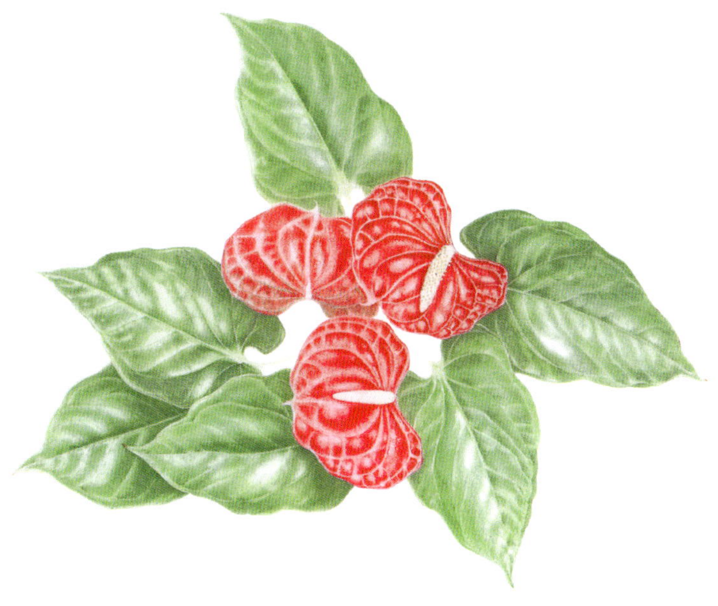

Step 4

Using your cream mix, paint the stems, the edges of the leaves and the veins more carefully, and darken the leaf tips with a light red-brown mix of Indian Yellow, Scarlet Lake and a little French Ultramarine. Blend into the lighter areas a combination of Sap Green and Indian Yellow, and use Sap Green with Prussian Blue and a touch of Permanent Carmine for the darker areas. When completely dry, give the leaves a wash of well-diluted olive green mix, taking it just over the edges of the highlights. Add a little Winsor Violet to your Sap Green and bring the leaves up to a darker and richer colour by stippling it on to the darkest and shadiest areas and the veins.

Step 5

Stipple the flowers with a deeper mix of Permanent Carmine with a little French Ultramarine, and in parts stipple some Winsor Lemon to sharpen and brighten. Finish with a stippled layer of Alizarin Crimson and Opera Rose, adding French Ultramarine to the mix where there is shadow and for the veins. Finally, gently remove the masking fluid from the spadix with your eraser, and use the cream mix with Scarlet Lake and a touch of the olive green mix to touch up around the clusters of pollen. For the stem, use the creams and greens that you used for the leaves, with a little red added.

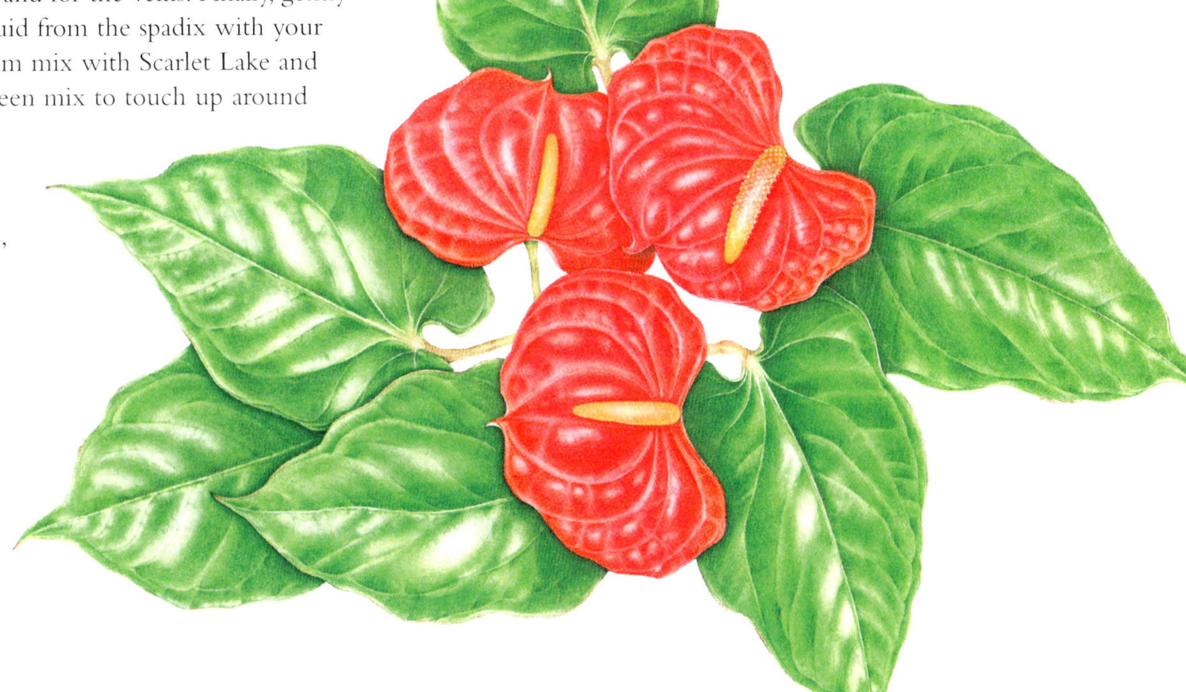

The tiny spadix in the top-left flower is shown larger in the final stage (above). This is because the artist thought it didn't look right as the picture neared completion, so she erased some of the spathe and painted in a larger spadix. Some watercolour paints are so staining that they can't be removed whatever you do, but it's usually possible to lift them off by flooding them with clean water and blotting with absorbent paper.

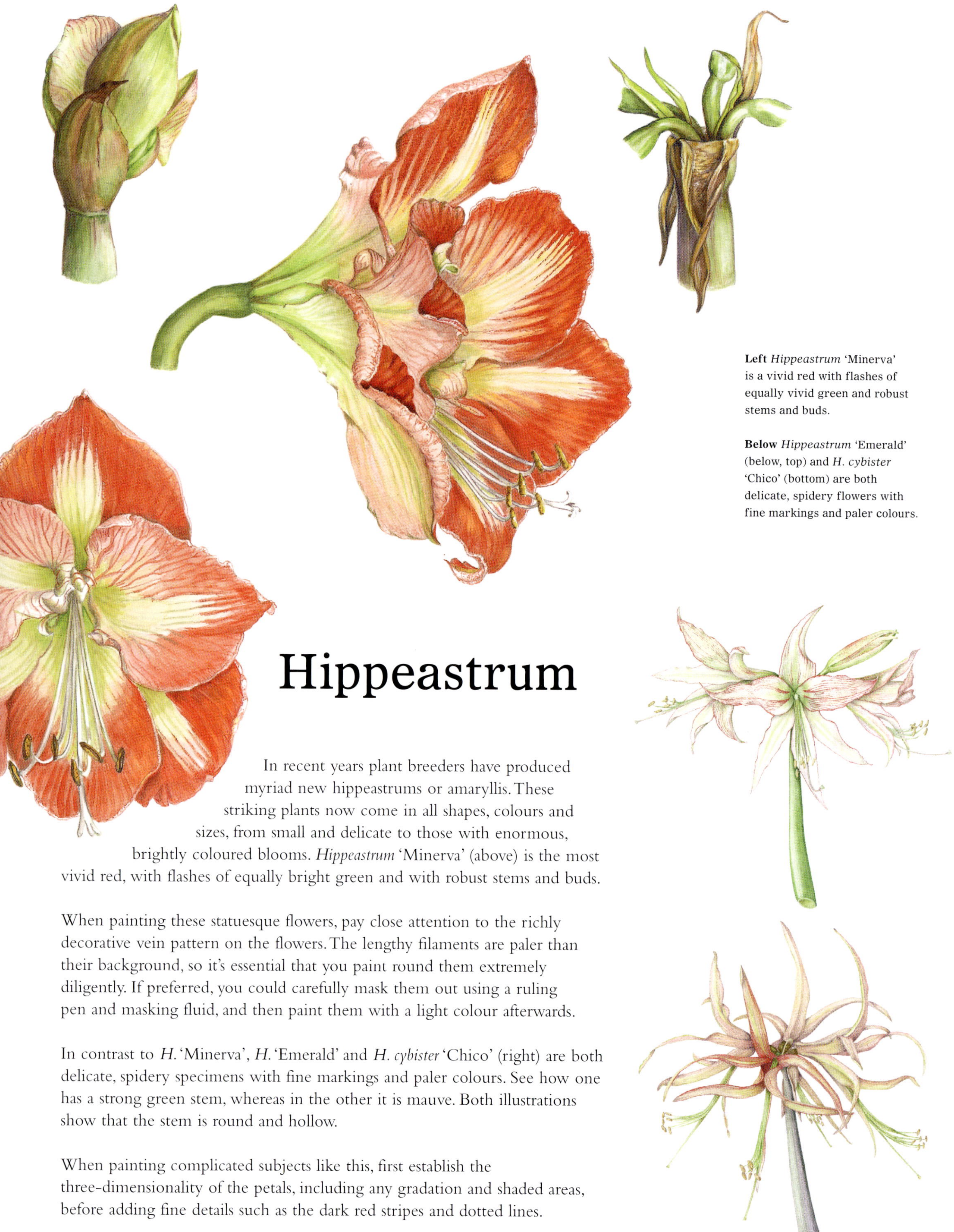

Hippeastrum

In recent years plant breeders have produced myriad new hippeastrums or amaryllis. These striking plants now come in all shapes, colours and sizes, from small and delicate to those with enormous, brightly coloured blooms. *Hippeastrum* 'Minerva' (above) is the most vivid red, with flashes of equally bright green and with robust stems and buds.

When painting these statuesque flowers, pay close attention to the richly decorative vein pattern on the flowers. The lengthy filaments are paler than their background, so it's essential that you paint round them extremely diligently. If preferred, you could carefully mask them out using a ruling pen and masking fluid, and then paint them with a light colour afterwards.

In contrast to *H.* 'Minerva', *H.* 'Emerald' and *H. cybister* 'Chico' (right) are both delicate, spidery specimens with fine markings and paler colours. See how one has a strong green stem, whereas in the other it is mauve. Both illustrations show that the stem is round and hollow.

When painting complicated subjects like this, first establish the three-dimensionality of the petals, including any gradation and shaded areas, before adding fine details such as the dark red stripes and dotted lines.

Protea

The two Proteas (right) have bold shapes but, in contrast, their leaves and flowerheads are quite delicately coloured. The backs of the leaves (top right) show the midrib in relief and the pink-edged leaves growing from a woody stem. The flowerhead of a protea is so detailed that you would benefit from spending some considerable time studying it before starting to draw. It might help to dissect it or pull apart a section of it to see how it works. A worksheet (below) would allow you to experiment, make notes and try out shapes and colours.

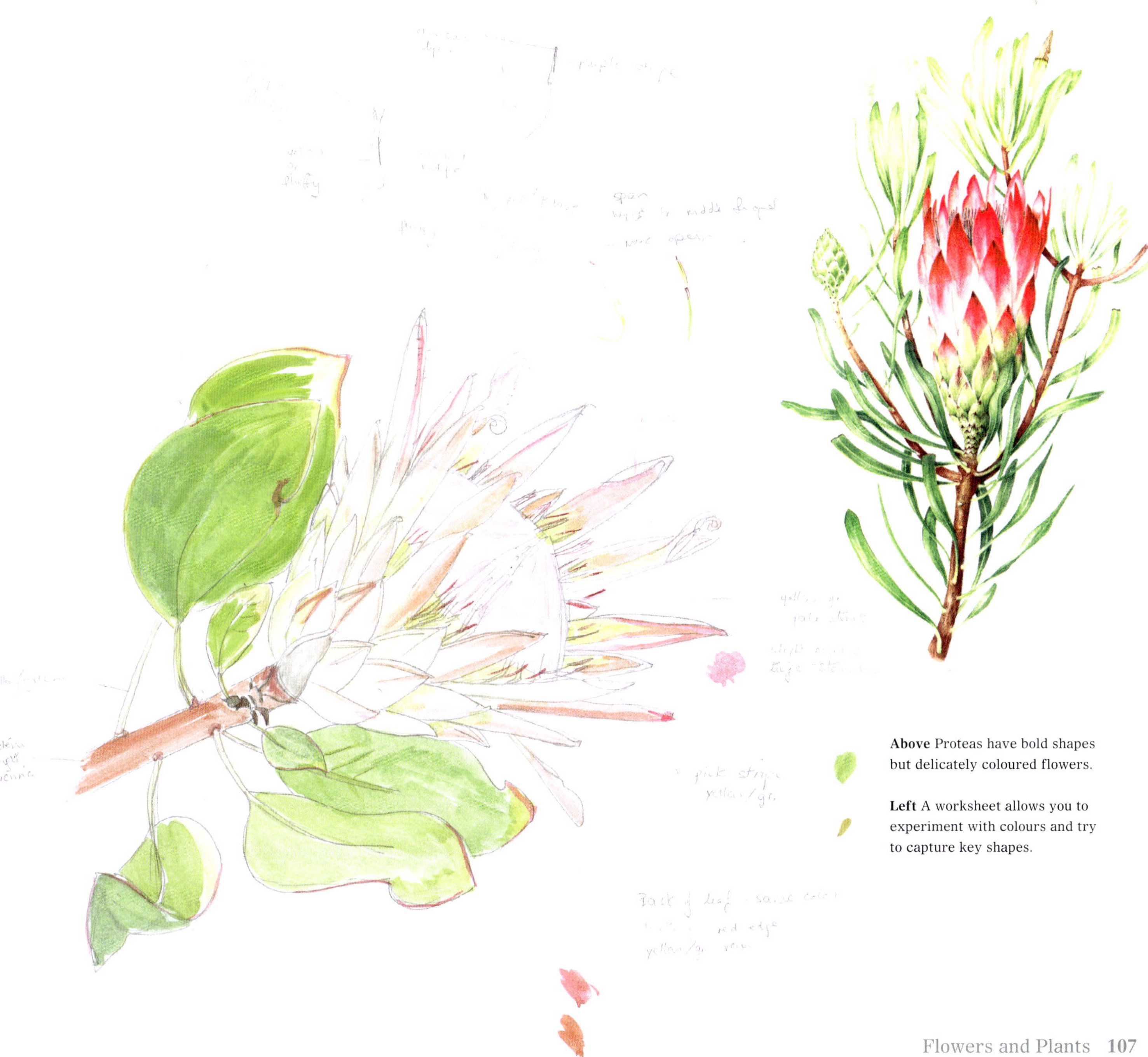

Above Proteas have bold shapes but delicately coloured flowers.

Left A worksheet allows you to experiment with colours and try to capture key shapes.

Exercise: Agapanthus

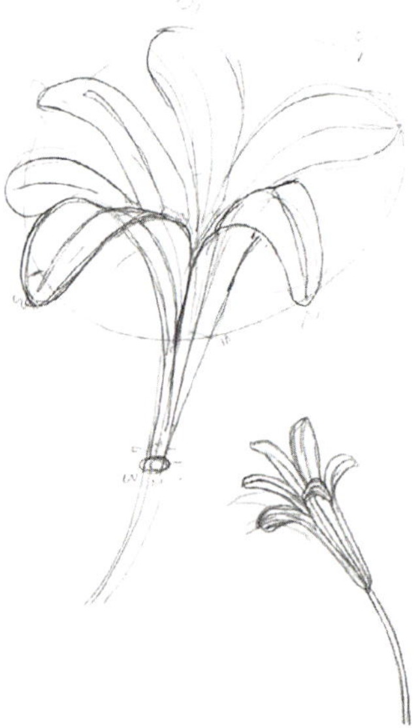

Step 1

To help you to understand your subject, use a worksheet to simplify the forms of florets and leaves. Here, the floret is based on an ellipse while a smaller ellipse forms the base of the petals. Observe carefully any foreshortening of petals, which will be found in most of the florets (see page 48).

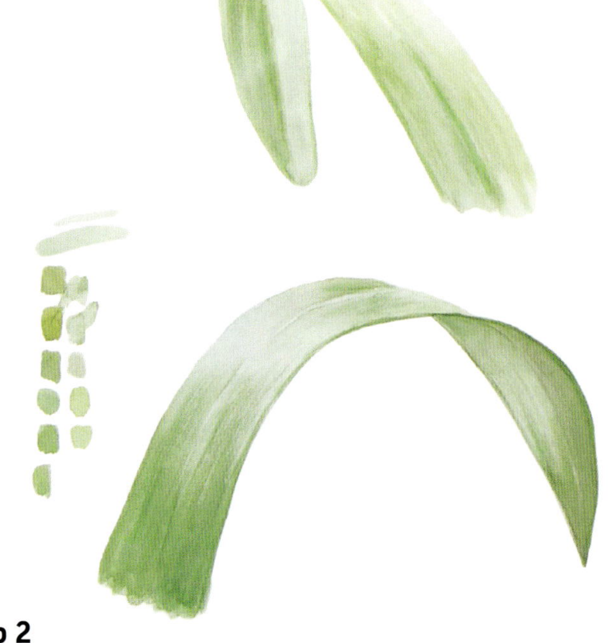

Step 2

Make studies of the leaves to show colour and shape as well as the fold and position of the disappearing midrib.

Step 3

Next make preliminary drawings of the flowerhead and indicate all overlapping stems. You might also like to remind yourself of areas of light and shade, as here, where yellow has been used to denote areas where the light hits the subject, and blue to show shaded parts.

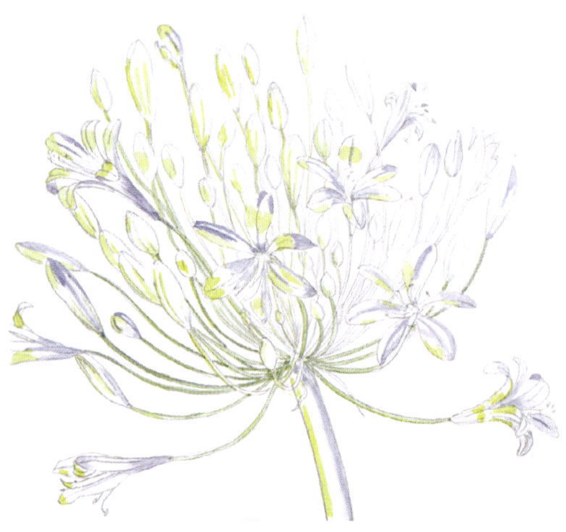

Step 4

Transfer your drawing to watercolour paper and paint it. The finished painting should show all the tiny stems accurately positioned, each bearing a blue bud or floret. Notice how, although they appear consistently blue, some of the florets or buds have areas of yellow or green (yellow under blue).

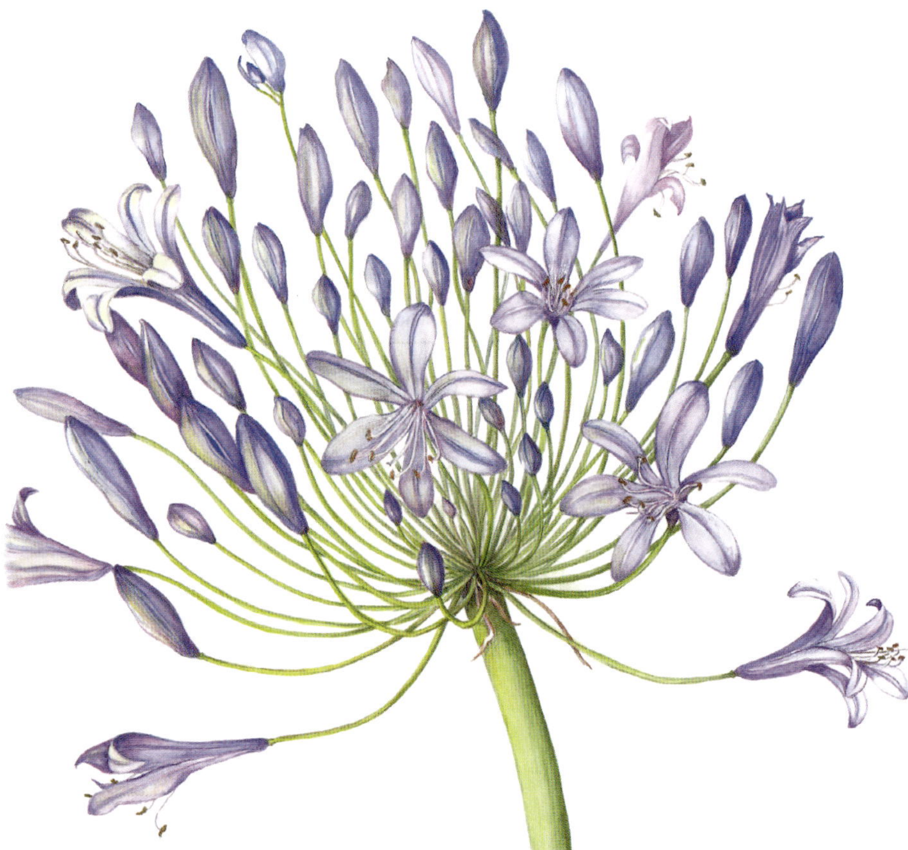

Gloriosa

This rather stylized portrait of *Gloriosa superba* 'Rothschildiana' or glory lily (right), gives a good idea of the character of the leaves (modified into climbing tendrils), the flower's six incurved petals, and the arrangement of reproductive organs that give it the appearance of a small, whiskery animal. Many of the final details on leaves and flower were stippled with a very fine, almost dry, brush.

Eucalyptus

A plant that is exotic mainly because of its shape and geographical range is the eucalyptus (right). Far from having flamboyant colours, it's a good example of the range of greys that can be found in nature. The leaves are subtle grey-greens, from very pale to very dark, and give the eucalyptus its soft, misty quality. Note the size and shape of the leaves, how they twist and overlap. The seedheads are round, hard, woody, rough in texture, and have a clearly defined, geometrical design that will repay careful attention.

Leucospermum

It's a matter of discussion whether or not to show animal or bird life in botanical painting (left). However, it's generally deemed acceptable if there's a strong connection between the plant and its pollinator.

Cape sugarbirds are native to the Fynbos region of South Africa and pollinate Proteaceae, the family to which *Leucospermum conocarpodendron* belongs. The bird's extremely sharp claws enable it to grip in even the strongest winds while it probes into the flowerhead to feed, thus pollinating the plant at the same time. Both bird and plant have been painted with great delicacy, with attention to individual characteristics. The fleshy leaves, the fine spindly filaments and the light feathery bird complement each other and make an interesting and informative composition.

Orchids

Orchids are probably the most widely available exotic plants for botanical artists to paint. They can be found in garden centres, nurseries, on the internet and even in supermarkets – although these last may not be accurately labelled with the correct name, or indeed any name at all. If you need to know the exact details, it is worth checking with a specialist.

Many orchids have a long, thin stem, with bulky leaves at the base and a large and colourful inflorescence at the top. This can present problems with composition, as there is not much of interest in the centre of the painting.

The paintings of the *Odontoglossum* (above right) and the pink *Phalaenopsis* orchid (right) are both good examples of how to make a tall, spindly subject fit comfortably on to a regular-sized piece of paper. Note how the artists have shown the leaves separately from the flower spike, while still showing the exact length of the stem, albeit in two sections.

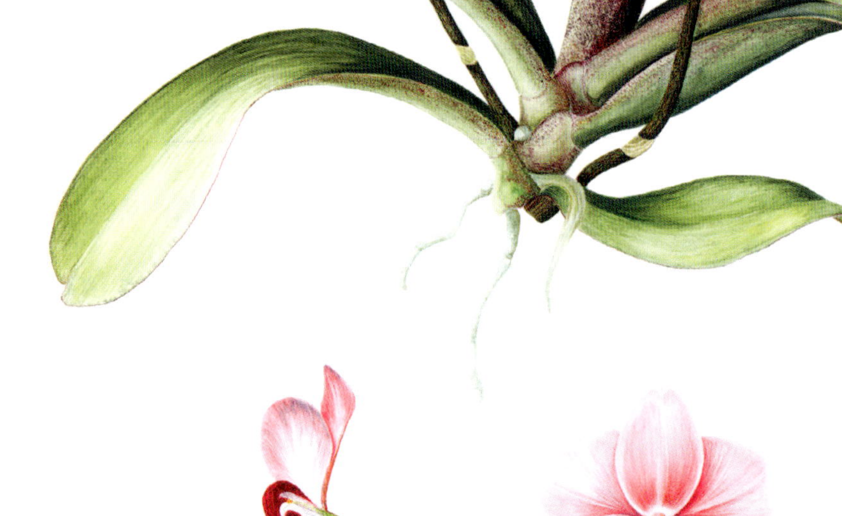

Right and above right The *Odontoglossum* (top right) and the pink *Phalaenopsis* (right) have both been presented in such a way that they fit neatly on to the paper.

These illustrations demonstrate a different treatment of slipper orchids (*Paphiopedilum*). The leaves and flowers have been shown in a similar fashion, but the artists have chosen to present the plants (particularly the stems) in the way that demonstrates how this orchid can grow.

Before you start to paint an orchid, spend some time studying it – they are complex plants with many tricky features. Look at it from all angles and try to discover how it might be pollinated, how the individual parts fit together and, if it has more than one flower, how they differ. You might like to show the whole plant, as in these illustrations, or you might choose to show a spray of flowers or just a single flower.

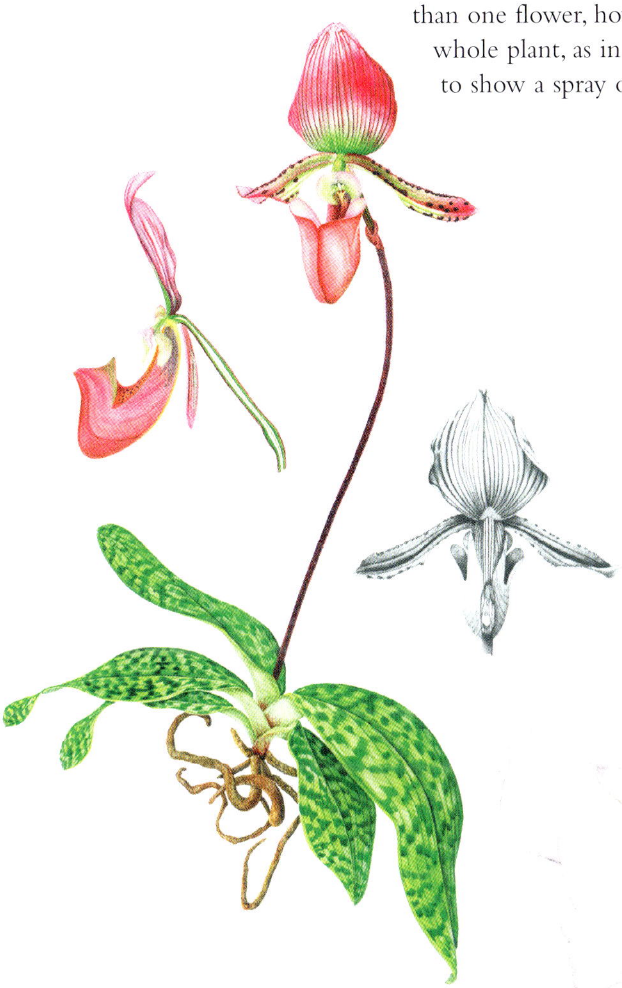

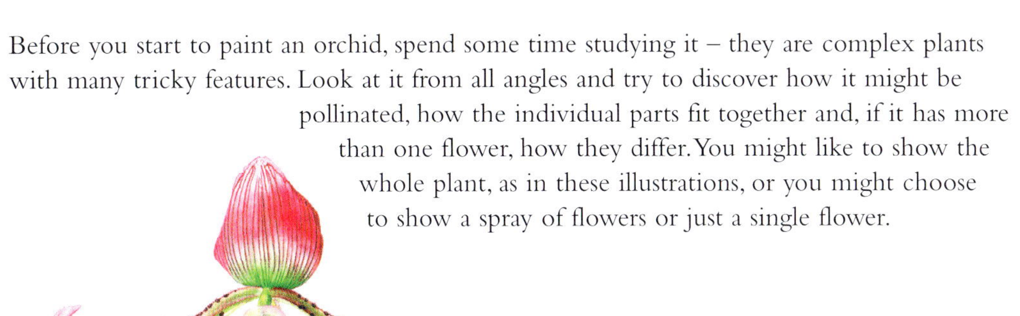

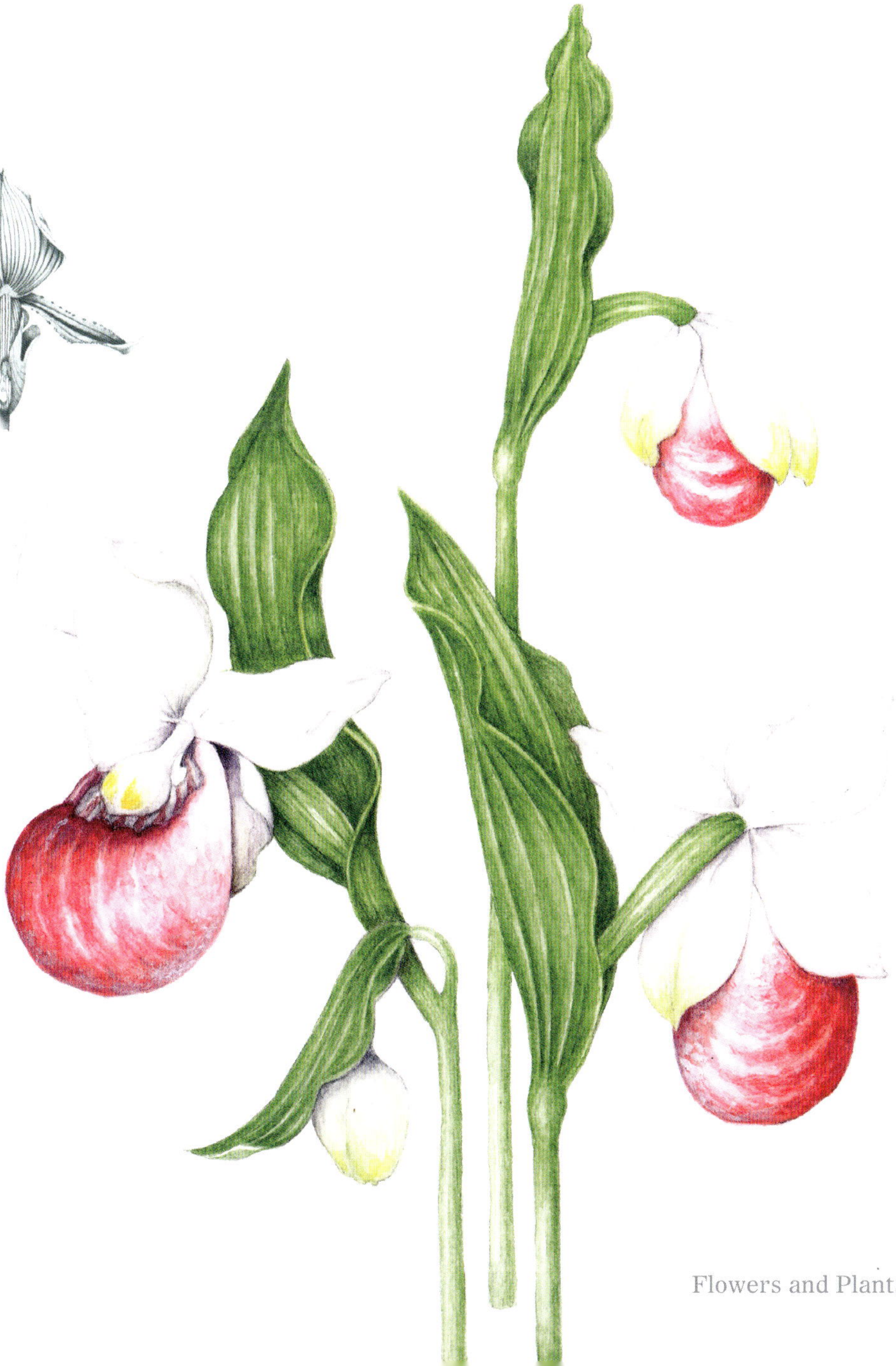

Above The slipper orchids on this page have been presented to show how this orchid can grow.

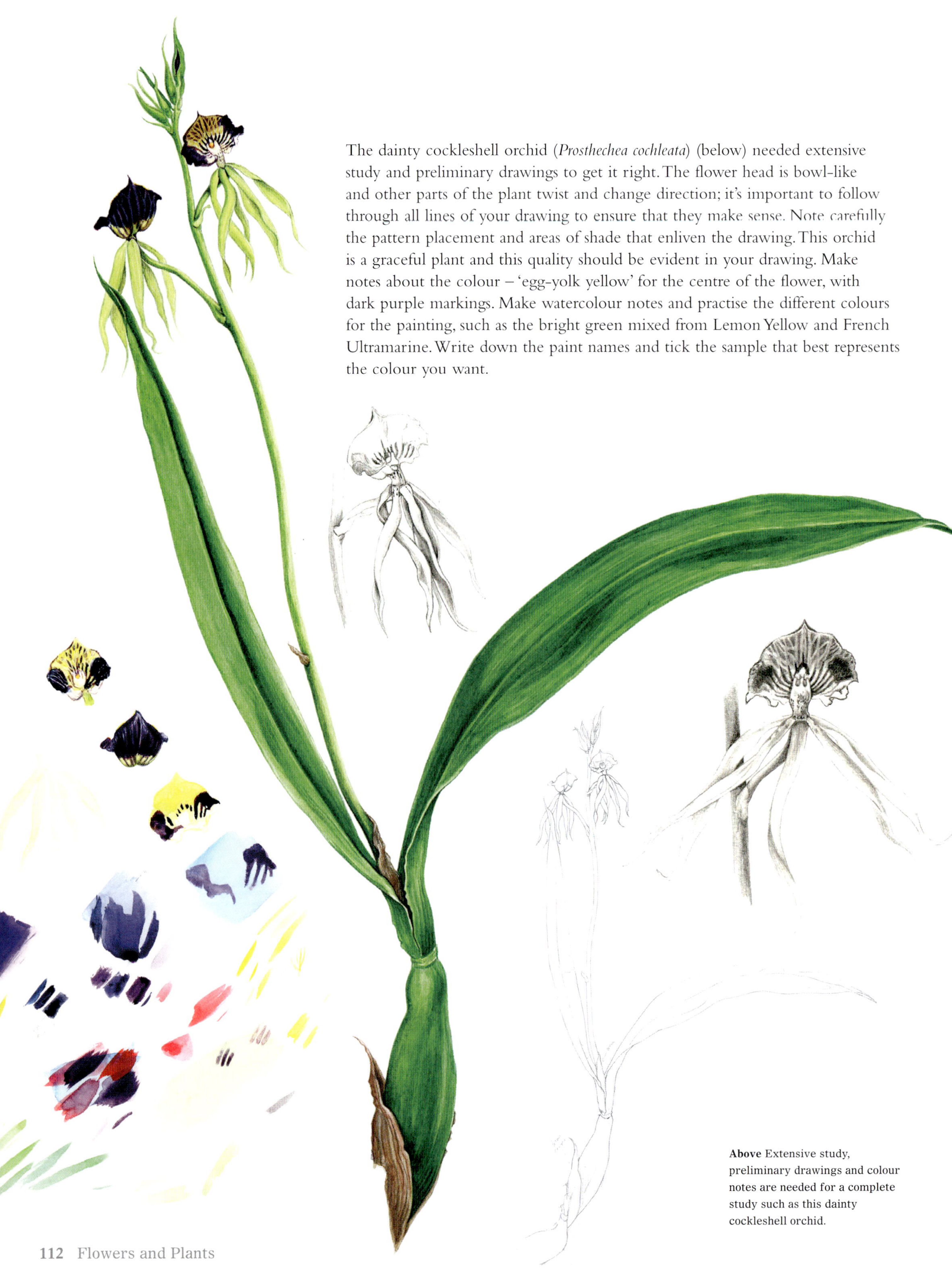

The dainty cockleshell orchid (*Prosthechea cochleata*) (below) needed extensive study and preliminary drawings to get it right. The flower head is bowl-like and other parts of the plant twist and change direction; it's important to follow through all lines of your drawing to ensure that they make sense. Note carefully the pattern placement and areas of shade that enliven the drawing. This orchid is a graceful plant and this quality should be evident in your drawing. Make notes about the colour – 'egg-yolk yellow' for the centre of the flower, with dark purple markings. Make watercolour notes and practise the different colours for the painting, such as the bright green mixed from Lemon Yellow and French Ultramarine. Write down the paint names and tick the sample that best represents the colour you want.

Above Extensive study, preliminary drawings and colour notes are needed for a complete study such as this dainty cockleshell orchid.

Exercise: Painting a slipper orchid

Start by making small drawings of different parts of the orchid until you are happy that you know how you will portray them (right). Look out for the roots, which are soft and hairy with smooth ends; notice how the dorsal sepal, or hood, appears to fold inwards, partly due to the shape and partly to do with the markings, which follow the shape; note any parts that reflect the light; look at what the markings do and how they follow the contours of the hood.

Make a good, clear and accurate pencil drawing of the orchid in your layout pad (below), tracing it carefully on to your watercolour paper. You will need warm and cool yellow, warm and cool red, and warm and cool blue, plus Winsor Violet and Sap Green.

Give the leaves a pale Sap Green wash. When dry, paint on the pattern with a darker green, softening the edges with a damp brush as you go. Add a pale primary mix wash of cream over the top of the leaves if the green is too intense. Lastly, stipple on a strong mix of Winsor Violet and Prussian Blue at the base of the leaves.

For the long petals on either side of the flower, with their hairy 'warts and bumps', start with a first wash of pale pink and green, dropped in wet-into-wet so that they merge slightly. Paint very fine light greenish-grey lines the length of each petal.

When dry, use a fine brush (size No. 1 or smaller) to paint the 'warts and bumps' with light centres, distinct highlights and dark edges. Using a lighter version of the colour for the 'warts', paint the very fine hairs. For these, always start the brushstroke at the 'wart' so that you can taper it towards the outer end. Paint the hairs on the stem in the same way, using a darker red for the ones on the edge of the stem and white for others.

The pouch and the dorsal sepal have a variety of pattern and texture – the pouch is shiny, the dorsal sepal is matt. To get the intensity of colour in the pouch, overlay washes of lemony green, deep red and yellow. Yellow over dark red will give a bronze colour. Add a greeny-blue to your deep red mix to bring the veins out darker. For the fuzzy stripes on the hood, either put in the dark red lines when the paper is still slightly wet, or paint on dry paper. Allow to dry and then run a damp brush over them.

Above Make small drawings of different parts of the slipper orchid, sample colours and test brushstrokes before you start the painting.

Exercise: Painting a white orchid

Although this orchid is obviously a white flower, if you study it carefully you will see that other colours are present, predominantly different versions of grey, giving it a three-dimensional quality. A well-painted white flower will appear even whiter than the paper around it. The colours you will use are warm and cool yellow, warm and cool red and warm and cool blue (see page 71).

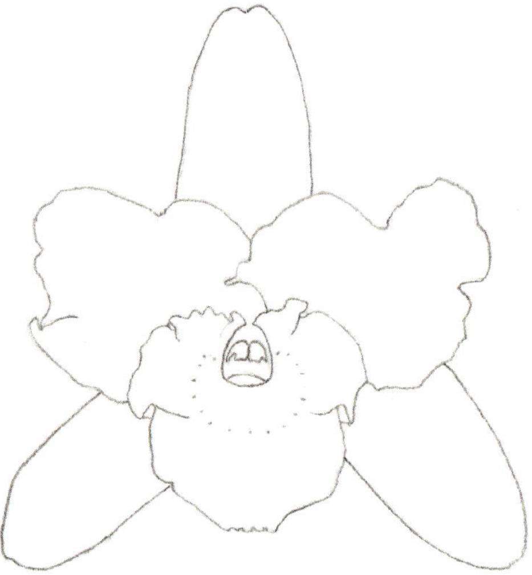

Step 1

Draw the orchid on layout paper and trace it on to white (not cream) watercolour paper.

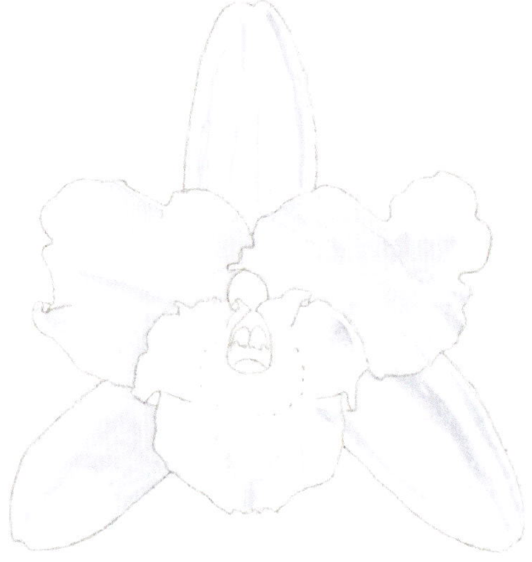

Step 2

Mix a well-diluted grey-blue and wash it on to any areas of shade or overlap, taking care not to over-paint.

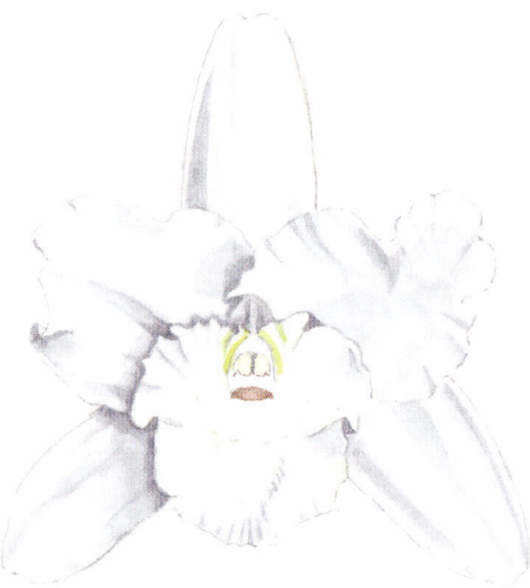

Step 3

Darken the grey-blue mix and heighten any areas of greater shade. Add some pale yellow towards the centre of the flower, and start to work up the recessed area in the centre with a deep red-crimson.

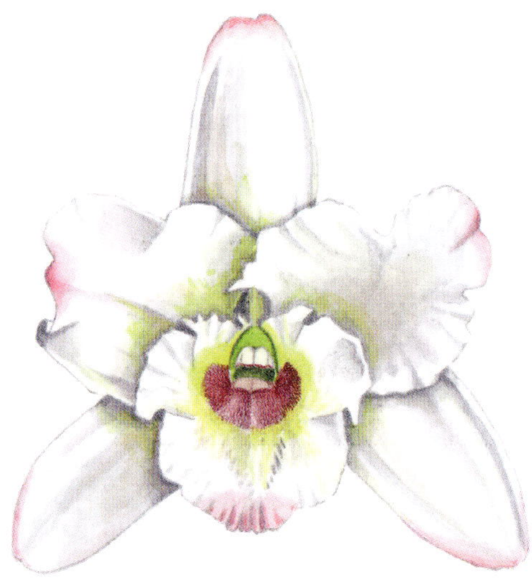

Step 4

Using a slightly stronger version of the grey-blue, deepen and strengthen shaded areas, indicate folds and pleats in the petals, and touch the petal tips with the diluted red mix, grading and blending to avoid hard lines. There's no need to make a continuous line around the petals as the shading will indicate the edges, but you might like to make a fine line of grey-blue on the shaded side of each petal.

Carnivorous plants

These brutal-sounding plants grow in wet and boggy areas where concentrations of mineral nutrients are low. As a consequence they have developed the ability to boost their nutrition by trapping insects and other small wildlife, including, in some instances, small birds, fish and frogs.

The flowers of most carnivorous plants are placed on long stems, far above the treacherous pitchers. This is to enable pollinating insects to perform their task without the risk of entering the deadly traps.

Sarracenia 'Beryl'

Sarracenia 'Beryl' (right) is a member of the Sarraceniaceae family of North American pitcher plants, which have evolved to operate statically – that is to say with no moving parts. The large, open, convoluted hoods allow rainwater into the pitchers. This hood is covered by bristly downward-pointing hairs. Insects cling to and slip from these hairs, which are wet with nectar, and drown in the water inside the pitcher. There they are largely decomposed by bacteria and other micro-organisms.

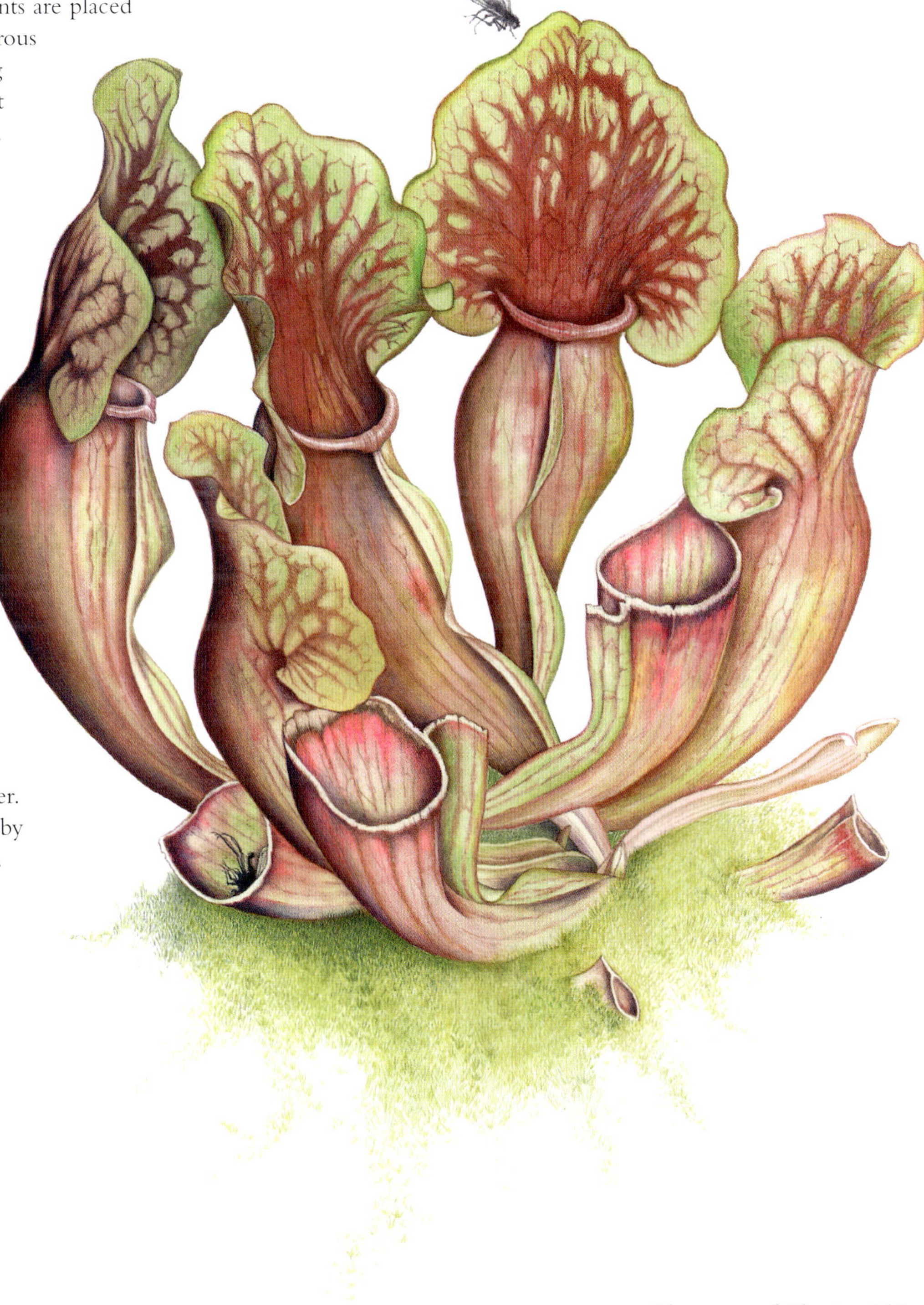

Right This painting of *Sarracenia* 'Beryl', the trumpet pitcher plant, is a good example of optical mixing.

Exercise: *Sarracenia* 'Beryl'

Construction

Geometric shapes mark out this complicated group. These will help to establish the main reference points of the subject. A cut-out card circle was placed behind the plant to contain the composition. This also assists in determining the relationship of the elements one to another and to the whole, and within a framework, allowing you to judge positioning and scale.

To place elements within the framework and to judge positioning, mark a series of dots to indicate distances from certain points to the outer circle and to each other. By plotting point-to-point, you will better understand the relationships of different parts one to another and to the whole.

Look also at the negative shapes. If they are wrong the drawing will not come together, because the positive and negative shapes are inextricably linked, forming the two parts of the jigsaw.

Drawing

Trace the basic drawing on to a sheet of cartridge paper (below). Information you will require later includes the full tonal range from light to dark, extensive markings, pattern and venation and the mossy habitat. All of these things will be a guide when you come to put paint on your finished drawing and you can refer to them at any time during the painting process. This is especially useful if the plant moves or changes.

Make the tonal changes definite but gradual – there should be no sudden jumps in tone. Observe carefully the differing perspectives and make the markings clear and specific.

Transfer your drawing to watercolour paper.

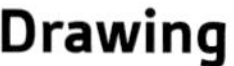

Above right The geometric shapes of this group are contained within a circle.

Right When drawing *Sarracenia* 'Beryl' – or any other botanical subject – make the tonal changes gradual.

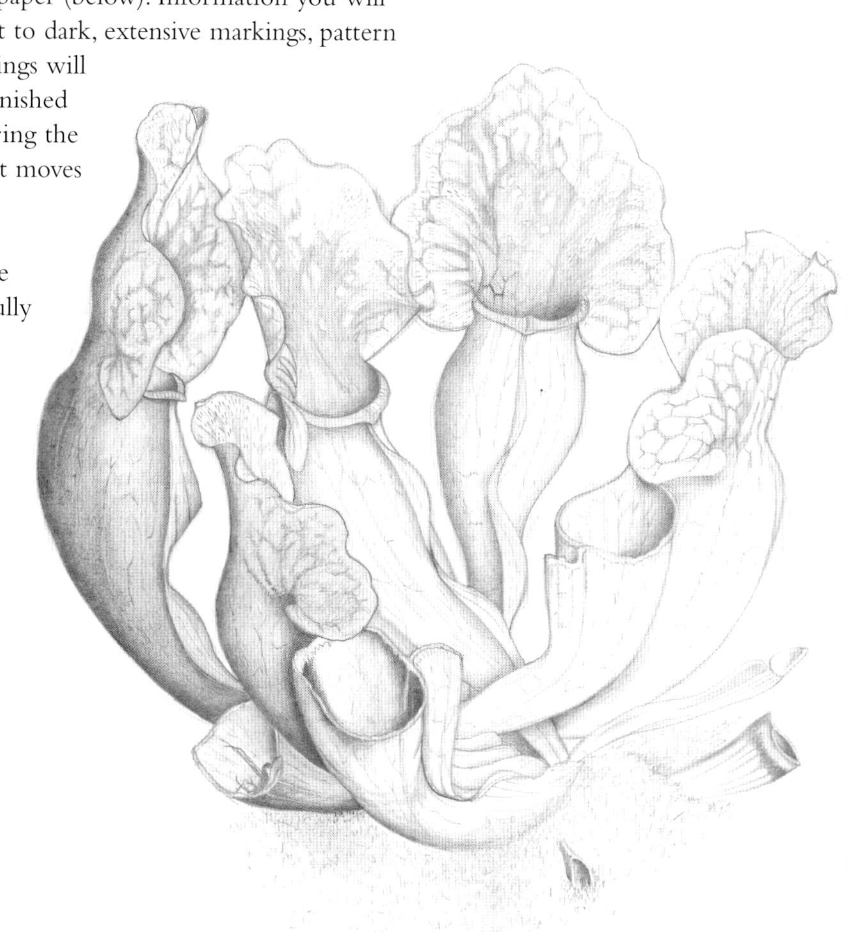

Painting

Colours you will need are Permanent Carmine, Lemon Yellow, Indian Yellow, French Ultramarine, Winsor Blue (Green Shade) and Opera Rose.

Practise overlaying, or superimposing, colours as shown on the worksheet (right and below). These are mainly reds on greens and greens on reds. Also try greens on greens and reds on reds. Make sure each layer is dry before applying the next.

Once you begin the painting itself, the initial washes are mostly wet-on-wet using two colours, red and green. When they are dry, add layers or glazes of green on red (wet-on-dry) then red on green, and repeat, applying as needed. Here and there, blend some strong Opera Rose on to the leaves.

The mossy habitat is as important as the plant. Start this at the initial wash stage, working with a light green (mixed from two yellows and two blues with a touch of Permanent Carmine). Blend the wash, or grade it out to nothing using a clean brush. For the markings on the hood of each trap, use cool red mixed with a little cool blue and a little warm yellow.

Other details to note:

- A spent trap is shown lying in the moss. This demonstrates the veining on trap bodies, and the layering of reds, greens and pink. To darken areas of extreme shadow use stippled greeny-blue.
- Blend the edges – a reddish-brown edge around the green hoods on the red/green wet-on-wet background is produced by painting a line then blending with a damp brush.
- Create depth inside the traps by increased tonal layering.
- Apply tone to the front 'pleated' part, to make it appear to curve or fold over realistically.
- All manner of insect life finds its way into the traps of carnivorous plants (below). Flies look most convincingly dead when they are on their backs – seen from the side they can appear to be hovering or alighting.

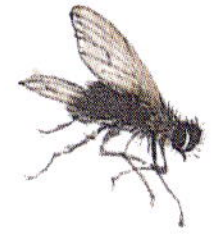
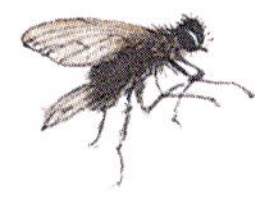
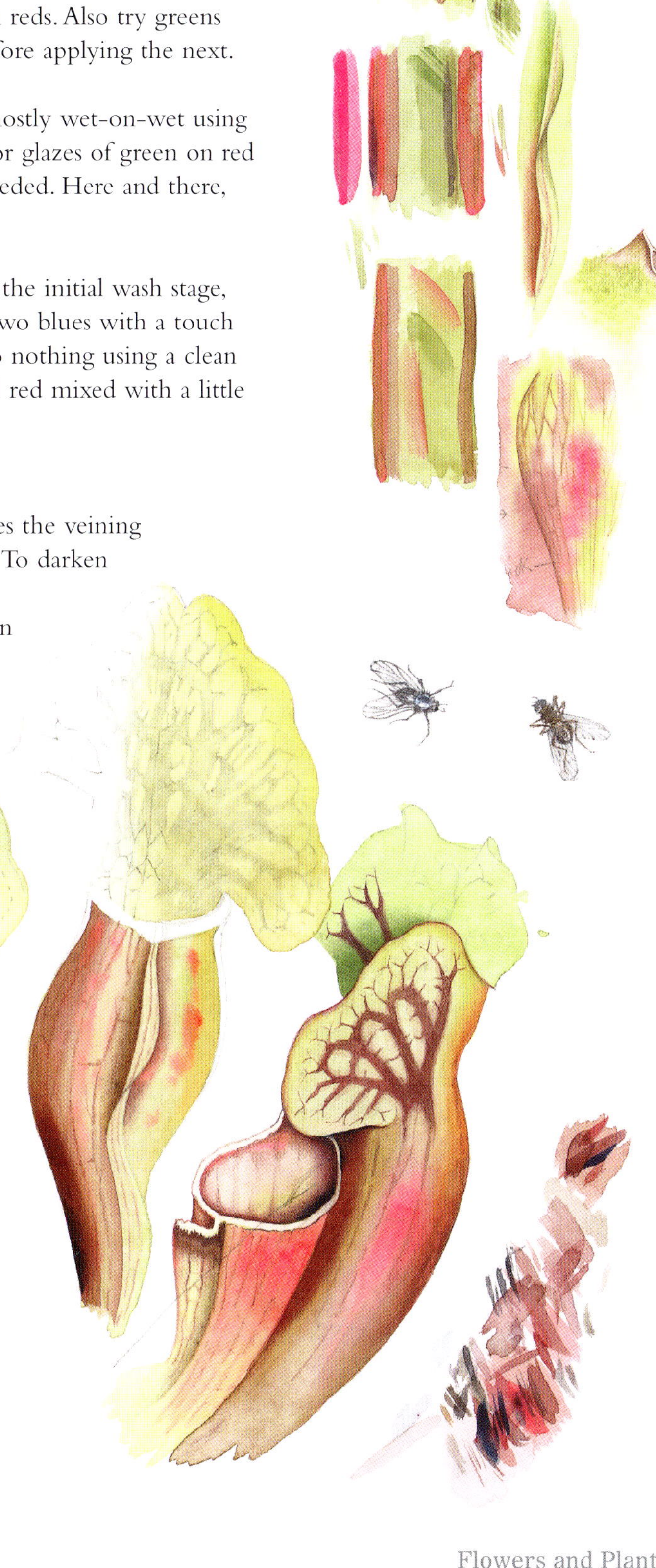

Exercise: Trumpet pitcher plant

This composition (opposite) of the trumpet pitcher plant, *Sarracenia* x *excellens*, shows two pitcher traps (centre and right) with a lower section on the left, which has split to reveal the insect parts as they collect after being digested.

The middle 'live' trap clearly shows the beautiful stained-glass effect around the hood and lip. It is easy to see from this example how the prey, once lured down to the lower parts, fail to find their way back up to freedom, and therefore succumb to the digestive enzymes emitted by the plant.

Colours used are Lemon Yellow, Indian Yellow, French Ultramarine, Winsor Blue (Green Shade), Permanent Carmine and Scarlet Lake. The following stages show the order of painting and the building-up process.

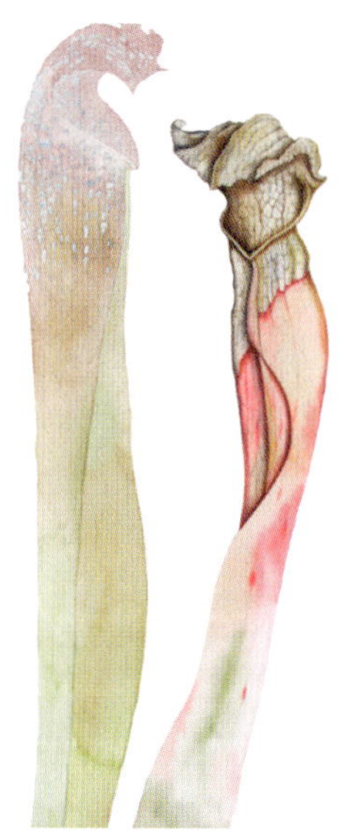 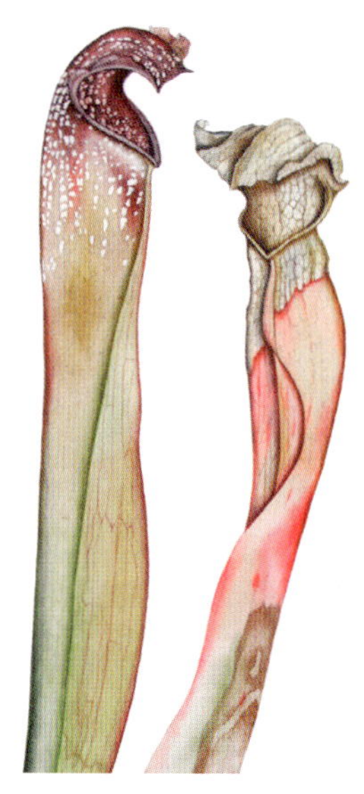 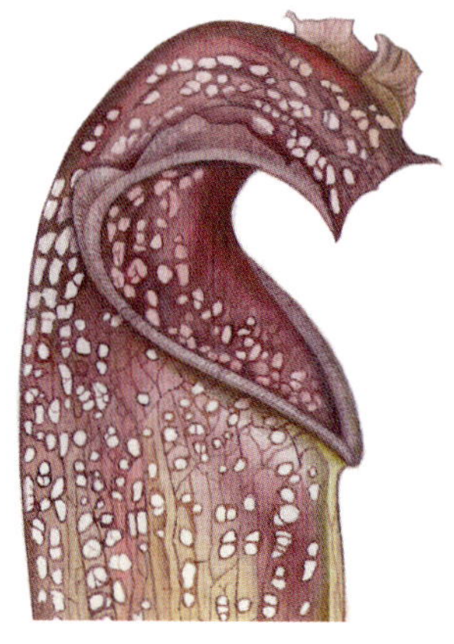 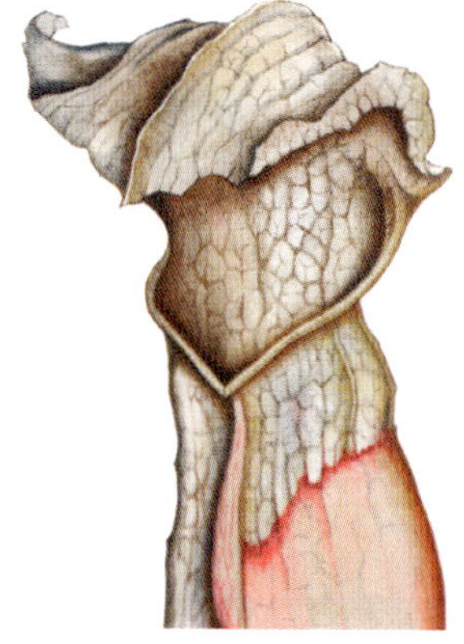

Step 1

Draw the plant carefully and transfer to watercolour paper. Use masking fluid to create the stained-glass effect on the middle trap. Once dry, apply a wet-into-wet wash over the whole stem. This would be impossible without the use of masking fluid.

Step 2

Once dry, add deeper shades of red, pink and green, blending them carefully with a damp brush.

Step 3

After all the deeper shades have been added, remove the masking fluid and paint the veins up to and around all the shapes left behind. Any further darkening must be done with care not to interfere with the masked spaces. Some of the shapes should be painted with a very light pink.

Step 4

The trap on the right should be painted wet-into-wet in two sections, upper and lower. Paint the hood and neck section first with mixed browns and greys. When dry, paint the lower section in pale browns, pinks and greens. The patch of brown at the bottom shows where the plant is decaying.

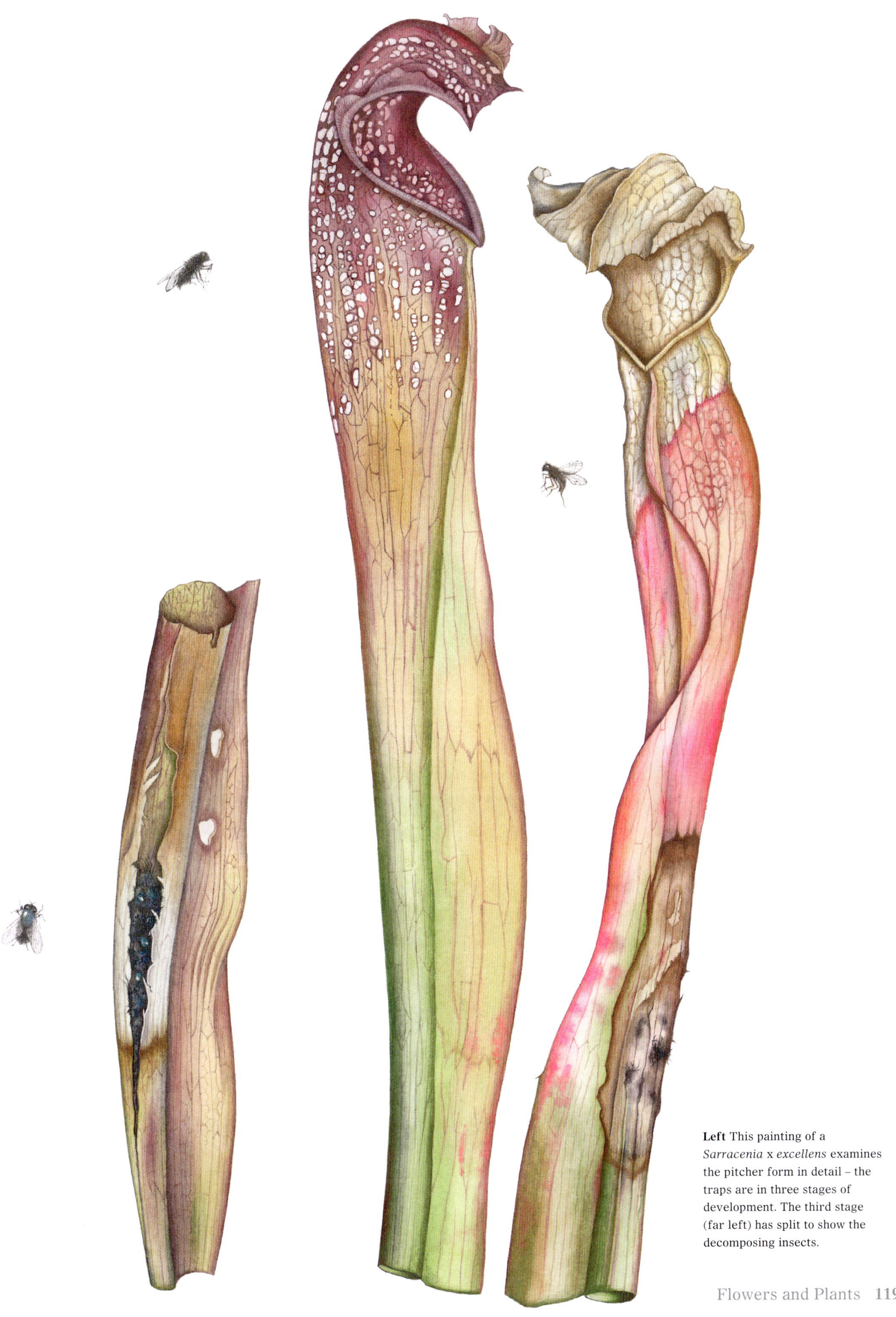

Left This painting of a *Sarracenia* x *excellens* examines the pitcher form in detail – the traps are in three stages of development. The third stage (far left) has split to show the decomposing insects.

Sarracenia minor var. *Okefenokeensis*

This wonderfully named carnivorous plant is a natural giant form found in the Okefenokee Swamp, one of the East Coast swamps that run from Florida to Carolina in the USA. The composition is very interesting in the way it reflects the plant's habit. You might think that the smaller traps resemble young snakes around their mother.

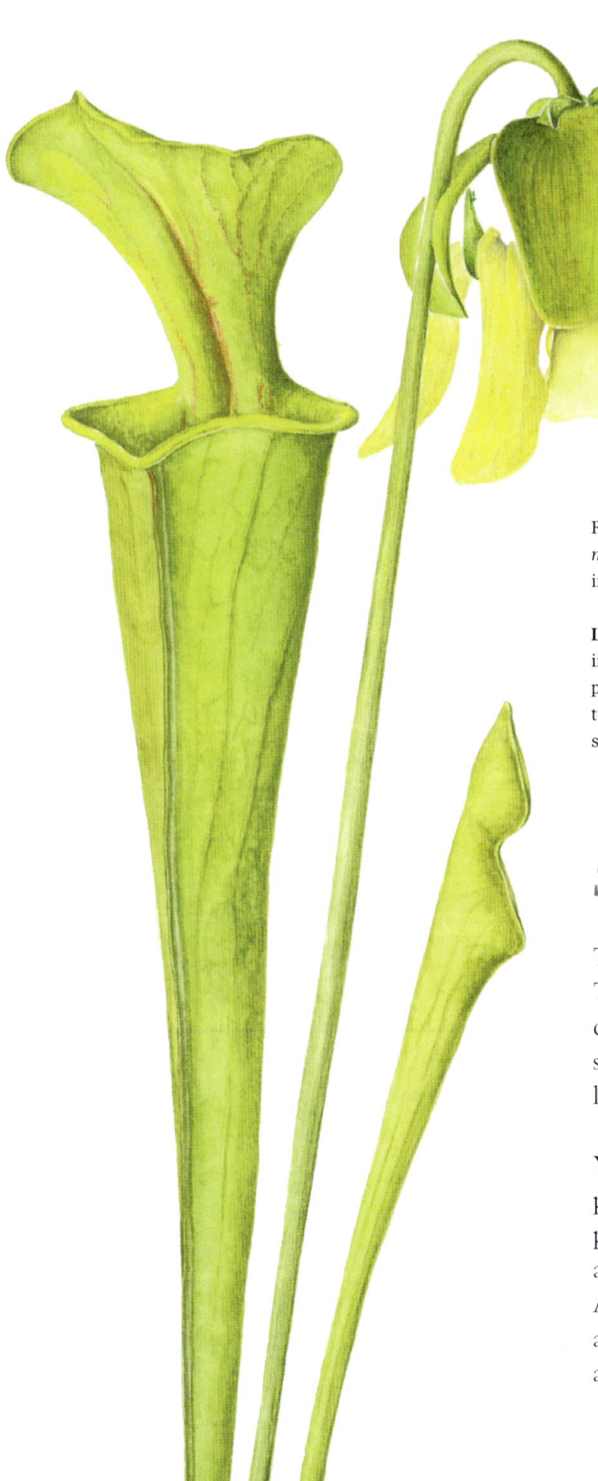

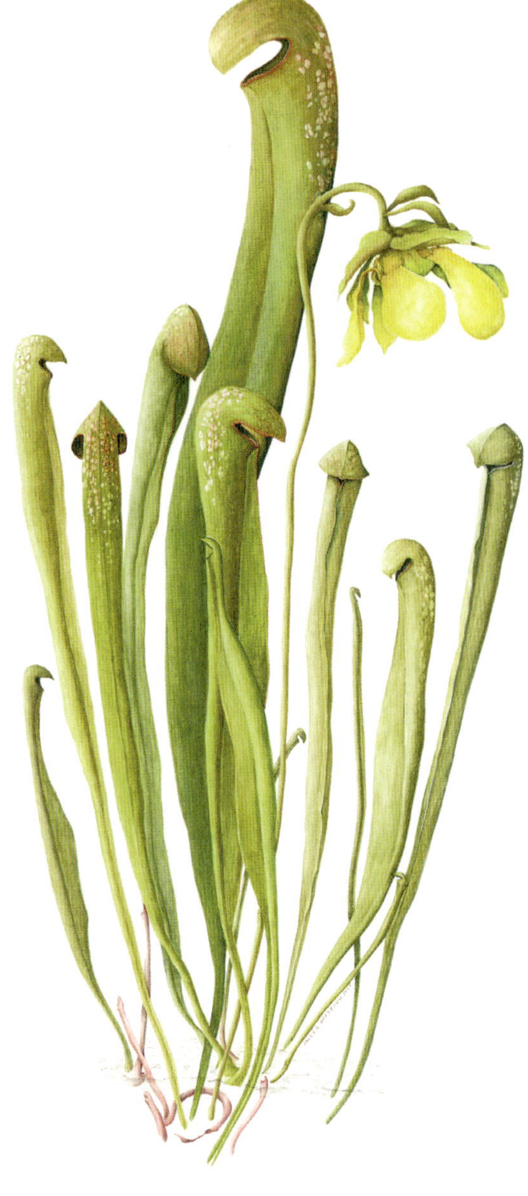

Right The carnivorous *Sarracenia minor* var. *Okefenokeensis* is shown in its natural habitat.

Left *Sarracenia flava* var. *maxima* in its full-sun colours. This pitcher plant was lit with very strong lights to mimic the colours seen in bright sunlight.

Sarracenia flava var. *maxima*

This intensely coloured plant personifies the lurid appeal of the genus. The specimen was lit unconventionally with very strong LED lights and daylight lamps quite close up to mimic the colours seen outside in strong sunshine. The plant turns a bright lime green with strong sun, and the lights aided the artist in achieving the tricky colour.

You could mix a green for the leaves, or use Sap Green as a base if you prefer, altering it with Lemon Yellow and some French Ultramarine in places. Winsor Blue (Green Shade) can be added carefully as well. To achieve tone and shadow on the green areas, use a little Winsor Violet. A tiny amount of Alizarin Crimson will add further reality to the greens, and should also be used for the detail of veins on the mature pitcher. Use a grey mix to paint the shaded areas on the yellow petals.

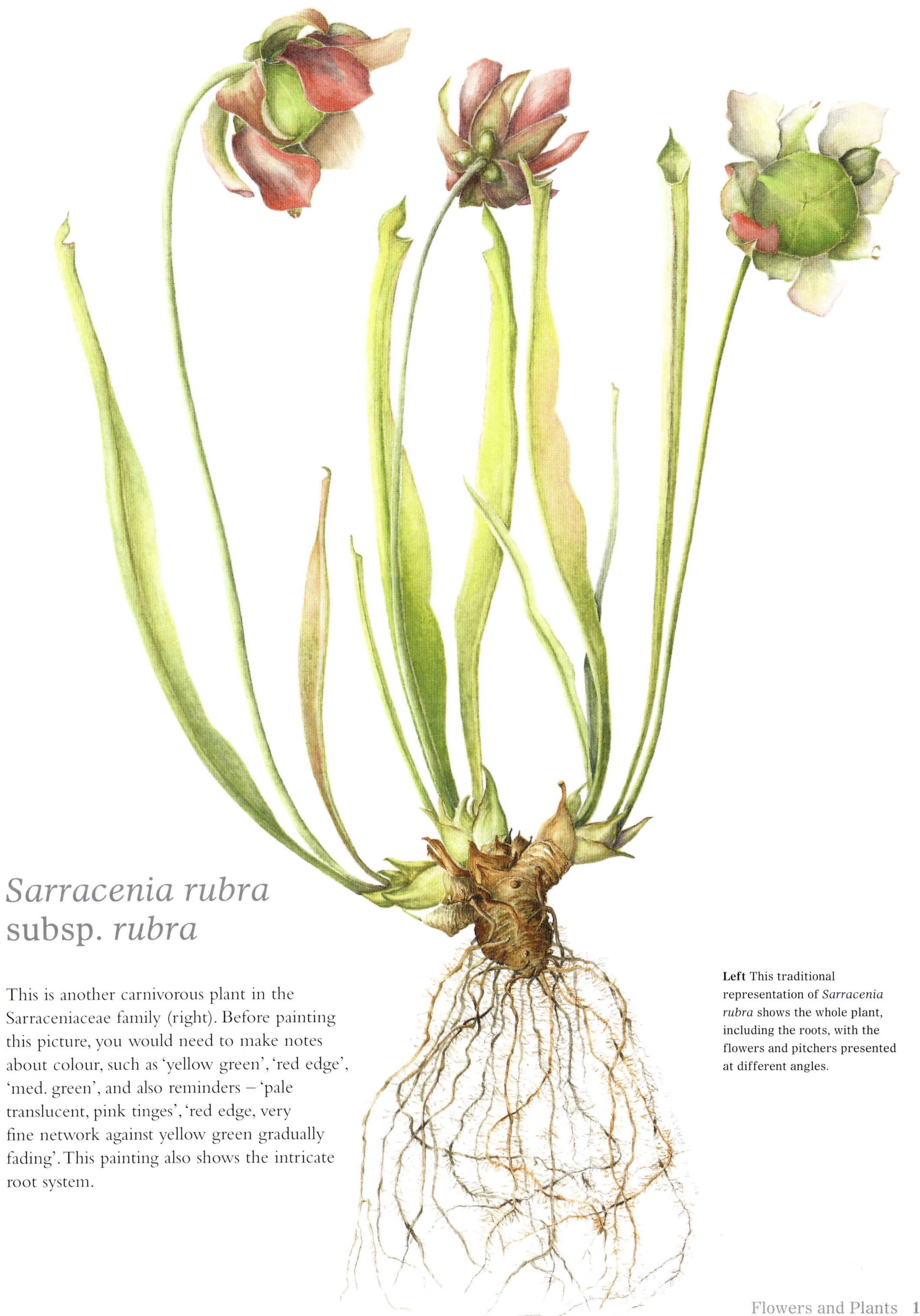

Sarracenia rubra subsp. *rubra*

This is another carnivorous plant in the Sarraceniaceae family (right). Before painting this picture, you would need to make notes about colour, such as 'yellow green', 'red edge', 'med. green', and also reminders – 'pale translucent, pink tinges', 'red edge, very fine network against yellow green gradually fading'. This painting also shows the intricate root system.

Left This traditional representation of *Sarracenia rubra* shows the whole plant, including the roots, with the flowers and pitchers presented at different angles.

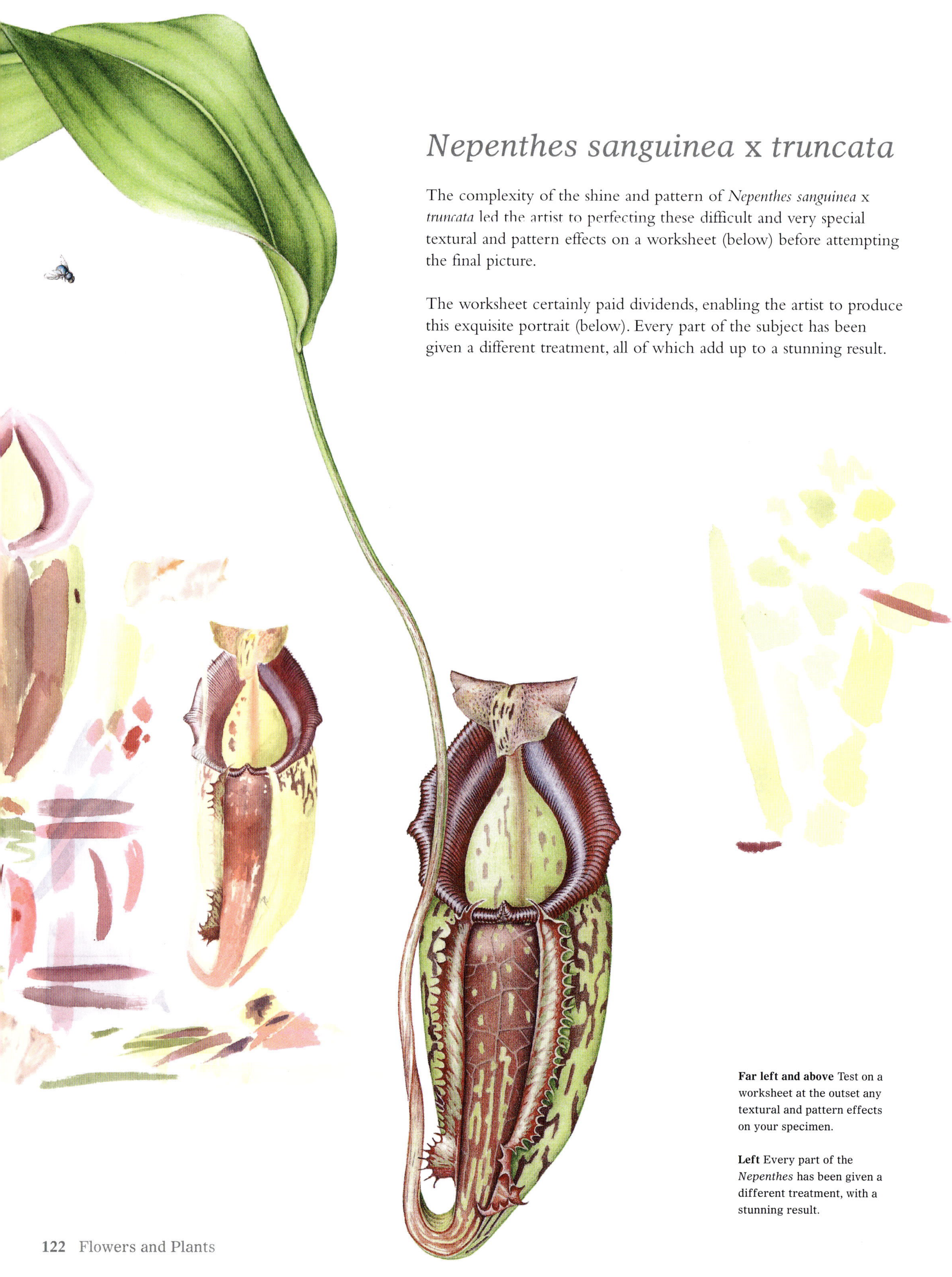

Nepenthes sanguinea x truncata

The complexity of the shine and pattern of *Nepenthes sanguinea* x *truncata* led the artist to perfecting these difficult and very special textural and pattern effects on a worksheet (below) before attempting the final picture.

The worksheet certainly paid dividends, enabling the artist to produce this exquisite portrait (below). Every part of the subject has been given a different treatment, all of which add up to a stunning result.

Far left and above Test on a worksheet at the outset any textural and pattern effects on your specimen.

Left Every part of the *Nepenthes* has been given a different treatment, with a stunning result.

Darlingtonia californica

Sometimes you will need to paint your subject in stages at different times, even if this means that you have to put your work on hold for a season to get another sample. The painting of *Darlingtonia californica* (below) shows the flowering cycle of the plant (clockwise from top left), recorded over two months. Once again, the flowers bear the distinctive red–green colouration of these strange and sinister plants, which have cobra-like pitchers.

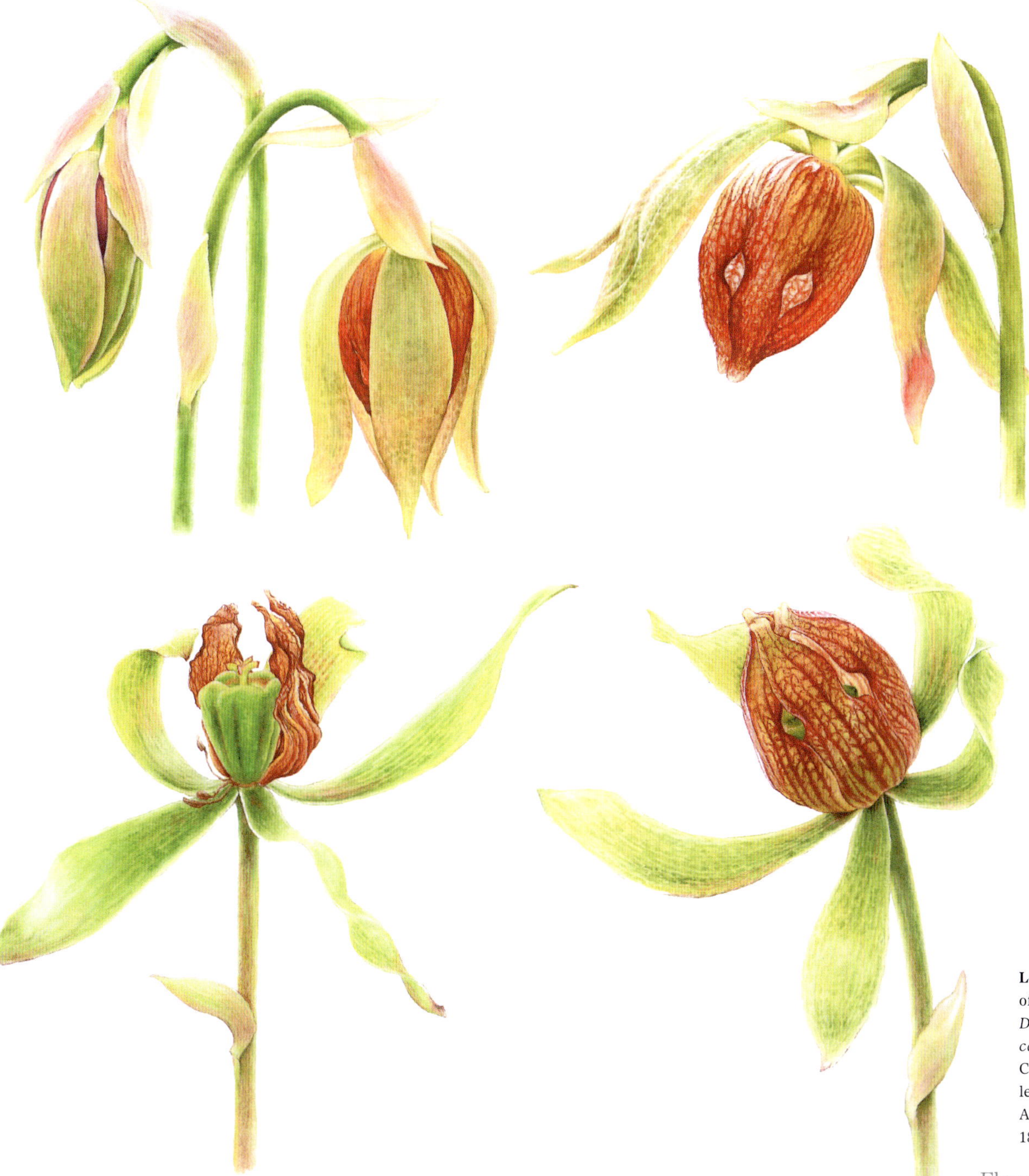

Left The stages of opening of *Darlingtonia californica* flower. Clockwise from top left: 17th April, 19th April, 25th May and 18th June (fully open).

Venus fly trap

Venus fly traps (*Dionaea muscipula*) vary in colour from green to red-purple, the reds genetically determined and enhanced by bright sunlight. A large part of the plant's diet is derived from insects trapped by its unusual fleshy leaves (lobes), each of which provides the two jaws of the trap that join along a flexible rib.

On each lobe a number of sensitive trigger hairs wait to be activated by an insect. When the prey moves over the trigger hairs the lobes spring shut and the imprisoned insect is digested by enzymes generated by the lobes. After between one and three feeds, the trap turns black and drops off, making way for a new trap to take its place.

This illustration shows the whole life cycle of the plant: open and closed traps, traps showing dehydrated husks of prey, traps waiting for prey to alight, dying and blackening traps, and a new trap emerging from the top of the group. Although this plant has white flowers on slender stalks, they are not shown here in order to make a more pleasing composition.

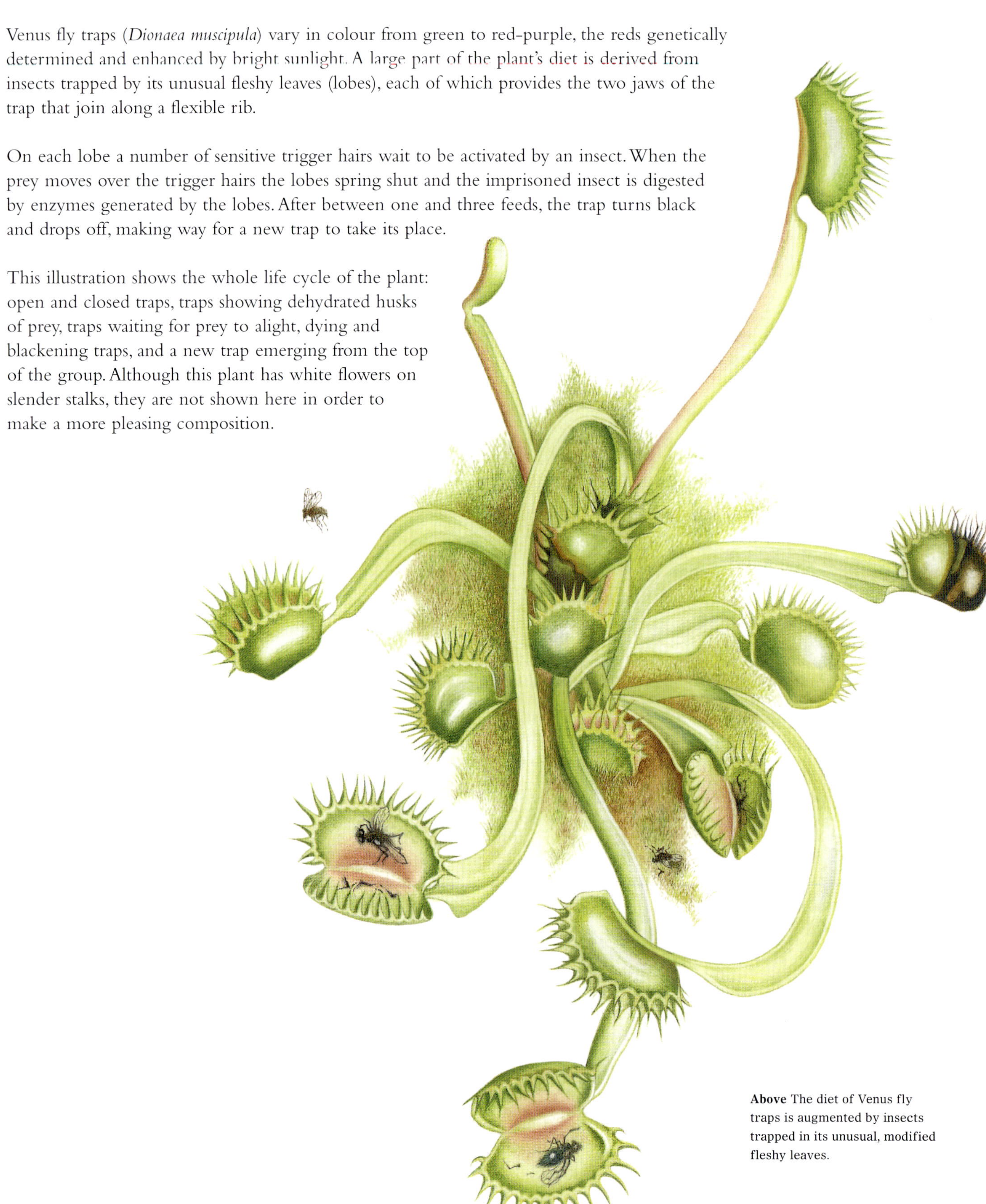

Above The diet of Venus fly traps is augmented by insects trapped in its unusual, modified fleshy leaves.

Exercise: Venus fly trap

The composition has been designed in such a way that the sinister, predatory nature of the Venus fly trap is very evident. It's acceptable to be selective in order not to overwhelm the viewer with an over-complicated composition, as long as you retain the true nature and attitude of the plant.

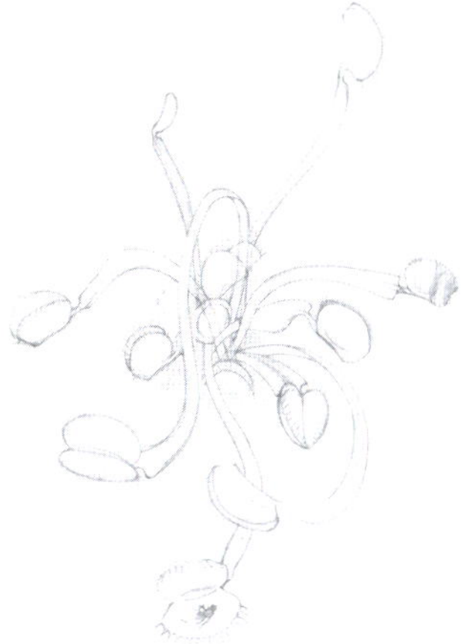

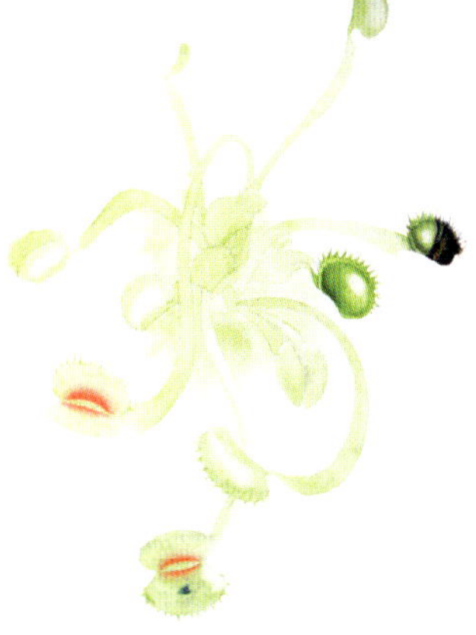

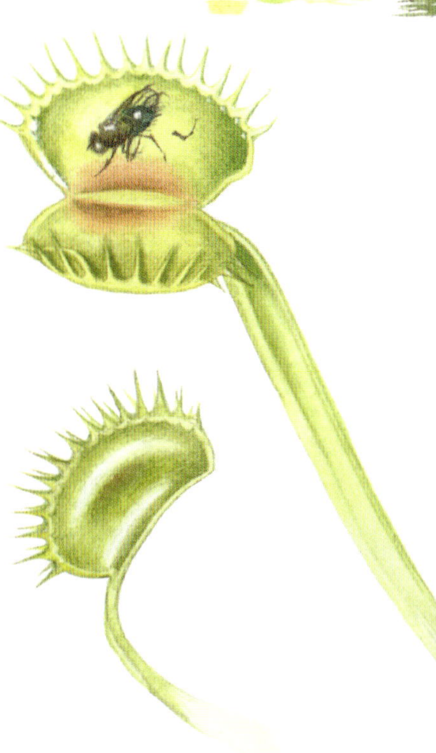

Step 1

Transfer your drawing on to watercolour paper. Determine your highlights and make sure you avoid them at each stage. They can be tinted with a pale wash of French Ultramarine at the end.

Step 2

Give a light yellowy-green wash (French Ultramarine, Lemon Yellow, Winsor Blue (Green Shade), Permanent Carmine and Indian Yellow). When dry, give the mossy areas a light green wash, wet-on-dry, with all edges being graded away to nothing. Remember to use clean water and a clean brush to avoid leaving hard lines or tidemarks.

Step 3

When dry, stroke on some bronze or terracotta (Indian Yellow, Scarlet Lake and French Ultramarine) in certain areas, blending it into the pale green background. Leave out the highlights at this stage.

Step 4

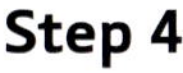

Outline the spikes to show three-dimensionality and the light source.

Gradually build up the greens from light to dark, first by blending and then, when the watercolour starts to lift, change to stippling the darker shades. Where the insides of the traps show pink, carefully stipple a little Permanent Carmine and Scarlet Lake in an arc shape. The spikes lining the edges of the traps should have extra yellow-green to emphasise their function of entrapment. Each spike is outlined on one edge with dark green to indicate shadow and to give a three-dimensional effect and thickness.

Work up the moss gradually with tiny brushstrokes of different greens and browns, using French Ultramarine, Lemon Yellow, Indian Yellow, Winsor Blue (Green Shade), Permanent Carmine and Scarlet Lake in varying amounts. Use the notes for *Sarracenia* 'Beryl' (see page 117) to paint the digested husks of prey waiting to be ejected from the open traps and for the spent fly lying in the moss.

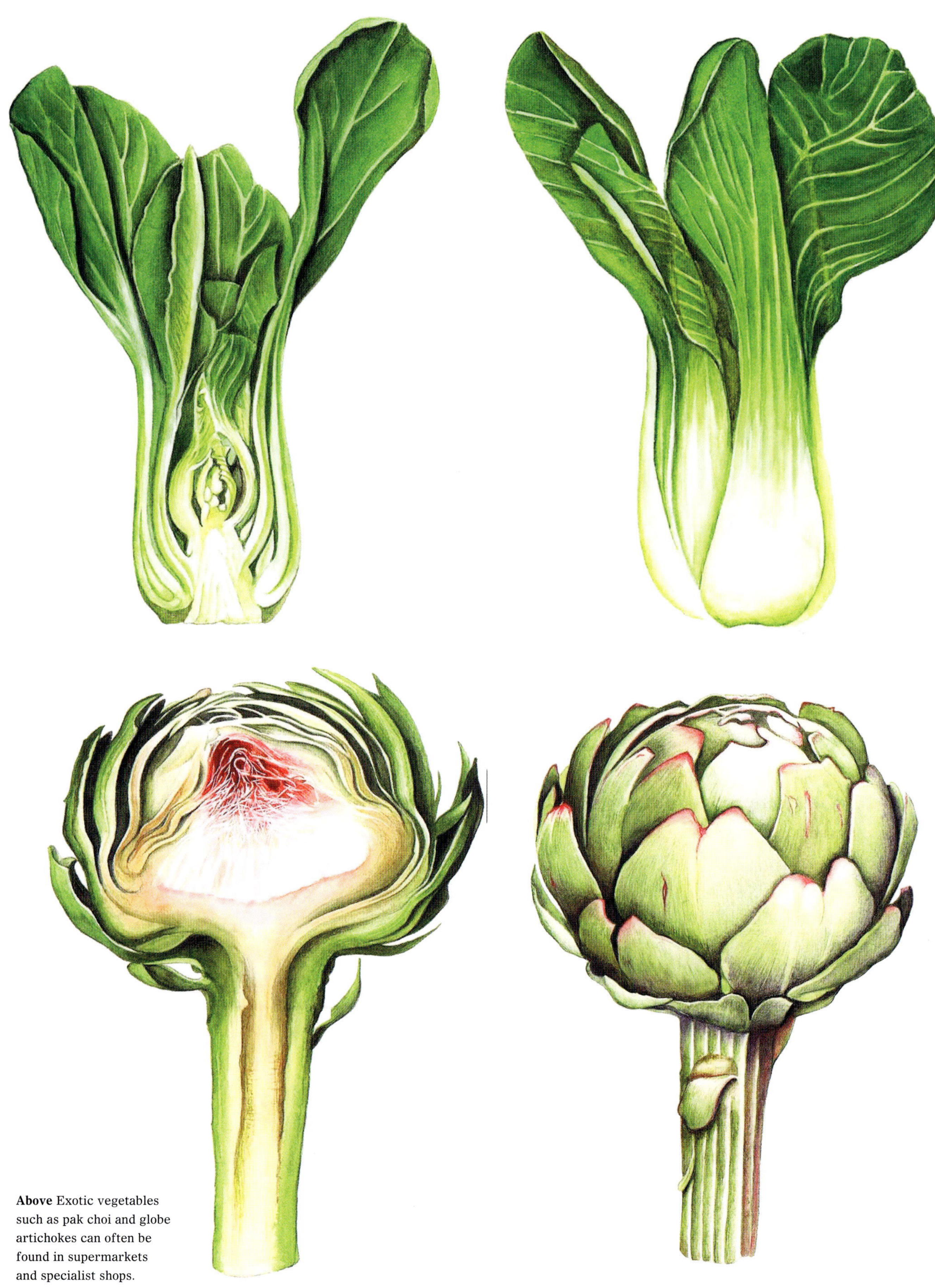

Above Exotic vegetables such as pak choi and globe artichokes can often be found in supermarkets and specialist shops.

Exotic Fruit and Vegetables

One of the advantages of painting fruit and vegetables is that they generally stay fresh for longer than flowers, with no petals to droop. They are also relatively easy to obtain – even exotic varieties can now be found in supermarkets and specialist shops, especially those catering for immigrant communities in large urban areas.

Squashes and pumpkins are widely available at the end of the summer and in the autumn, especially in the run-up to Hallowe'en. Although they could be considered commonplace, they are exotic by virtue of their range of colours, exciting shapes and sizes.

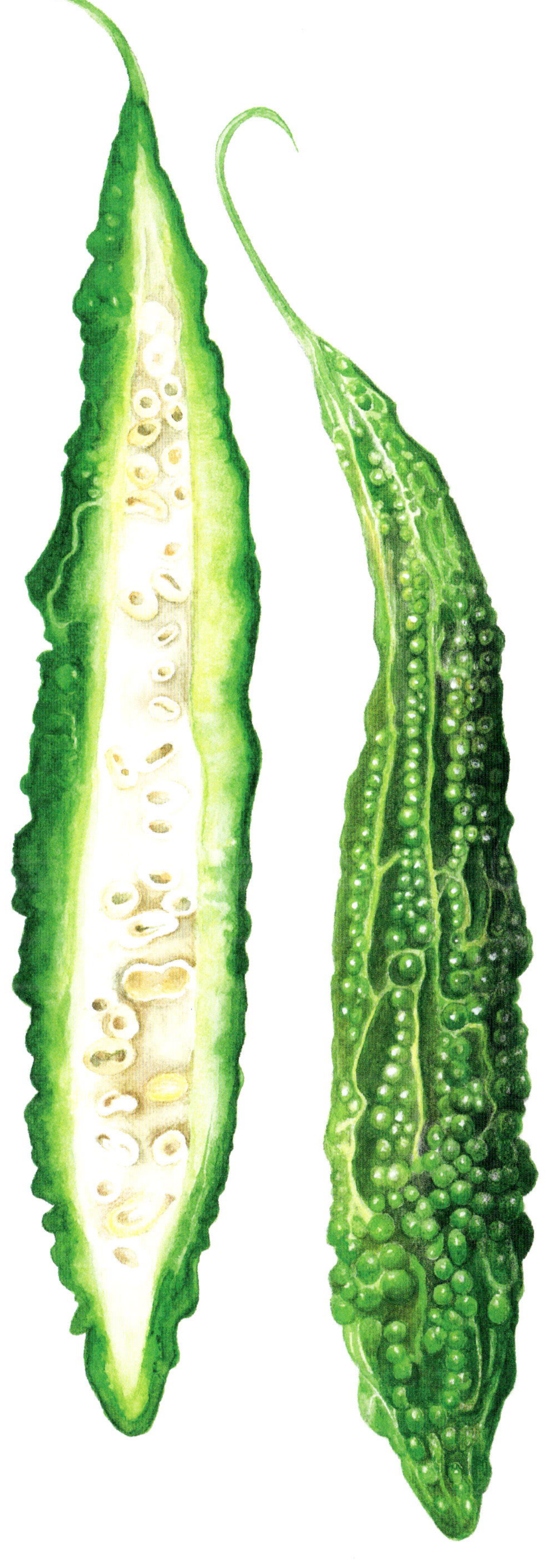

Right Some fruits and vegetables, such as this bitter melon, karela, can stay fresh for longer than flowers.

The banana

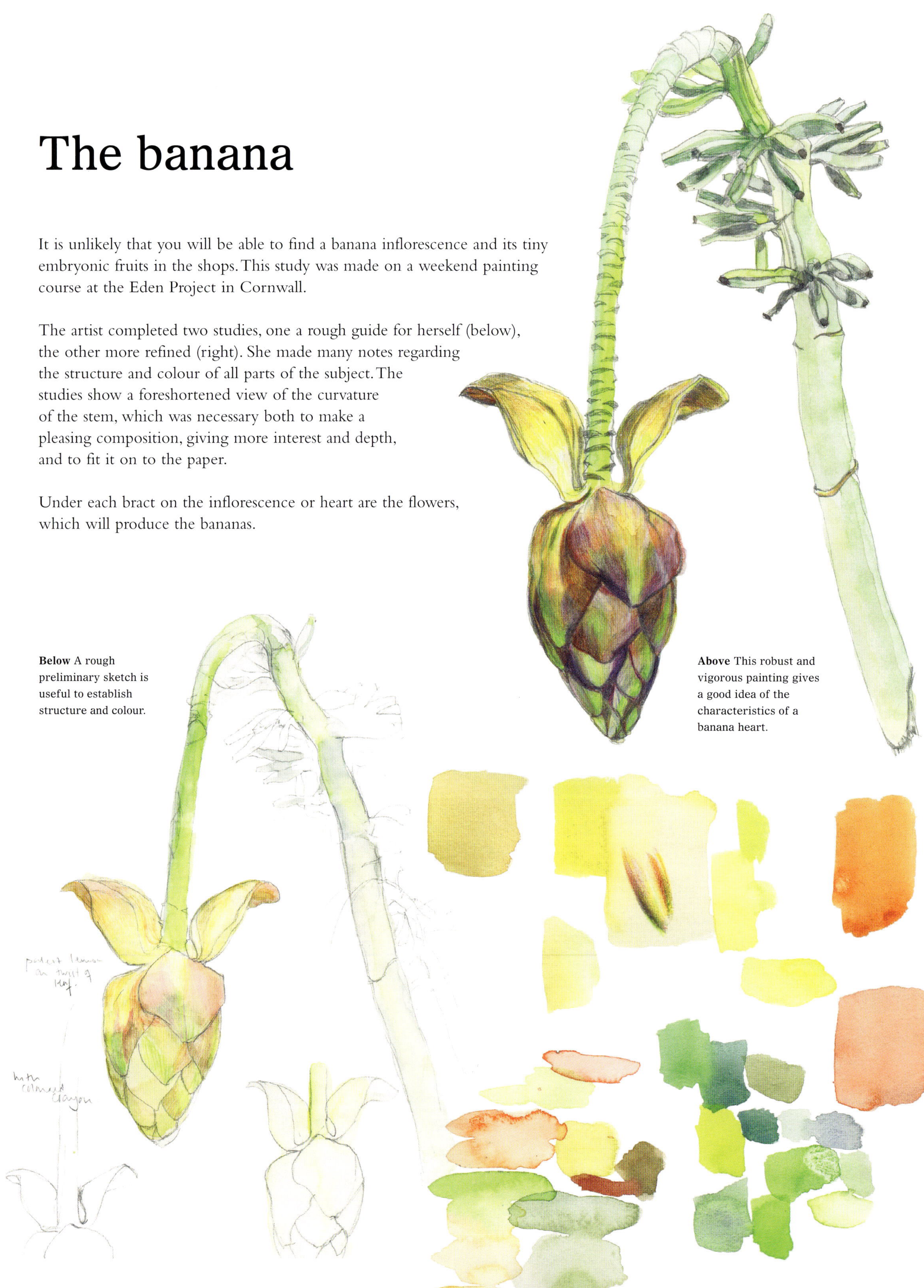

It is unlikely that you will be able to find a banana inflorescence and its tiny embryonic fruits in the shops. This study was made on a weekend painting course at the Eden Project in Cornwall.

The artist completed two studies, one a rough guide for herself (below), the other more refined (right). She made many notes regarding the structure and colour of all parts of the subject. The studies show a foreshortened view of the curvature of the stem, which was necessary both to make a pleasing composition, giving more interest and depth, and to fit it on to the paper.

Under each bract on the inflorescence or heart are the flowers, which will produce the bananas.

Below A rough preliminary sketch is useful to establish structure and colour.

Above This robust and vigorous painting gives a good idea of the characteristics of a banana heart.

Exercise: A hand of bananas

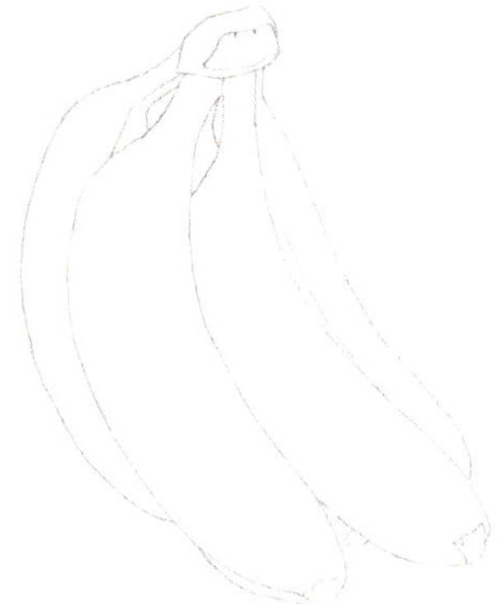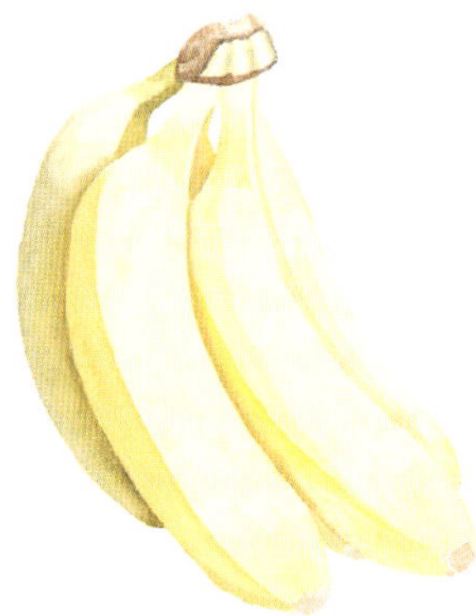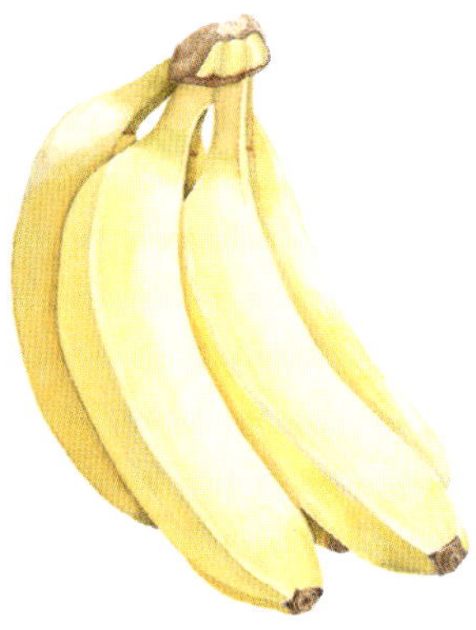

Step 1

Arrange the bananas in the most pleasing position and make a clear outline drawing on layout paper, tracing it on to watercolour paper when you are happy with it.

Step 2

Mix a light wash of the palest colour, using Lemon Yellow and Indian Yellow. When the first coat is dry, darken the paint and apply to the shaded areas as a wet-on-dry wash. Keep the washes smooth so as not to show any brushstrokes.

Step 3

Mix some Alizarin Crimson and French Ultramarine into your yellow wash to make a grey and deepen the shaded areas. Add a little more Alizarin Crimson for the broken sides of the stem and the tips of the fruit.

Step 4

Build up the colours and shading, being careful to keep strong lines between light and dark areas.

Step 5

Use mixes of grey, purple and brown to deepen the shaded areas, to add blemishes and to enhance the shape of the individual fruits. This is best done by stippling with a fine brush. Notice how the paint has been kept away from those parts that have an almost luminescent glow from reflected light. You could use coloured pencils at this stage if you prefer.

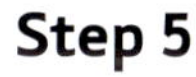

Squashes and pumpkins

The members of the squash tribe are familiar vegetables to most people, but the sheer range of shapes and colours makes them attractive and eye-catching subjects for painting. Painted en masse, they make a very pleasing composition, as shown below.

Unusual varieties with unexpected colours and features can provide exotic subjects for the botanical artist. The traditional orange Hallowe'en pumpkin has a very familiar form and colour, whereas the squashes shown below right are a complete contrast, their pale colour and strange structure lending themselves to delicate treatment. Colours don't necessarily have to be bright to be unusual; these pale squashes are a good example of subdued and subtle shades used to accentuate the strange 'wings', giving a horned and sinister appearance to an otherwise rather unassuming fruit.

Note the changing tones of the summer squash shown right, indicating the extreme contrasts that can be achieved with thoughtful lighting.

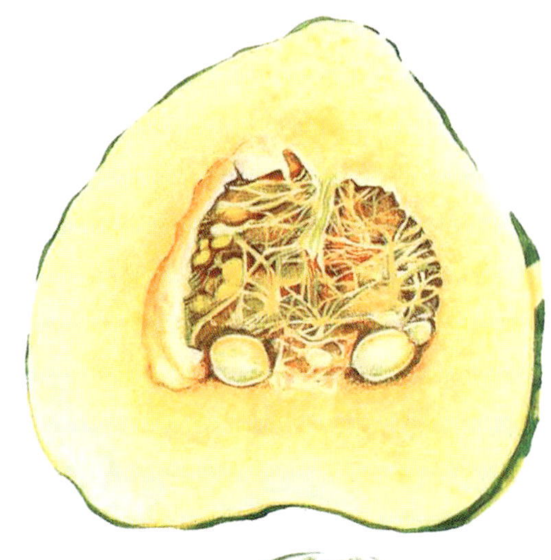

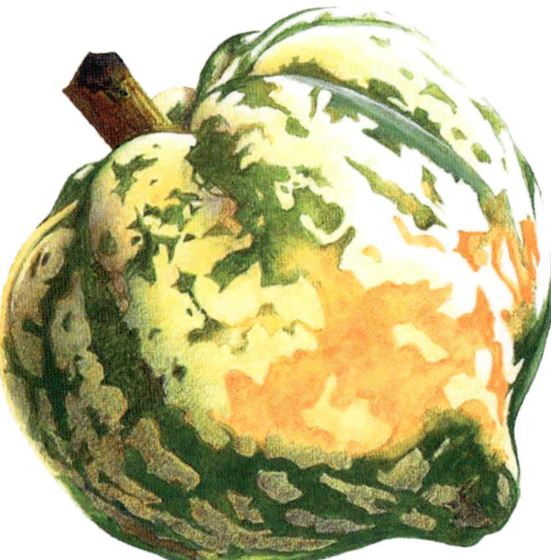

Below Squashes and pumpkins come in all shapes, sizes and colours.

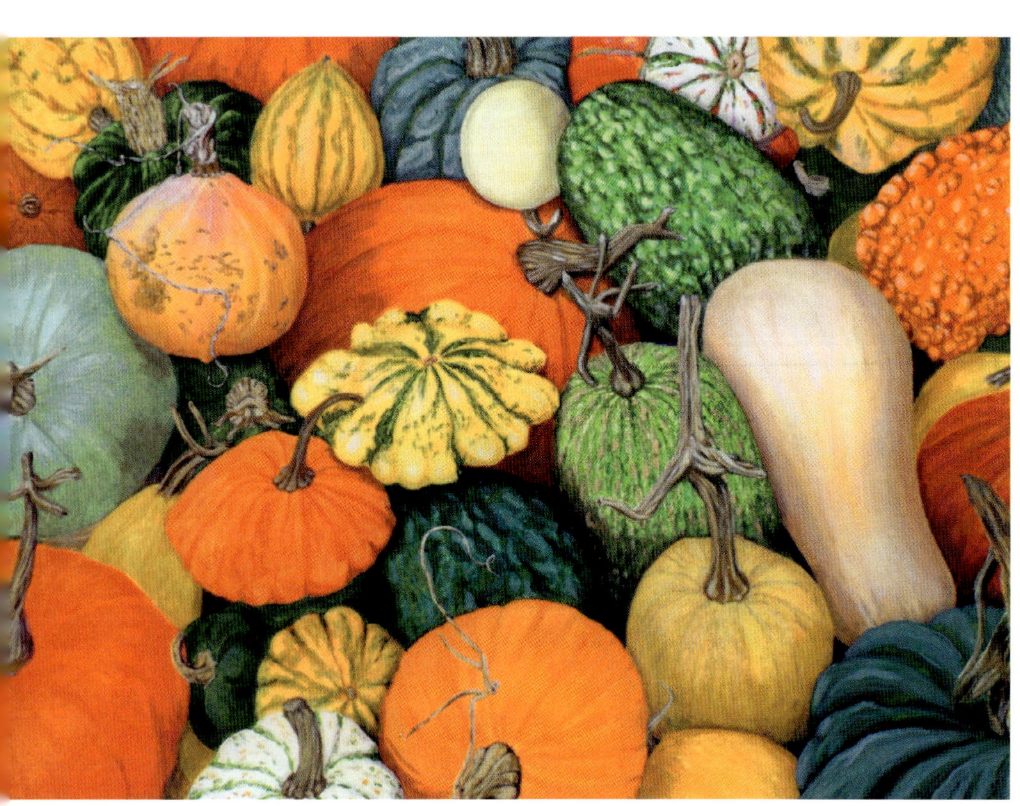

Above Contrasts in tone can be achieved by the thoughtful use of lighting.

Exercise: Painting a pumpkin

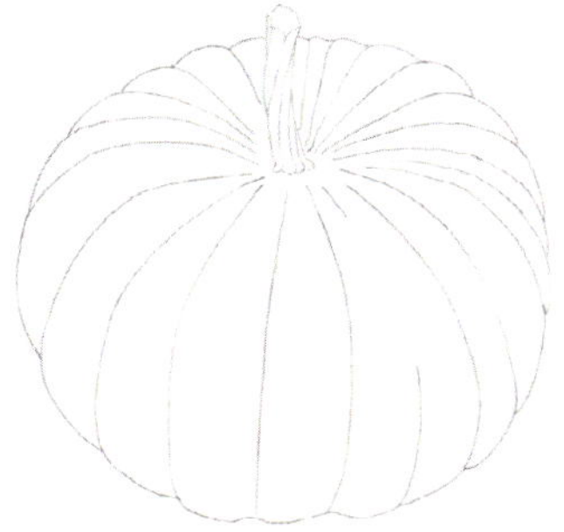 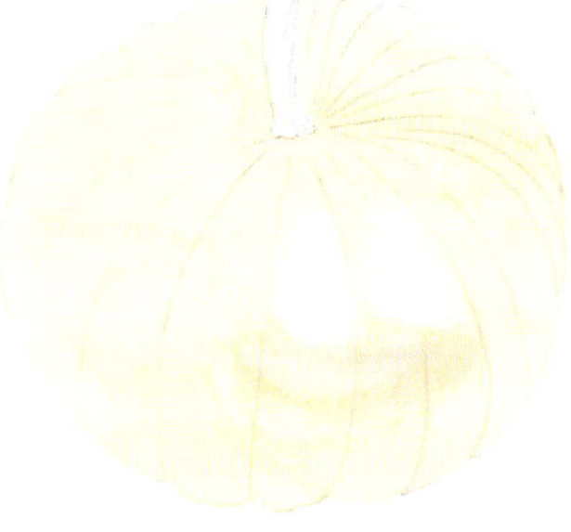 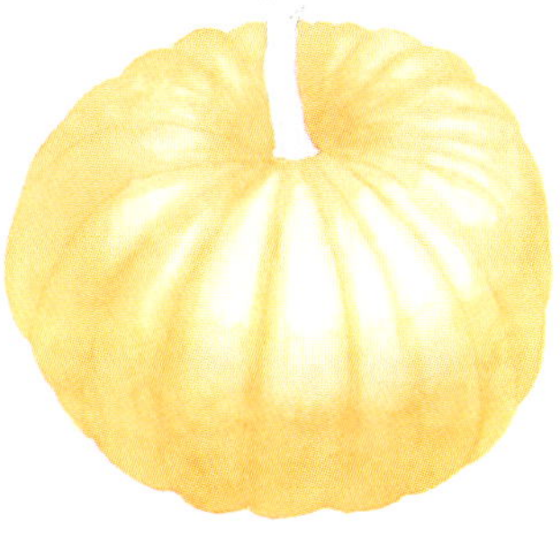 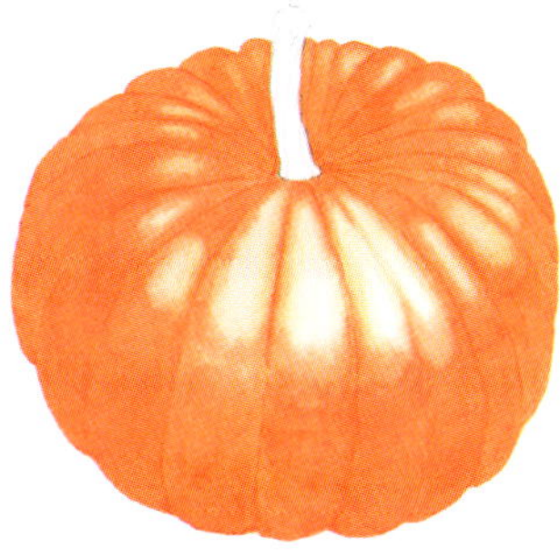

Step 1

Draw the pumpkin on layout paper, using an HB pencil. Make your lines clear and unambiguous, taking care with the overall shape and the relative width of the segments. Trace the image lightly on to your watercolour paper.

Step 2

For the first wash, mix Indian Yellow and Lemon Yellow and add plenty of clean water. Lay it on, wet-on-dry, leaving sections of highlight and blending the edges. While the paint is still wet, drop in some pale pink made from Opera Rose and a very small amount of Scarlet Lake.

Step 3

Working on one segment at a time, enhance the shape with a stronger wash of Indian Yellow mixed with a tiny amount of Scarlet Lake. Do not totally cover the previous two washes.

Step 4

Build up the colour on each segment using a mixture of Scarlet Lake, Indian Yellow and Alizarin Crimson, again leaving some of the previous washes untouched.

Step 5

Deepen the colour of the indentations between the segments and darken the shaded side of the pumpkin and the points where one segment disappears behind its neighbour. Using a pale greeny-brown colour (your yellow mixture from Stage 3 tinted with a bit of French Ultramarine), wash over the stem, deepening the colour in the shaded areas once it is dry. If you find the highlighted areas too harsh, lightly wash over them with a pale orange mix, taking care not to leave hard lines or disturb the underlying paint.

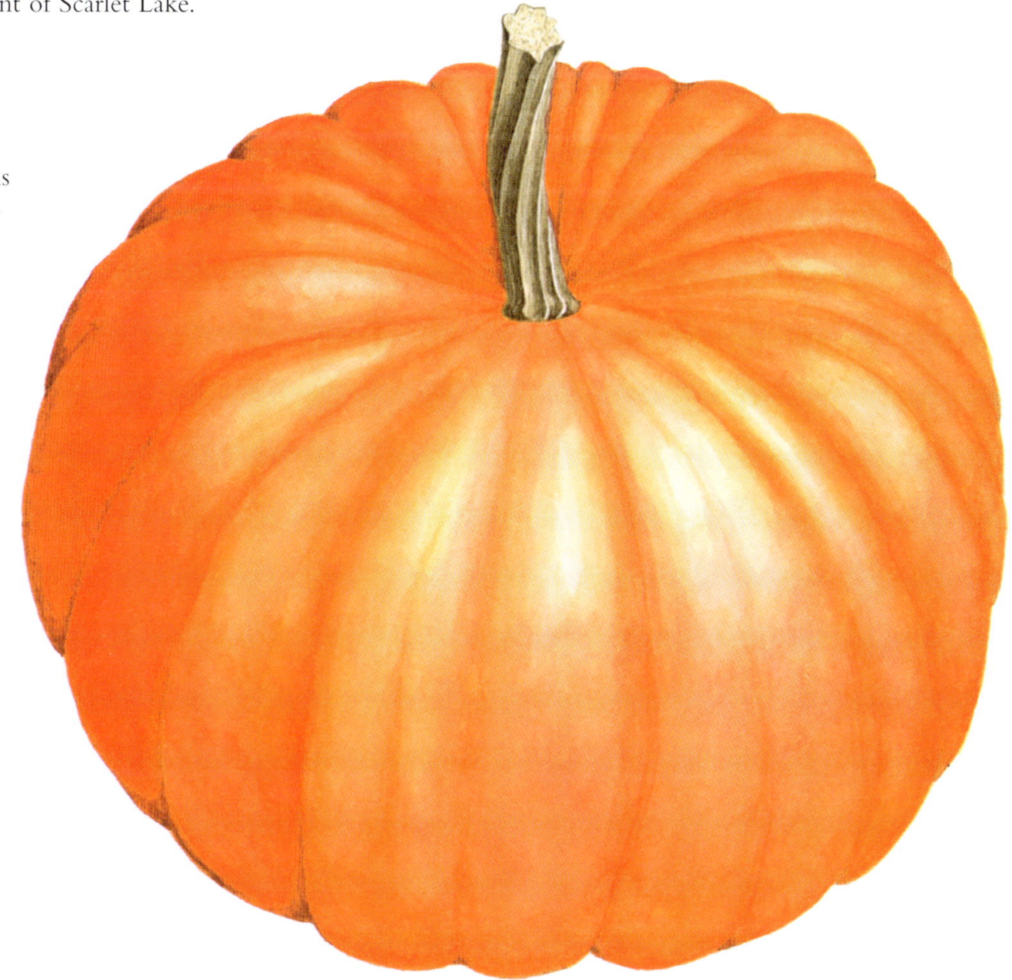

Strong colours and forms

Be adventurous with your paintings of fruit and vegetables. Trawl the supermarket shelves and local greengrocers to find unusual subjects; try compositions that are a bit out of the ordinary; put wildly different elements together; and assemble groups of subjects of different shapes, textures, sizes and colours.

Cocoa pods from the cocoa tree, *Theobroma cacao*, come in all colours, from pale yellow to dark red and a wide range of greens, but inside they are much the same. The illustrations below show two different treatments. The green pod was first drawn in sepia ink, then filled with watercolour in a way that gives life and vigour to the fruit. The knobbly red pod and its dissection were painted in the traditional botanical way: first lightly drawn, then painstakingly coloured using watercolours and fine brushes.

Red onions (opposite) are relatively easy to come by, and many people would not think them particularly exotic. However, this painting is a lively, stirring composition and it turns what could be considered a mundane subject into a vibrant portrayal. The painting outlines the different elements – the dry stalks, whiskery roots, smooth glossy bulbs and the contrast in light and shade. Complementary colours violet and yellow also have their part to play.

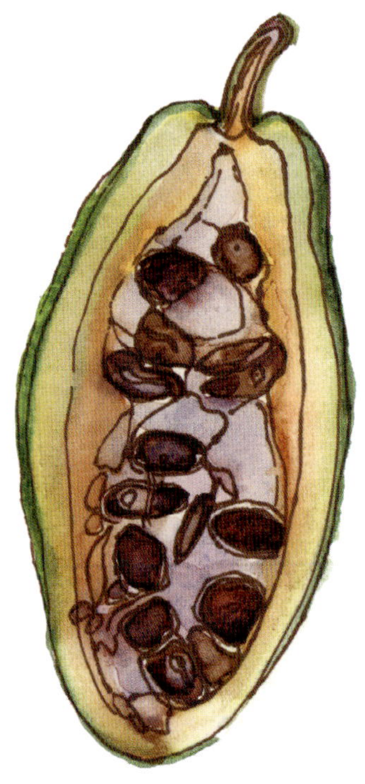
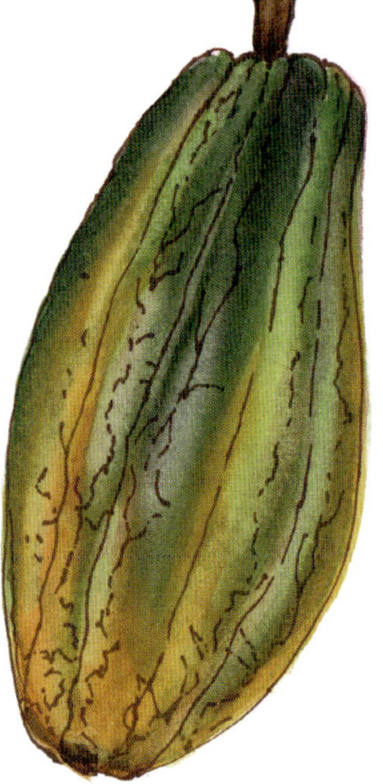
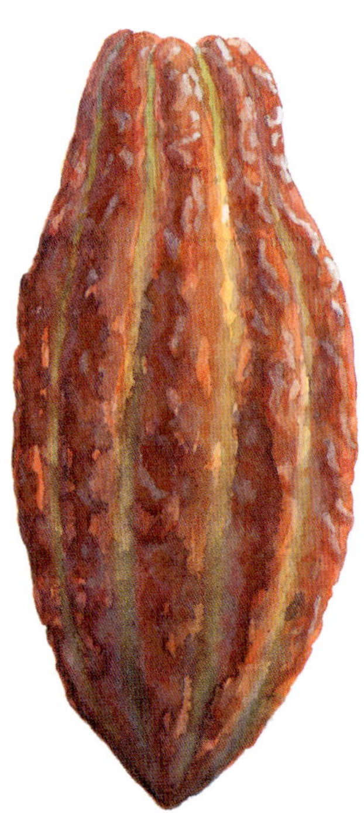
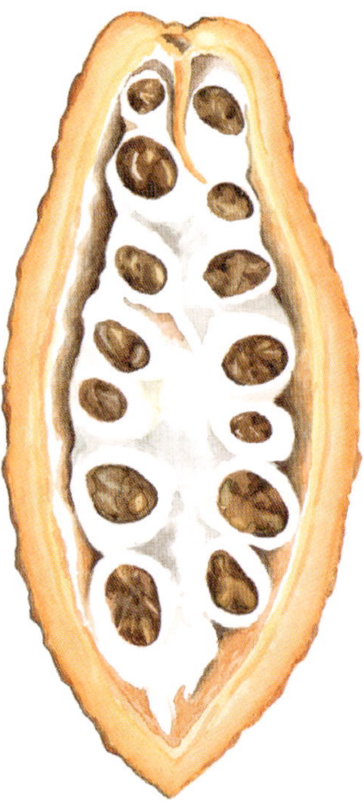

Below Two different treatments of cocoa pods and dissections.

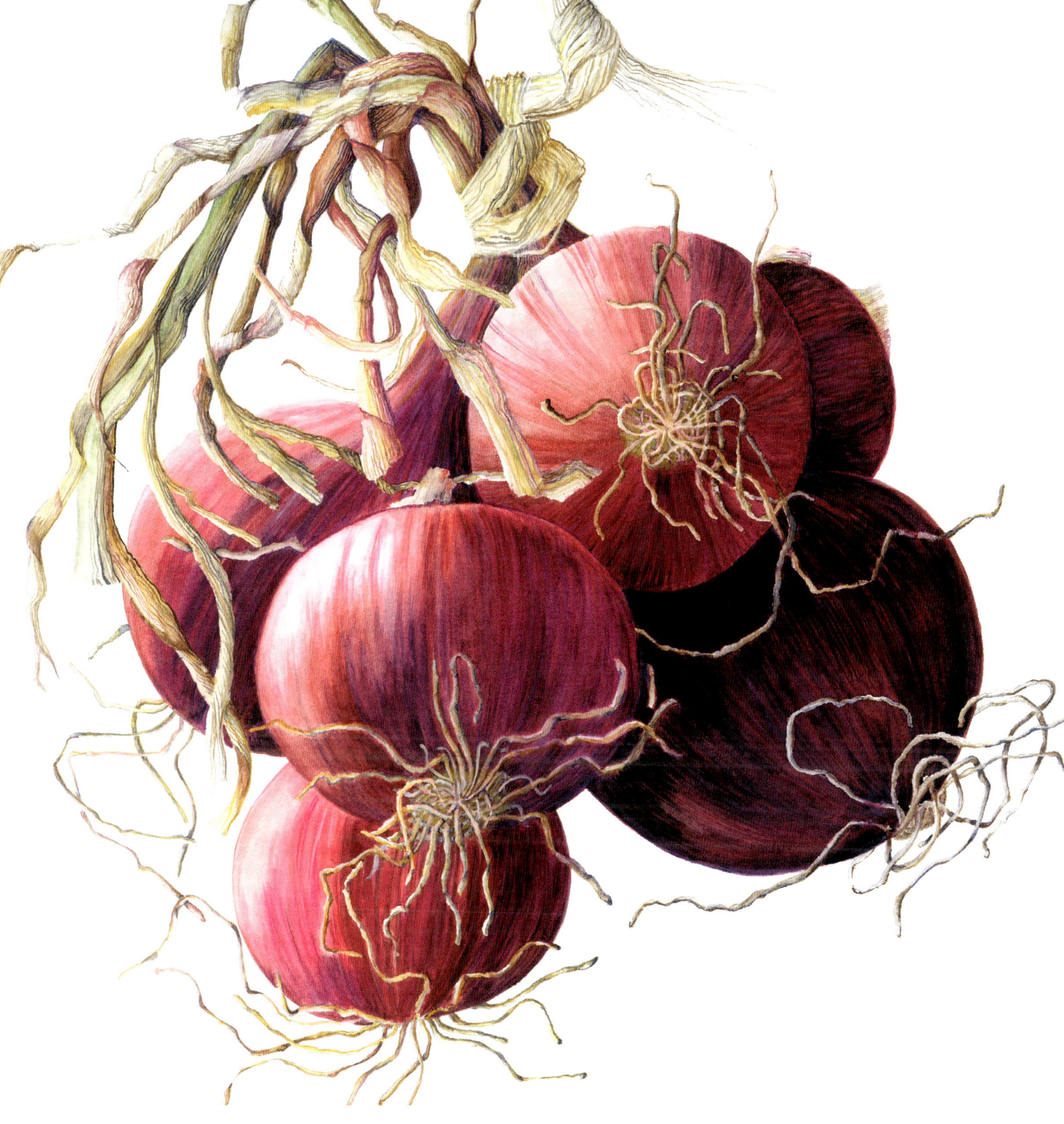

It's all an illusion, as is all botanical painting – creating a two-dimensional portrait of a three-dimensional subject. But if your picture has a feel of weight and solidity about it – if you can imagine holding and weighing the piece of fruit, or the vegetable, in your hand – then you have done exceedingly well.

Above All botanical painting is an illusion, turning a three-dimensional object into a convincing two-dimensional portrait. These red onions are a superb example.

Complex Forms

This chapter deals with complex structures, the most familiar of which, in the plant world, are probably pineapples and pine cones. Such structures tend to follow the Fibonacci series of numbers, which can be found in many natural objects. Leonardo Fibonacci (c.1170–c.1250) was the first mathematician in the Western world to record the sequence of numbers that is named after him, although they were already known in India. To put it simply, each number is the sum of the two preceding numbers: 0+1=1, 1+1=2, 1+2=3, 2+3=5, 3+5=8, 5+8=13 and so on.

Fibonacci numbers demonstrate the mathematical formula for aspects of natural growth, showing how nature assembles petals, leaves, seeds and many animal forms in the most efficient way possible. Seedheads such as sunflowers (*Helianthus*), spiral shells and goat's horns are all examples of arrangements that follow the Fibonacci sequence.

Exercise **Pine cone**

Make an outline drawing of the base of a pine cone and then colour in the spirals in each direction (right). In the diagrams shown right, the spirals are shown in red and white, and you will see that there are eight one way (four red, four white) and thirteen the other. Both are Fibonacci numbers.

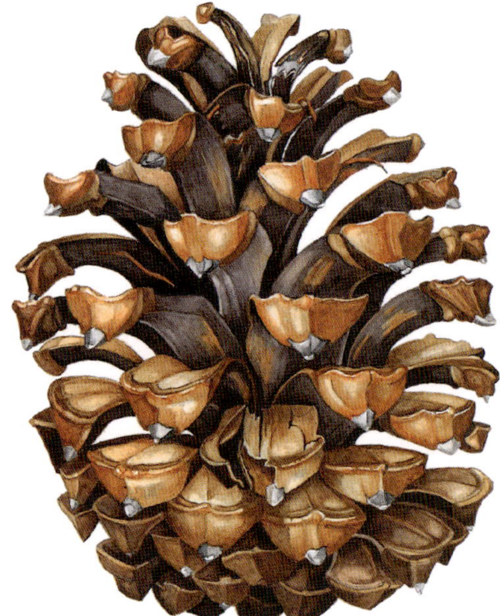

Above Pine cones have eight spirals in one direction and thirteen in the other, both Fibonacci numbers.

Below The simple pine cone becomes a study in resonant browns and greys.

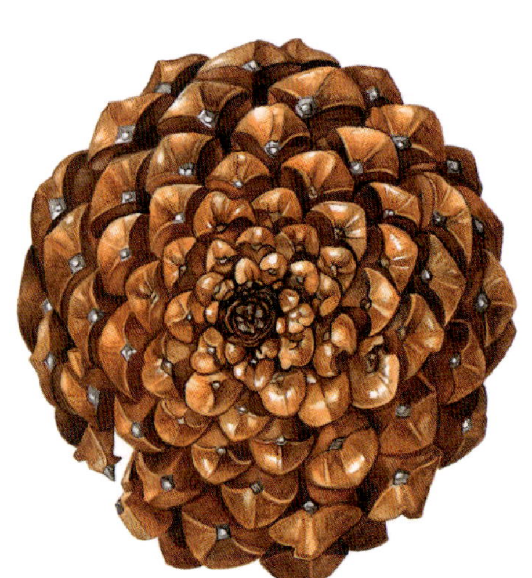
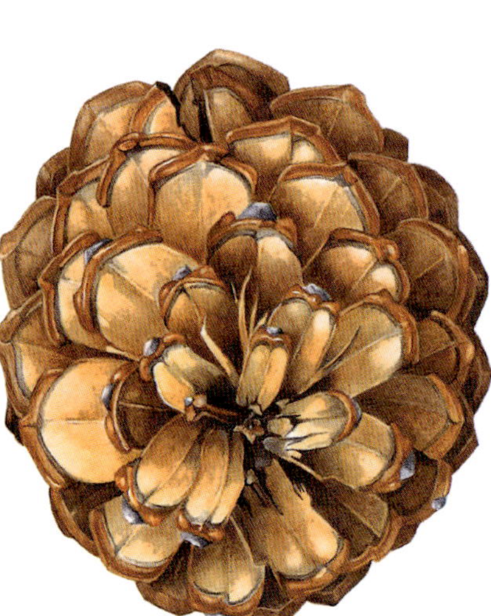

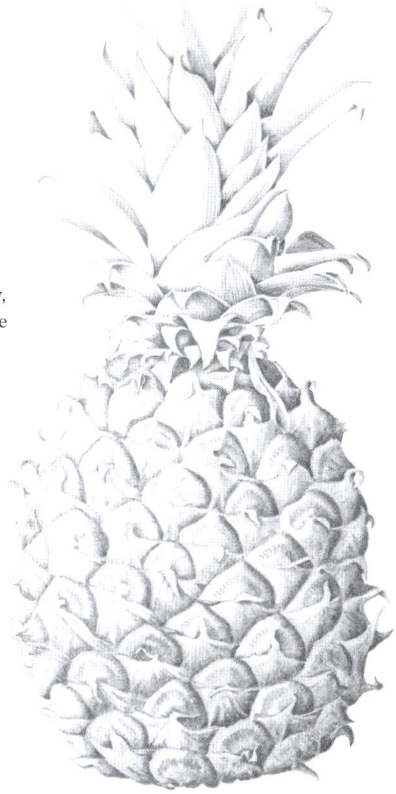

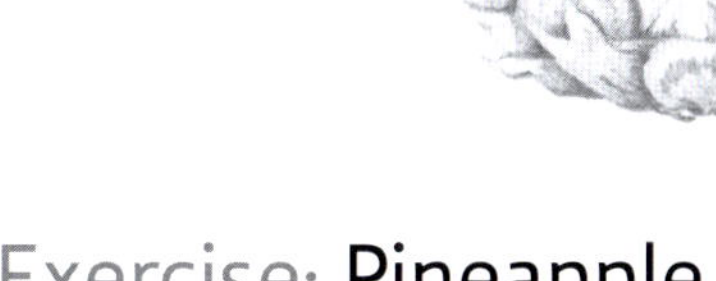

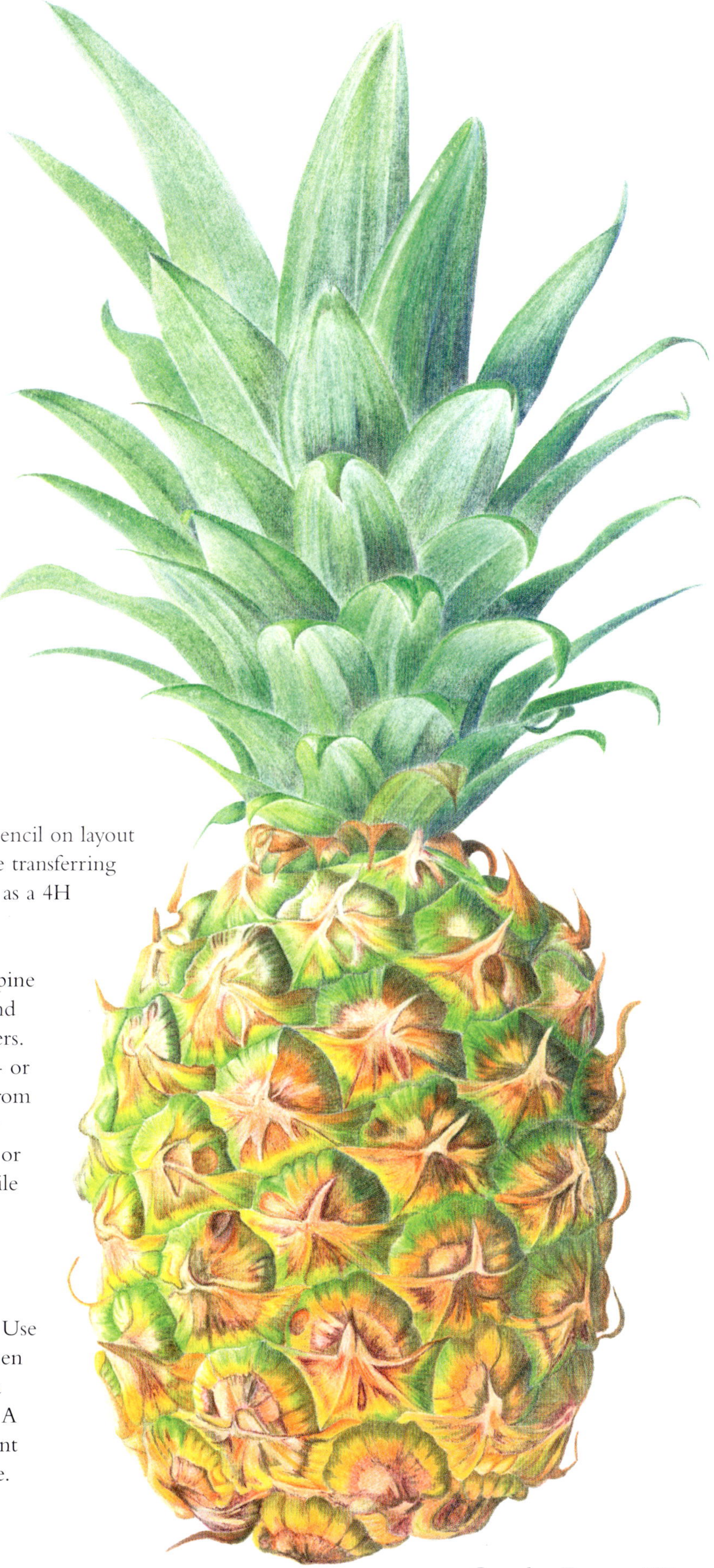

Exercise: Pineapple

First make a very careful line drawing using an HB pencil on layout paper, getting all the shapes absolutely accurate before transferring to watercolour paper. For this, use a hard pencil such as a 4H very lightly to avoid indenting the paper.

Note the direction and shape of the spirals. Like the pine cone, pineapples have eight spirals in one direction and 13 in the other – these are adjacent Fibonacci numbers. Although the segments are all roughly the same four- or five-sided diamond-like shape, each one is different from its neighbours. Unless you identify them as you draw them you are likely to get into a muddle, so use pins or tape to identify each section as you go, and again while you are painting. The closer the segments are to the outside of the shape the more distorted they appear, because they are foreshortened.

Start painting with a first wash of the lightest colour. Use a pale blue-green for the leaves and a pale yellow-green for the segments, and then work on one segment at a time, making sure that you achieve the correct tones. A final touch-up with a fine brush and some darker paint will give life and three-dimensionality to your picture.

Exercise: Indian wax ginger

Indian wax ginger, *Tapeinochilus ananassae*, has bright red flowerheads made up of stiff, waxy bracts enclosing small, bright yellow flowers. It is a native of Malaysia, Indonesia and northern Australia and grows on bamboo-like stems to a height of up to 2.5m (8¼ft). The colours you will need are French Ultramarine and Prussian Blue, Lemon Yellow and Indian Yellow, Scarlet Lake and Alizarin Crimson.

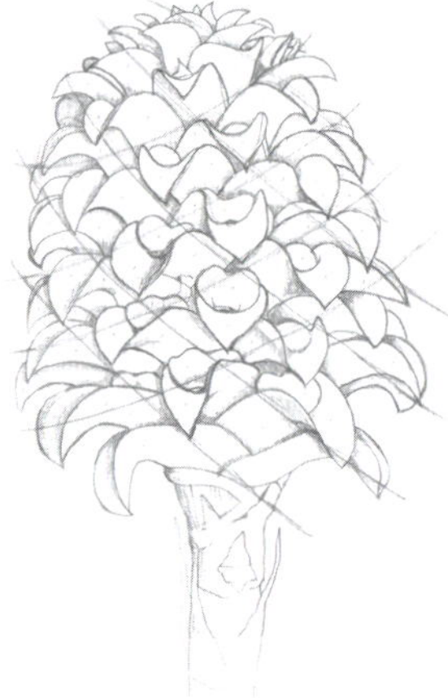 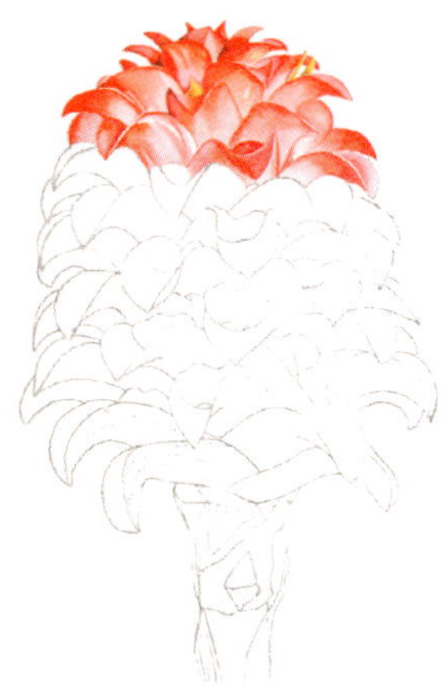 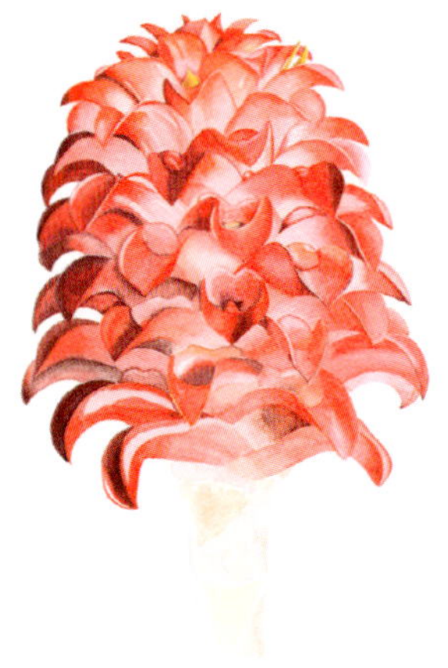 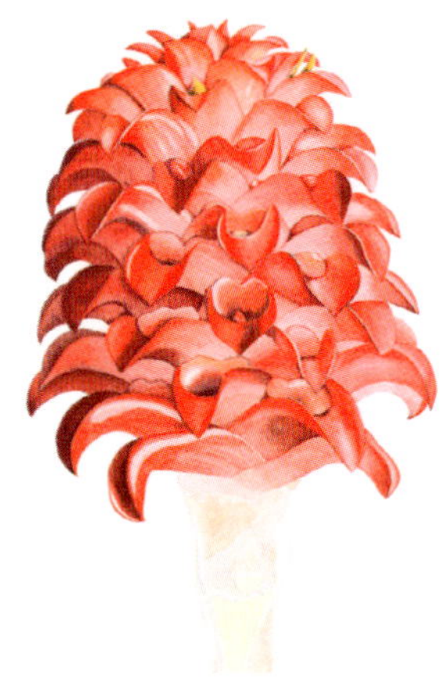

Step 1
Block out the general shape then indicate the spirals. Sketch in the different bracts – you might like to start with the one at centre top with the bright yellow bud, because that is the easiest to identify. Adding small areas of shading will give you a useful reference later on. Mark each area of highlight with a lightly dotted line so that you remember not to paint over it. You can erase this at the end.

Step 2
You might prefer to paint each section individually and therefore begin with the darker paint, one section at a time, grading and blending colours where necessary.

Step 3
Notice how the bracts on the side away from the light source are darker. To achieve this darker red, try adding some blue. Block in the stem with light washes of brown, yellow and green where appropriate.

Step 4
Deepen areas of shade and consolidate the paler parts to give a more cohesive look to the whole painting.

Step 5
Continue to accentuate the shaded areas. Brighten the tips of the bracts to make them appear to project forwards and paint the fine lines on their under surfaces. Paint the stem using washes of green mixed with red and blue for the darker areas. Using a fine brush, paint the fine lines on the stem's papery leaf bracts and bring out the shadows with a reddish black mixed from the colours on your palette.

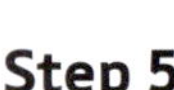 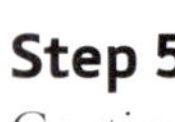

Exercise: Anthurium

The name anthurium comes from the Greek for 'tail flower', a description of the fleshy, flower-bearing spike (spadix), which rises from the spathe, a waxy, modified leaf. Anthuriums come from tropical America and are much prized by florists and others for their long-lasting flowers and ornamental leaves.

Make a careful drawing of the flowerhead (right), taking care with the pattern on the spadix – this is another example of Fibonacci spirals (see page 134). Draw the patterning first, from left to right and right to left, thus forming a criss-cross pattern. Then add the little seeds, which appear to form in a random way.

You may find the spathe more difficult, so make plenty of trial drawings and paintings on your worksheet first (below right). Notice how irregular the veins are, and also give thought to where the highlights and lowlights are placed.

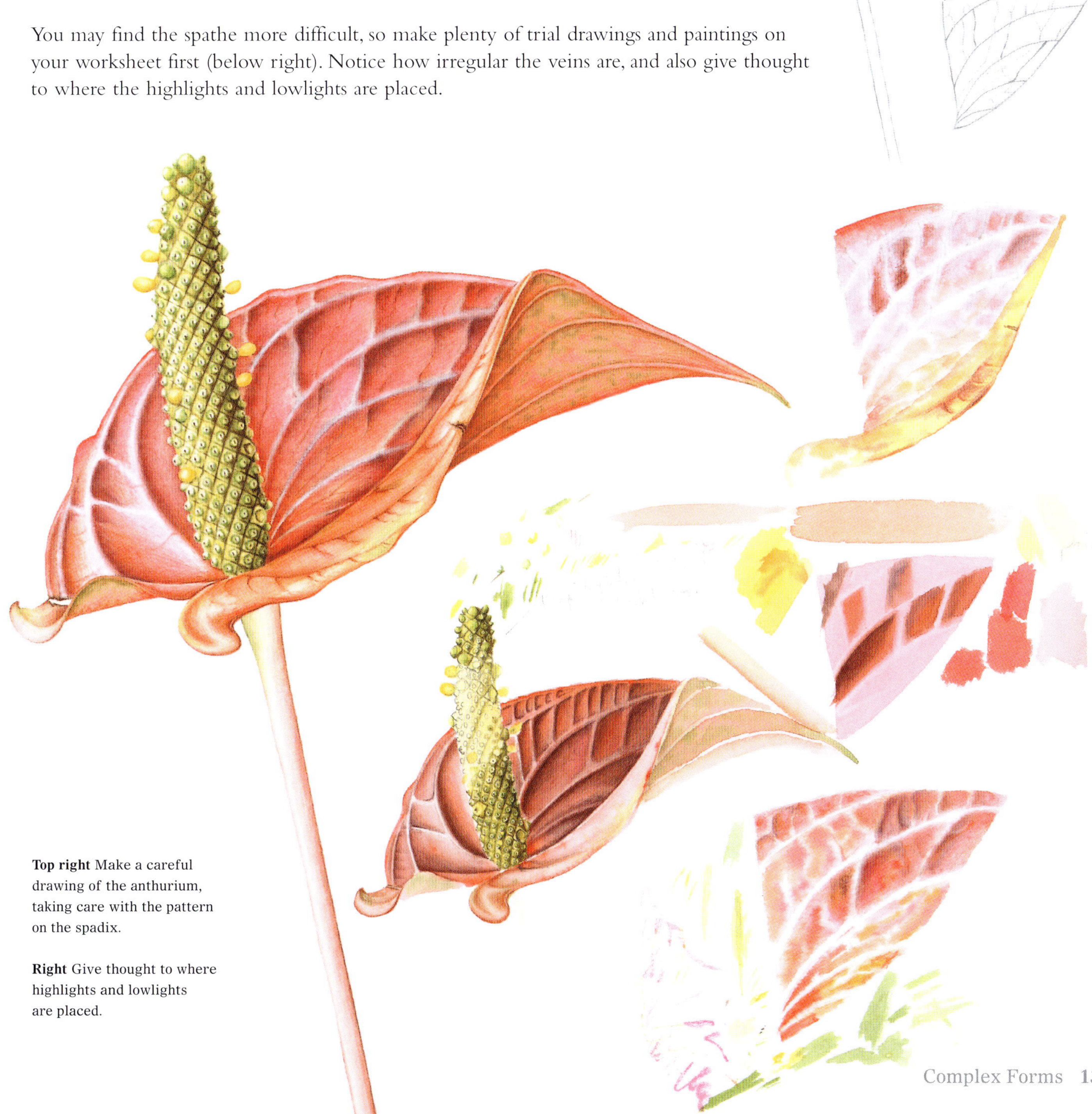

Top right Make a careful drawing of the anthurium, taking care with the pattern on the spadix.

Right Give thought to where highlights and lowlights are placed.

Phacelia tanacetifolia

Originating in the USA and Mexico, *Phacelia tanacetifolia* is an annual herb that grows up to 1m (3¼ft) high, with hairy inflorescences and long stamens. It is considered by many botanical artists to be a difficult and complex subject to draw and paint.

The specimen shown here, like other images from this artist, could be described as a drawing with paint applied; it has a spiral of colour woven into its structure which mimics the curving growth habit of the plant.

Attention to small detail is paramount in a subject like this. Start by making a detailed drawing, life-size (bottom right). Draw one or two full blooms or buds, noting the arrangement and relative size of the stamens and the shape of the anthers. The actual size of this specimen was 4 x 6cm (1½ x 2½in), and it was scaled up by x5.5. Thus the stamens, which measured 1.5cm (¾in), were portrayed in the final work at 8.2cm (3¼in). Note also the actual distance between the flowers on the stem (2mm), which scales up to 11mm (⅜in).

Make an enlarged drawing (right), scaling up each element in turn. On this, make notes on the colour of the anthers (blue and purple), the two stigmas (very light lilac colour) and the five stamens (a deeper purple colour); note that the petals are a paler lilac colour at the base, with purple veins; that the stamens turn brown as they die, as do the flower petals lower down the stem, and that the yellowy-green seed pods overlap in places. All sepals are hairy, some quite thickly covered. The young ones in the centre are a lemony-green, whereas the older ones become redder.

Transfer your drawing to watercolour paper and finish it. The form of the specimen opposite was enhanced with a colour spiral, but you might prefer to work the whole plant in colour. Either way, you will have a most interesting, testing and eye-catching painting.

The diversity of plants

This chapter, indeed this whole book, has shown you examples of a range of botanical subjects, from minuscule to huge, from colourful to plain, from complex to simple. By studying their diversity you will have realized that there are many different ways of looking at and portraying plants, and that a study of even the most seemingly simple subject can give you deeper insight into the wonderful world of nature and influence how you choose to portray it.

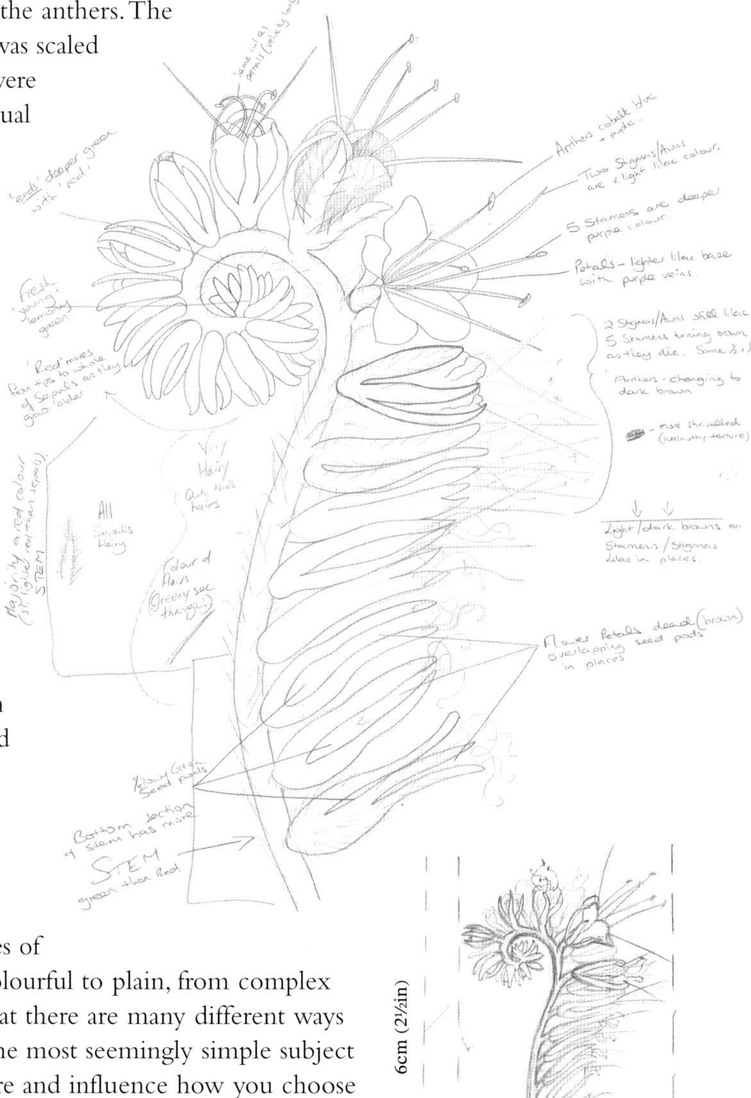

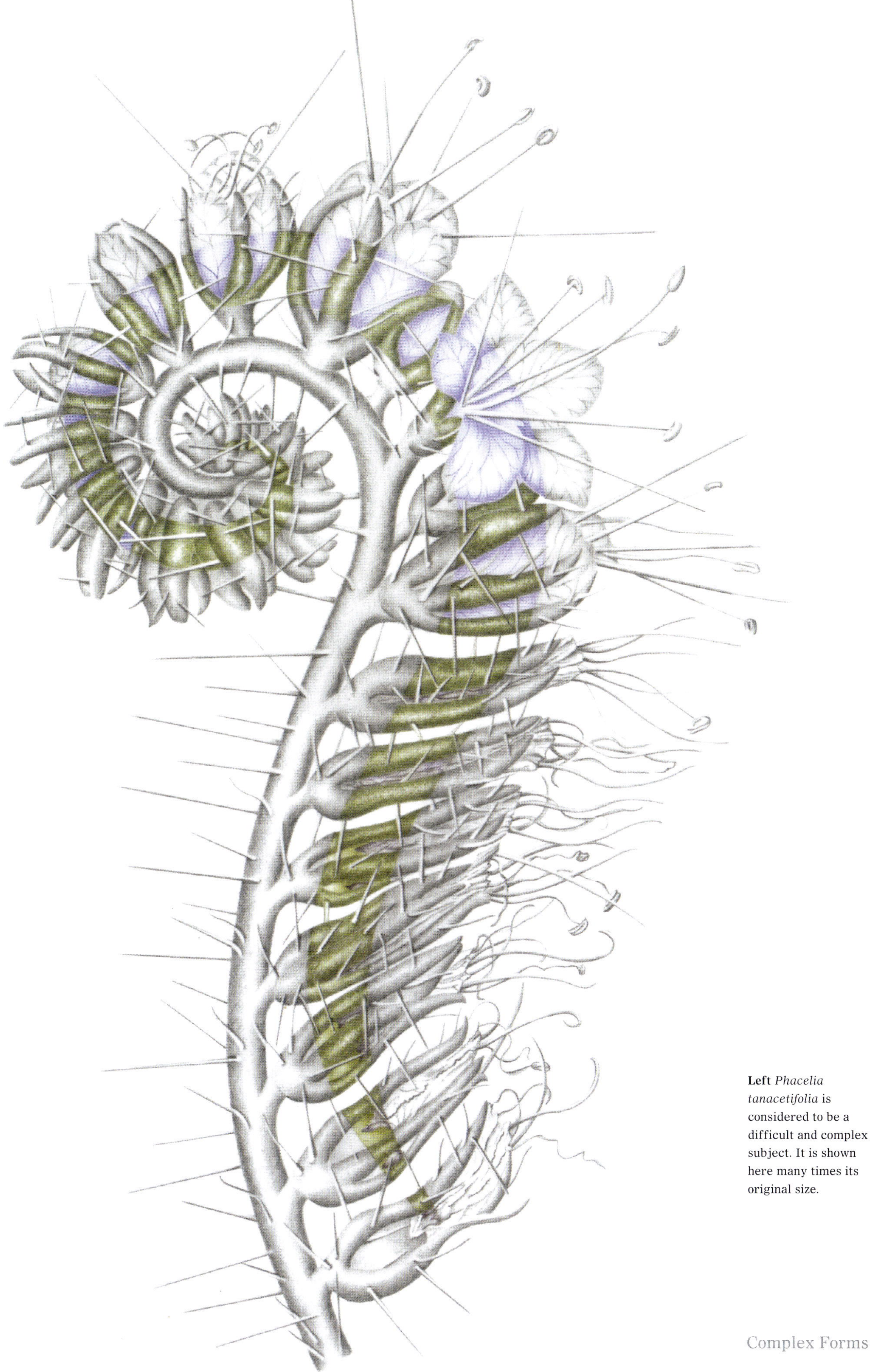

Left *Phacelia tanacetifolia* is considered to be a difficult and complex subject. It is shown here many times its original size.

Suppliers and Useful Addresses

L Cornelissen & Son, Artists' Colourmen
105 Great Russell Street
London WC1B 3RY
tel: 020 7636 1045
www.cornelissen.com

Dick Blick Studio
PO Box 1267
Galesburg
Il. 61402-1267, USA
tel: 1.800.828.4548
www.DickBlick.com

Falkiner Fine Papers
76 Southampton Row
London WC1B 4AR
tel: 020 7831 1151
www.falkiners.com

UK Coloured Pencil Society
www.ukcps.co.uk

Jackson's Art Supplies
1 Farleigh Place
London N16 7SX
tel: 08444 998430
www.jacksonsart.co.uk

Ken Bromley Art Supplies
Unit 13, Lodge Bank Estate
Crown Lane
Horwich
Bolton BL6 5HY
tel: 01204 690114
www.artsupplies.co.uk

Eden Project
Bodelva
St Austell
Cornwall PL24 2SG
tel: 01726 811911
www.edenproject.com

South West Carnivorous Plants
Blackwater Nursery
Culmstock
Devon EX15 3HG
tel: 01823 681669
www.littleshopofhorrors.co.uk

Desert to Jungle
Lower Henlade
Taunton TA3 5NB
tel: 01823 443701
www.deserttojungle.com

South West Society of Botanical Artists
www.swsba.org.uk

Rosie Martin
www.syberist.talktalk.net

Meriel Thurstan
www.merielthurstan.co.uk

Materials

Paper
Hot Press (HP) (see page 12 for qualities)
Arches Aquarelle 300gsm (140lb)
Fabriano Artistico traditional 300gsm (140lb)
Fabriano Artistico Extra White 300gsm (140lb)
Fabriano 5 300gsm (140lb)
Magnani Corona Smooth 310gsm (140lb)
Royal Watercolour Society (RWS) 300gsm (140lb)
Saunders Waterford 300gsm (140lb)
Sennelier 300gsm (140lb)

Graphite Pencils
Caran d'Ache Technograph
Faber-Castell 9000
Staedtler Mars Lumograph 100
Staedtler 480
Derwent Graphic

Kolinsky Sable Brushes
Winsor & Newton Series 7 Round
Da Vinci Maestro Series 10 or 35
Raphaël Series 8404
Isabey Series 6228
Escoda Series 1212

Watercolour Paints
Schminke Horadam
Winsor & Newton Artists'
Old Holland Classic
Lefranc & Bourgeois
Holbein
Sennelier

Coloured pencils (not water-soluble)
Caran d'Ache Pablo – quite soft, 120 colours
Derwent Artists – medium-hard, 120 colours
Derwent Studio – hard, fine points, 72 colours
Derwent Signature – intense, lightfast, 60 colours
Faber-Castell Polychromos
Lyra Rembrandt Polycolor
Prismacolor Verithin (USA) – hard, very fine points, good
for detail, 40 colours
Prismacolor Premier
Swan Stabilo Luminance

Supports for coloured pencil work
HP 300gsm (140lb) watercolour papers (see above)
Bristol board – very pure white surface, very smooth
Cartridge paper – smooth, white, 220gsm (120lb) or heavier
Illustration board and museum board – expensive but good
for detailed work

Pencil sharpeners
Rapesco.com
Helix.co.uk

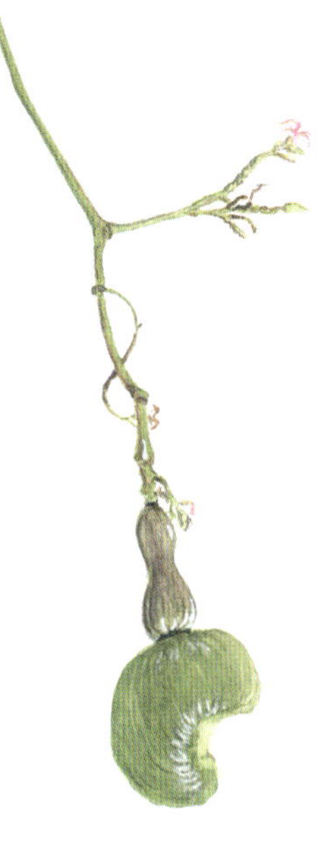

Right The tree of the cashew nut, *Anacardium occidentale*, grows at the Eden Project in Cornwall.

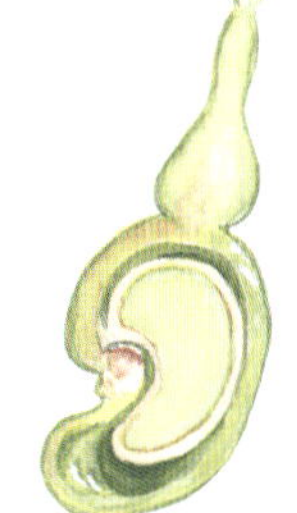

Further Reading

Cummings, Robert and Porter, Tom, *The Colour Eye* (BBC Books, 1991)

Cowling, Richard and Richardson, Dave, *Fynbos, South Africa's Unique Floral Kingdom* (Fernwood Press, 1995)

Finlay, Victoria, *Colour: Travels Through the Paintbox* (Hodder & Stoughton, 2002)

Hockney, David, *Secret Knowledge* (Thames & Hudson Ltd, 2001)

Itten, Johannes, *The Art of Colour: The Subjective Experience and Objective Rationale of Colour* (John Wiley & Sons, 1974)

RHS Plant Finder (The Royal Horticultural Society/Dorling Kindersley, produced annually)

Martin, Rosie and Thurstan, Meriel, *Botanical Illustration Course* (Batsford, 2006)

Martin, Rosie and Thurstan, Meriel, *Contemporary Botanical Illustration* (Batsford, 2008)

Martin, Rosie and Thurstan, Meriel, *Natural History Painting* (Batsford, 2009)

Sherwood, Shirley, *Contemporary Botanical Artists: The Shirley Sherwood Collection* (Cross River Press, 1996)

Swan, Ann, *Botanical Painting with Coloured Pencils* (Collins, 2009)

Zomlefer, Wendy B., *Guide to Flowering Plant Families* (Atlantic Books, 1995)

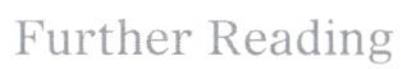

Acknowledgements

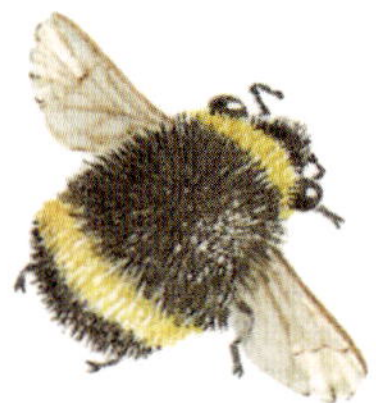

Breeders and custodians of exotic plants are, we have found, the most kind and generous of people. We would particularly like to thank Tim Pettitt and Katie Treseder, who hosted a day for some of the contributing artists in the Jungle Biome at the Eden Project; Maureen Newton, also at the Eden Project; Rob Gudge of Desert to Jungle; and Alistair and Jenny Pearce of South West Carnivorous Plants.

To all those friends who willingly lent plants to be painted and to Jane Erith and Anne Bebbington for checking our facts – a big thank you. Some of the artists were extra generous with their time and expertise, giving us information about how they set about their work or even completing lengthy special assignments for us. Very special thanks, therefore, to Kate Barling, Jessie Carr, Judith Carter, Ros Casares, Georgia Danvers, Catherine Day, Ros Franklin, Pam Hargreaves, David Lewry, Sue Linton, Fran Patterson, Sarah Poat, Eliza Price, Vivienne Rew, Liz Rousell, Hamilton Sampford, Jessica Rosemary Shepherd, Julia Trickey and Kate Wilson.

Botanical painting is one of those subjects where one never stops learning, whether it is from books, from demonstrations or from one's students. There are many people whose names either were never known or have been lost in time, from whom we have garnered many little titbits of information. To them we say a sincere thank you, whoever and wherever you are.

To all the artists and to Kristy Richardson and all at Anova Books for being willing to work with us yet again, we owe a huge debt of gratitude. Without all of these people this book would not have come about.

Artists:

Lyn Aldridge 18 (bottom), 130 (bottom left), Kate Barling 2, 64 (2nd row centre), 79 (bottom left), Deborah Barton 96, 99 (top and right), 101 (right), 128, 132 (left), Anne Bebbington 52, Mary Bedford 141, Jenny Booker 39, 133, Nonn Bound 45 (left), Phil Bound 72 (part), Anton Bradburn 72 (part), Valerie Bradburn 120 (top), 121, Debora Cane 72 (part), Jessie Carr 73, 87, 122, 137, Bernard F Carter 44 (top), Judith Carter 9, 106 (top), 107 (bottom), 108, Ros Casares 101 (top), Mike Cawthorne 64 (2nd row left), 79 (bottom centre), Susan Clark 72 (part), Georgia Danvers 30, 32, 33, 37, 40, 41 (right), 113, 138, 139, Catherine Day 5, 6, 28 (bottom), 36, 41 (bottom left), 64 (top left and 3rd row right), 76 (top), 83 (main picture), Ros Franklin 120 (bottom), Jane Goodson 8, 110 (bottom), 135 (bottom), Pat Gunn 72 (part), Pam Hargreaves 104, 105, Susan Hillier 34 (bottom), 38, 97 (top), Carole Howie 14 (top), 18 (top), Ann Jelley 27 (top), Moira King 20 (bottom left), Tricia Leftwich 19, David Lewry 62 (bottom left), 64 (top right), 90, 92, 93, 94 (top), 126, 127, 130 (top), Sue Linton 123, Rosie Martin 17, 48, 49, 54, 56, (bottom), 57 (bottom), 63, 64 (bottom left), 65 (top), 66, 74, 75, 76 (details), 81, 83 (details), 98 (top), 115, 116, 117, 118, 119, 124, 125, 129 (final details using coloured pencils), Jessica Middleton 20 (bottom centre and right), Fran Patterson 14 (bottom), 15, 88, 89, 106 (right), Sarah Poat 11 (bottom right), 35 (bottom), 53, 65 (bottom), 82 (top), 112, Eliza Price 64 (bottom centre), 91, Vivienne Rew 56 (top), 102, 134 (bottom), Liz Rousell 86, 103, Hamilton Sampford 100 (top), Sally Sewell-Alger 72 (part), Judith Shelley 72 (part), Jessica Rosemary Shepherd 35 (top), 44 (bottom left), 84, 85, Sarah Sollom 27 (photos), Sylvia Sroka 3, 16, 111 (top and left), Meriel Thurstan 7, 11 (bottom left), 13, 20 (top), 26, 29, 45 (right), 47, 51, 58, 59, 60, 61, 62 (top and bottom centre), 64 (2nd row right and 3rd row left), 67, 68, 69, 70, 71, 77 (bottom left and top), 78, 79 (right), 80, 82 (right and bottom left), 95, 98 (bottom), 99 (bottom left) 109 (top), 110 (top), 114, 129, 130 (bottom right), 131, 132 (right), 134 (top), 135 (top), 136, 144, Julia Trickey 10, 11 (top), 21, 23, 31, 41 (top left), 43, 62 (bottom right), 77 (bottom right), Karina Weeks 50, Julie Wilson 34 (top), 42, 44 (bottom right), 46, 57 (top), 107 (top and centre), 109 (centre and bottom), 111 (bottom), Kate Wilson 64 (top centre, 3rd row centre and bottom right), 94 (bottom), 97 (bottom), 100 (bottom) Joe Yunnie 24, 28 (top)

Index